I dedicate these memoirs to my very dear
children and grandchildren

Published in 2015 by Mercer Books
www.mercerbooks.co.uk

Copyright © Therese Sidmouth 2015

The right of Therese Sidmouth to be identified as the author of this work has been asserted in accordance with the Copyright, Designs & Patents Act 1988.

Every effort has been made to contact copyright holders of material reproduced in this book. If any have been inadvertently overlooked, the publishers will be pleased to make restitution at the earliest opportunity.

All rights reserved. No part of this publication may be reproduced, stored in or introduced into a retrieval system, or transmitted, in any form, or by means (electronic, mechanical, photocopying, recording or otherwise) without the prior written permission of the author. Any person who does any unauthorised act in relation to this publication may be liable to criminal prosecution and civil claims for damages.

A CIP catalogue record for this book is available from The British Library.

This book is sold subject to the condition that it shall not, by way of trade or otherwise, be lent, re-sold, hired out, or otherwise circulated without the author's prior consent in any form of binding or cover other than that in which it is published and without a similar condition including this condition being imposed on the subsequent purchaser.

ISBN 978-0-9557127-9-1

THE STORY OF
A COLONIAL FAMILY
1909 – 1947

Therese Sidmouth

Contents

Preface

PART 1: IN THE BEGINNING

Introduction to Part 1		1
1	The Most Courageous Railway in the World	3
2	Birth of a Colony	9
3	The Land Grab	11
4	Settling In	17
5	Taming the Wilderness	20
6	Grogan and Delamere	24
7	Law and Order	31
8	How the British came to Colonise East Africa	34
9	The Sultans of Zanzibar	40
10	Sir Ali bin Salem	48
11	Conclusion to Part 1	54

PART II: ORPHANS OF EMPIRE

12	I meet my sister Helen	63
13	I am part of a large Family	66
14	Kenya	69
15	Dar es Salaam Remembered	73
16	Nursery Life in Dar es Salaam	78
17	The Voyage	86

18	The Convent	95
19	August in Greyshott	102
20	Back to School	106
21	Willesden Again	112
22	Holidays	115
23	Return to Brittany	123

PART III: NOSTALGIA FOR AFRICA

24	Freedom	135
25	Wartime Travel	139
26	Kenya Revisited	148
27	The Daughters of the Chief Justice	153
28	Lumbwa	160
29	Escape from Nairobi	170
30	The Coast	177
31	I Spread my Wings	186
32	Rhodes University	191
33	The Journey Home	200

Epilogue

Bibliography

Preface

The Macaulays and Sheridans: Love Stories of Long Ago

My story starts many miles from equatorial Africa in another corner of what was then the British Empire – the West of Ireland. My family's roots lie on the banks of the River Moy in the shadow of Croagh Patrick and by the waters of Loch Conn. My mother came from Ballina and my father from nearby Castlebar, so they were virtually neighbours.

By the time I was born in Nairobi in 1927, the only one of my grandparents still living was my mother's mother Grandma Macaulay. I remember her as an indomitable woman who spoke forcefully in a rich brogue. She was, I recall, held in affectionate respect by her extensive family. I sensed, though, that she was not at ease with small children. Bridge and hats were her passion. She liked to dress in the Edwardian manner adopted by Queen Mary; and being tall and upright, this suited her well. At the age of sixteen, despite being rather plain in appearance, she had captured the heart of a doctor from Ballina in the west of Ireland. Roger Macaulay was not only considerably older than her, but was engaged to another woman at the time. He broke off the engagement after falling deeply in love with my grandmother, Louisa, and as a result, had a breach of promise case brought against him. Possibly this was the reason why his marriage to his beloved Louisa Treston was such a quiet affair. Instead of being in Dublin, where her family came from, it took place in a small country church in Mayo. The first Dr Macaulay's housekeeper knew of the marriage was when she was told to put a second pillow on his bed! Whatever the reason, it proved to be a singularly happy marriage. They made their home in Francis Street, Ballina. It was here that they brought up their fourteen children, and where Roger indulged his passion for thoroughbred horses. The lady he had forsaken married a Mr Fogarty, a wealthy sugar baron. She remained in love with my grandfather, however, for the rest of her long life and always considered herself to be our adopted grandmother. We knew her as Nanny Fogarty and used to enjoy visiting her in her Dublin house. Her granddaughter, Elizabeth, who married a descendant of Daniel O'Connell, became a close friend of mine, and I was delighted to be godmother to her daughter, Kate.

The Macaulays were, politically speaking, nationals and even rebels. My mother's uncle, Thomas Macaulay, joined a cell of the Irish Republican Brotherhood while at university. He ended up serving a life sentence in Mountjoy Prison for attempted murder after involvement in what became known as the Crossmolina Conspiracy. The Sheridans, by contrast, were supporters of the Crown. They chose to emigrate, to join the army, or become involved in the business of Empire. My father's brother, Henry, enlisted as a second lieutenant in the Connaught Rangers, and was killed at the Battle of the Somme in 1916. There was, however, one thing my grandparents had in common: their ruthless determination in pursuit of true love.

My paternal grandmother, Margaret Murphy, known as 'Little May', was loved by everyone, but the fond diminutive was deceptive. Her sweet demeanour concealed an iron will. Her love affair with her first cousin, Alfred Sheridan, was frowned on by the church, as the relationship fell within the bounds of consanguinity. The marriage therefore could not be sanctioned. Bitterly disappointed, Little May fled to America, 'sailing before the mast'. Her family's entreaties fell on deaf ears. She refused to come back unless she could marry Alfred. Her parents had an anguished discussion with the parish priest. He in turn approached the bishop, and the bishop passed the matter on to Rome. Finally a dispensation was granted and Little May joyfully set sail for home. Meanwhile Alfred, through the influence of one of his Protestant friends, a member of the Bourke family, had been appointed County Court Registrar. He had also acquired a small estate, Spencer Park, on the outskirts of their home town of Castlebar (now the site of a housing estate). This is where he brought his intrepid bride after the wedding, and where they lived happily with their six children.

It was the popular music of the day, the Edwardian ballads, the Irish folk songs and the melodies from the light operas of Franz Lehar and Johann Strauss that brought the two families together. My parents met at a benefit concert given in the local psychiatric hospital in Castlebar. Recent medical research had revealed that mentally disturbed patients in institutions showed significant improvement when exposed to music. This had been adopted in England, and Dr Macaulay, always a progressive, was anxious to follow suit. With this in mind, he helped organise an evening of light entertainment in the hospital. It was also an occasion for him to show off his bevy of pretty daughters. My mother had recently returned from finishing school in Rome, where, among other accomplishments, she had become a competent pianist. The Sheridans were invited and my father was asked to bring his music. While studying law at Trinity College he had become interested in singing, and had had lessons. As a result, he was much in demand to give recitals. He seldom refused, for he loved singing. My mother was asked to accompany him. He stood beside her at the piano, tall and slim, with the dark good looks that give credence to the notion that shipwrecked Spaniards from the Armada intermarried with the people of Connaught. He waited while she confidently rippled through some opening arpeggios, flexing her fingers before leading him into the melody. Was it 'Kathleen Mavourneen', or 'Believe Me if All those Endearing Young Charms'? Whatever it was, his voice and her hands wove a love song that came straight from the heart. Their romance blossomed: picnics on the shores of Loch Conn; tennis parties; cycle rides through the boreens at the foot of Mount Nephin; expeditions to Achill Island and jolly outings in the jaunting car to the windswept beaches and sand dunes of Enniscrone. It seemed that before the year was out Muriel Macaulay would have agreed to become Mrs Joseph Sheridan.

But the course of true love is seldom predictable. My father, after being called to the Irish Bar had joined the Connaught Circuit. After a year he became restless and was tempted by the prospects open to young lawyers prepared to help the British Government administer the new territories in East Africa. He applied to the Colonial Office and was accepted. All this was before he met my mother. When he proposed to her he had to explain that he would be leaving soon to take up an appointment as Assistant Attorney General in Nyasaland (Malawi), and that he would not be back for three years. My mother was only eighteen – nine years younger than my father – and he felt he could not hold her to a formal engagement over such a long period of time. So he promised he would ask her again when he returned. They parted with heavy hearts.

Nothing in his previous experience could have prepared him for life in the dark heart of Africa. Blantyre, on the marshy shores of Lake Nyasa, is a place still rife with malaria and other tropical diseases. Before long he fell ill with blackwater fever. How often, in his weakened state, must he have thought of Muriel and wondered if she still loved him.

It was also a testing time for my mother. She was the prettiest of Dr Macaulay's daughters and this, coupled with her passion for horses, marked her out as his favourite. He was understandably proud when she was chosen as one of the first women to ride in the Dublin Horse Show. There were pictures of her in the papers riding side saddle, clearing the jumps with a graceful ease. Inevitably, she was courted by many an ardent beau. My grandfather must have hoped she would abandon the idea of life in far away Africa and choose, rather, to settle down with someone locally. But this was not to be. True to his word, Joe Sheridan returned in 1913 to renew his courtship. He was as handsome and debonair as my mother remembered him, and she gladly accepted his proposal.

They were married in December. Unlike my grandparents' wedding, this was a stylish occasion, with the Archbishop of Dublin officiating. The ceremony was held in the University Church on Stephen's Green (the church commissioned by Cardinal Newman and designed by his friend, John Hungerford Pollen – a forebear of my husband, Francis Pollen). The reception was at the fashionable Shelbourne Hotel. There was no honeymoon; but early one morning, before leaving Ireland, they climbed Croagh Patrick for a Mass of thanksgiving in the little chapel on the summit. The sight of the dawn breaking over the islands of Clew Bay warmed their hearts against the winter cold and remained stored in their memories over the years to come.

They sailed for Mombasa, where my father had been posted as Resident Magistrate. They had little furniture, so packing cases were pressed into service. My mother's notion of geography must have been poor, for she seemed to have had no idea of how close they were to the equator. In her trousseau she had packed, not only chilpruf combinations, but also a new pair of skates! In the beginning, her homesickness was overwhelming. Their house in Mombasa was out by the lighthouse on English Point. Overwhelmed by homesickness, she would watch the ships sailing out of the harbour, her dark blue eyes shrouded in a mist of tears.

Before long however, the Magistrate's pretty young wife became the toast of the town. She learned to smoke, to dance the cha cha, and to manage her African servants so that she could entertain with style. Later, when my father moved to Nairobi as a High Court judge, her riding skills were noticed by the Governor, Sir Edward Northey. He not only allowed her the pick of his fine stables, but arranged for her to accompany him and his wife on safari. She proved to be an excellent shot and, I am sorry to say, seldom missed her target. At least two leopards, shot by her, ended up as rugs under our feet, and later as evening capes. When they returned home to the West of Ireland on leave, her siblings were at first irritated and then bored by her tales of adventure. She spared them no detail in her accounts of dining with the rich and famous at Government House. The story of her evening at the Muthaiga Club when she danced with the Prince of Wales fell on deaf ears. Soon the couple discovered that, apart from nostalgia, they had little in common with the people of Ballina and Castlebar.

Their glamorous life, however, was overshadowed by tragedy. On their first visit back to Ireland in 1917, their two children, Dermot aged three, and Peggy, a baby of eighteen months, contracted polio. Baby Peggy recovered unscathed; but Dermot, their little boy, was cruelly crippled for life. The bitter memory of their journey back to Africa remained locked forever in my mother's heart. The manner in which both my parents and Dermot triumphed over this disaster speaks volumes for their strength of character.

In their public life, Muriel and Joe could be relied upon to enliven the dreariest of official functions. No one could match my father's wit. His speeches, which he loved giving, were a tour de force. He relished my mother's interruptions. 'Sit down, Joe, you've been speaking long enough,' would be greeted with, 'My wife, whose judgement I have learnt to respect over the years, is urging me to reclaim my seat beside her. This of course, I am delighted to do, but not before I have mentioned...' and he would return seamlessly to his theme. His audience loved it. He would introduce my mother with the words, 'My wife, who as you all know, is well able to speak for herself is, I am delighted to say, with us tonight to keep me in order'. He was always at ease; had a wonderful delivery; seldom used notes, and spoke with commanding authority.

At home, he was not so sure-footed. Though the bonds of love remained rock solid throughout their life, there was, as with many marriages of that period, a tension born of incomprehension. My mother never saw the point of his jokes. He was a notable squash player, but at a loss to understand my mother's passion for all things equestrian. She was continually worried about money, and counted every penny. He, by comparison, was generous to the point of foolishness. While he over-tipped, she upset many a waiter by demanding half the tip back. Travelling with him had its problems. Ever conscious of the need to uphold the probity of the judiciary, he would present customs officials with a lengthy list of items he felt should be declared, including Lourdes water. Bored by the catalogue of innocent goods, the official would wave them both through, giving my mother the chance she had been hoping for of slipping her cases through unopened. To my knowledge she was never caught, but later she could run into trouble with Joe when he discovered the packets of undeclared De Reszke cigarettes in her luggage.

Despite their differences, their devotion to each other never wavered. It was at its most evident when she accompanied him at the piano as he sang. They never seemed to lose that moment when they first met at the concert in Castlebar. 'Believe me if All Those Endearing Young Charms' was sung for her alone, and she knew it. Tragically, he became a victim of clinical depression, brought on by the part he was called upon to play as the presiding judge in the murder trial of Lord Erroll. In those days the treatment for depression was through electric shock therapy, and, if that failed, frontal lobotomy. My poor father endured both of these. As a result he became a shadow of his former self.

Their old age was a dismal affair spent in rented rooms, first in London and then on the South Coast. Their attempt to settle in the West of Ireland had been disastrous. They could not adapt, and resented being looked upon as outsiders. They were living in Hove at the time of my father's death. He fell downstairs at the age of eighty-two, while on a Saint Vincent de Paul mission, visiting the sick. He broke his leg, and never recovered. He died in Brighton General Hospital in 1964. Every day for four months my mother had toiled up the hill from the bus stop to the hospital to bring him home-cooked meals. I saw him a few days before he died. It was Christmas time and the window beside his bed had been decorated with blobs of cotton wool. The Mayor of Brighton, in his ceremonial regalia, accompanied by Santa Claus, visited the ward. Their cheery voices wishing him a happy Christmas and a prosperous New Year were not able to rouse him from his coma. That afternoon, in wild, wet, windy weather, my mother and I chose a burial plot for them both in Brighton Cemetery. When I got home to Henley my sister Mary telephoned. Her sharp wit could always be relied upon to lighten the gloom. 'I hear you have been doing some Christmas shopping', she said, 'and that you have bought a double decker!'. He died on Boxing Day – the feast of Saint Stephen. The readings for the Mass for that day are particularly appropriate. 'I see heaven thrown open, and the Son of Man standing at the right hand of God'.

We arranged for my mother to be looked after by some nuns who had a convent at Hare Hatch, not far from Henley. She didn't stay there long. She was much too independent to submit to being looked after. She found herself a tiny flat in Kensington, Cranmer Court. Here she spent three tranquil years before cancer caught up with her. On a beautiful summer's evening in July, she died in St George's Hospital. She was seventy-six. As we tried to comfort her in her agony, we could see from the window of her room the guests from a Buckingham Palace garden party queuing for taxis – a scene she would have enjoyed so much. To the end of her days she remained an ingénue, unashamedly excited by the glamour of Life.

Part One

In the Beginning

Introduction to Part One

Empires are the story of world history, and the most astonishing story of them all is that of the British Empire. In terms of human history there never was another empire that had so much influence on political reform, cultural exchanges and way of life for so many people. At one time this small country ruled over a quarter of the world's population. It lasted for nearly 400 years.

At the time I was born, in 1927, this country was known throughout the world as Great Britain. The politics of the day were shot through with imperialism. It was a matter of pride to have been born British. At that time, the nation believed passionately that its greatness was due to civilisation underpinned by Christianity and the rule of law – British law of course. It went without saying that the people of Great Britain had a duty to civilize the underdeveloped nations of the world, while at the same time introducing them to the business of world trade. This was the background to my father's and my brothers' professional lives.

Today we are uncomfortable with the concept of empire. Contemporary politics is about human rights and democracy. Civilization is put in inverted commas, indicating we are no longer sure what it stands for. The distinction between right and wrong now has little to do with Christianity and everything to do with personal opinion. In short, the world has moved on.

From this changed position, we judge the past using the criteria of today. We are ashamed of Britain's involvement with the dreadful business of the slave trade, but are not prepared to acknowledge the fact that we were the first nation to abolish it and the only nation to police the oceans of the world to eradicate it. We view Britain's policy of colonisation, its class structure and the various crimes of its past in isolation, with no regard for the political and social structures of the time. We make our accusations in the fond belief that man's flawed nature is a thing peculiar to the past; something from which our generation is immune. Now, we assure ourselves, we know better. Do we really?

What is forgotten is the legacy left to the world by the British Empire: Westminster as 'The Mother of Parliaments', the invention of the steam engine and its use for the expansion of world trade and communication, the rule of common law, world sport, and the lingua franca of the world – the English language. The list continues. To quote from the world's greatest playwright, William Shakespeare: 'The evil that men do lives after them. The good is often interred with their bones.'

It was the two emerging superpowers of the 1930s who were responsible for the opprobrium that has been heaped on the Empire. Both the U S A and the Soviet Union were out to destroy it. Imperialism did not sit well with democracy or communism. President Roosevelt made the dismantling of the Empire a condition on America entering World War II. The Soviets meanwhile opened a school in Moscow for political activists from the colonies, people like Jomo Kenyatta, who were plotting rebellion. 'Colonialism' became a dirty word. The mud, sadly, has stuck.

As an octogenarian grandparent I stand at the junction of these conflicting ideas. This I believe is where the importance of grandparenthood lies. For us, placed in this pivotal position, the past is not a foreign country, and the present we see as living proof of mankind's adaptability and innovative skills. Such a viewpoint fills us with hope for the future. The hardships my parents had to face (my mother in particular – for she is the heroine of my story) – would have been easier to bear if they had had access to the internet, mobile phones, jet airplanes and all the other marvels of contemporary life that we take for granted. So it will be in the future: the struggles of today will find their resolution in the inventions of tomorrow.

There is, one thing that remains constant, and that is the human spirit with its emotions of love, jealousy, grief, hatred and all those other components that make us sentient beings. The script may alter, the scenery change, the costumes and props look different throughout the ages, but our ceaseless quest for happiness remains forever the same. 'Our spirits, Lord, are restless until they find their home in you'.

Therese Sidmouth
Bath 2013

Chapter 1

'The Most Courageous Railway in the World'

The wide, dusty road leading out of the commercial sector of Nairobi to the railway station was bordered by straggly eucalyptus trees, planted in 1900 by Jim Ainsworth, the enthusiastic first Sub-Commissioner of the Protectorate. They had been imported from Australia, and were as alien to Kenya as the station building itself. With its gothic clock tower and ugly brick façade, it pleaded to be in Middlesborough or Sheffield, rather than here in the sharp African sunlight. A few ancient rickshaws were parked haphazardly near the entrance, together with one or two battered trucks and Ford saloon cars. This was 1941 and petrol was scarce.

Once through to the platform, all gloom was dispelled by the noise, the excitement and the heat of the seething crowd. The Africans loved the train. They never missed an opportunity to greet its arrival. It was a golden opportunity to barter their produce and exchange news. The men pushed their bikes along the platform with branches of bananas swaying from the handlebars. The women struggled with kikapus (baskets) filled with vegetables and live chickens. Jostling, laughing and shouting, they accosted the bemused traveller leaning out of the train window. Stout Indian women in brilliant saris, smelling of cheap perfume, could generally be seen arguing with the Sikh station master, probably insisting that one ticket was sufficient for all their family; while wide-eyed children gazed in wonder at the big, maroon coaches, each with the Imperial Crown and the letters K.U.R.& H (Kenya and Uganda Railways & Harbours) painted on the side. Bare-foot Askaris (African police), smarter than any English policeman, in their dark blue jerseys with khaki epaulettes and tall, black fezes, attempted to keep some kind of order. Porters threaded their way to the front of the train, their trolleys piled high with duffle-bags full of linen for the first-class passengers. Here, away from the flies and the melée clustered around the third-class coaches, stood small groups of Europeans; the women, cool and elegant in their afternoon dresses; the men, by contrast looking hot and crumpled in their tropical suits and old school ties. A few were in khaki, for two theatres of war were uncomfortably close: the Italians in Abyssinia, and the Japanese threatening the Indian Ocean. Occasionally a pretty young WREN, like my sister, Mary, might be glimpsed boarding the train for the return journey to the coast, after a spell of leave in Nairobi.

Had we been travelling, my younger sister, Helen would have been found settling our dachshunds into the Dog Box. This was a unique feature of the train. It was extremely popular with up-country settlers, but not regarded with the same enthusiasm by the railway staff. Lord Delamere loved to tell the story of how he had on one occasion asked the station master at Nakuru to telegraph Lady Delamere informing her that he would be arriving with their dog and her three puppies. The message she received read: 'The Lord is on the train with a bitch and three sons of a bitch'!

As we moved towards the Chief Justice's coach, did any of us give a thought, I wonder, as to how this railway was constructed, and what the circumstances were that led to its being dubbed 'The Lunatic Express'? The history of this particular railway is the story of how the British Empire felt committed, at the end of the 19th century, to making one last push to set its boundaries still wider, and so acquire its last Colony.

In 1888, William MacKinnon, a Glaswegian shipping magnate, formed the Imperial British East African Shipping Company for the purpose of opening up the country between the East African coast and the Kingdom of Uganda for trade. In doing so, he stumbled on the horrors of the Sultan of Oman's slave trade. It had been going on for centuries. Forays would be made by the coastal Arabs into the heart of Uganda. Here slaves were selected, chained together and, with awful cruelty, marched through extremely hostile terrain to the coast. The survivors of this grim trek were loaded onto dhows and shipped to the Arabian Gulf, where they were sold to the highest bidder.

Back home in England MacKinnon's account of what he had witnessed was greeted with outrage. Thanks to William Wilberforce, slavery was now illegal. The British navy patrolled the oceans of the world, intercepting ships thought to be carrying slaves, setting them free, and arresting the crews. McKinnon addressed meetings up and down the country, giving graphic accounts of what he had seen. His audiences responded with passion: 'Uganda must be saved', they cried. 'This is the time', urged Lord Salisbury, 'for responsible imperialism'. He was also, of course, conscious that other European nations, notably Germany, were seriously engaged in the scramble for Africa. Great Britain was not only anxious not to get left behind, but she also had a vested interest in checking the Germans, who were cunningly and deviously making their way through Uganda to the recently discovered source of the Nile. Just as in Napoleon's day, the British government was wary of anyone wanting to control the Nile, for whoever controlled the Nile, controlled Egypt, and whoever controlled Egypt, threatened India: India, the Jewel in the Imperial Crown! The Empire was therefore, under threat. Action must be taken immediately. A Railway must be built.

To the Victorians, a railway was the answer to almost all political problems. It was their newest toy and they revelled in its construction. In this case it would rule out any armed conflict. After the Indian Mutiny and the Zulu Wars in South Africa, the British were chary of the use of force. A railway 'would be a suitable expression of British humanitarianism' proclaimed Lord Salisbury, and as such would be a powerful deterrent to the slave traders and at the same time would checkmate the Germans. So overcoming the opposition in the country of The Little Englanders, who had scathingly dubbed the train 'The Lunatic Express', the Government embarked on one of the most ambitious feats of engineering ever to be carried out on the Continent of Africa. The year was 1896.

Labour and rolling stock were ordered from India, which is why the currency in Kenya was for many years, the rupee. The gauge too, was Indian, proving to be unfortunate in later years, when attempts to link the East African railway with the South African had to be abandoned because of the disparity in the width of the two tracks. The route chosen followed the one used by the Arabian caravans. Starting in Mombasa, the plan was to approach Uganda through the waste land of what would in time be known as Kenya.

The first hazard they encountered was the Taru desert. For me, Taru was a disappointment. It did not fit my idea of a desert; for though the heat was terrific, there were no rolling sand dunes, just miles and miles of red earth with dust devils playing through the grey-green scrub. When my father travelled through it by car, his white hair would become Titian-red in a matter of moments.

Back in 1896, water was a major problem for the railway construction team. It had to be severely rationed. And then came the drama of the two man-eating lions at Tsavo. Work was brought to a halt for ten months, during which time one hundred and forty members of the labour force were killed. One official, Charles Ryall, met a particularly grisly death. One of the lions broke into his carriage while he was asleep.

With a single blow from his massive paw, he broke the poor man's neck, and then dragged the body out through the window on to the track, where he set about eating it. The situation became so desperate that a worldwide appeal went out for big-game hunters. This was the origin of Kenya's subsequent reputation as a big-game hunter's paradise. It attracted many wealthy Americans, amongst them Theodore Roosevelt. His celebrated safari in 1909 was particularly bloody and today sends shock waves through the ranks of our conservationists. It was Lt-Col Patterson, an engineer on the railway project, who ended the nightmare at Tsavo, by bravely shooting both lions. Once work resumed, the engineers were faced with a climb of 6000 feet on to the Kikuyu Escarpment. Here, on swampy land, a railhead was established. The huddle of shacks and tents erected at this point was the foundation of what would become the capital, Nairobi.

The next step involved a further climb of 2000 feet to the summit of the escarpment. This was achieved with two wood-burning engines; one in front, the other behind. Even in the 1940s, I remember a great deal of shunting and huffing and puffing and whistle blowing at Nairobi Station, in order to get the two engines in place. The busy noise created a sense of anticipation of the difficult task that lay ahead. After this, there was the sharp descent on to the floor of the Great Rift Valley. When crossing this valley, I would gaze with fascination at the sinister bulk of the extinct volcano, Loganot. It appeared to me to be an intrusion in the vast emptiness of the plain. The train seemed to take hours to pass it; and as the sun illuminated its ridges and crevices, it was easy to imagine red-hot lava pouring from its crater.

In May 1900, the weary platelayers made the difficult ascent out of the valley, and up the craggy ravines of the Mau Escarpment. The line was now 9000 feet above sea level, and the temperature frequently fell below zero. Few tribes could endure the cold, so this part of equatorial Africa was almost entirely deserted. However, a few miles further on, at a place called Lumbwa, an advance survey party encountered the first serious opposition to the incursion of the white man and his railway into Africa. The juniper forests, that clothed the surrounding hills, were home to the hardy Nandi tribe. Unlike the Masai, who believed the prophecy about an 'iron snake' bringing prosperity to their country, the Nandi were not only unimpressed by the white man and his 'iron snake', they were also enraged by the Indian work force who, they suspected, were playing fast and loose with their women. To make matters worse, they considered the supplies of telegraph poles and copper wire to be heaven-sent gifts for fashioning weapons and ornaments. Spearmen made continual hit and run raids, forcing the railway committee to call a halt, while they negotiated a peace settlement. The delay was frustrating. The enterprise was tantalisingly close to completion. From this point, they could glimpse the waters of Lake Victoria in the distance.

After some weeks, a truce of sorts was made with the laibon of the tribe and the platelayers could continue the work of laying the track down the west side of the Mau, towards the shore of the lake. The work was painfully slow: not only were the Nandi continuing to harass them, but over half the labour force became ill with malaria and dysentery.

What Elspeth Huxley described as 'the most courageous railway in the world' reached Lake Victoria on 21st December 1901. A smudgy photograph records the little ceremony that marked the event. Florence Preston, the young wife of the chief engineer, is laying the last plate on a bleak, grassy knoll by the lake. Five men and two dogs watch her. They look so quintessentially British under their topees. Mr Preston even carries an umbrella! It had taken them six years to cover 582 miles from the coast. They had constructed 35 viaducts and over 1000 bridges. The cost of this noble folly was 5.5 million pounds; to be paid by the British taxpayer.

And what was this noble folly for? By 1901, the problem of the slave trade was over after the blockade of Zanzibar by the British Navy; also, the Germans no longer posed a threat. They had been happy to forfeit their interest in Uganda in exchange for Heligoland. William

McKinnon's rhetoric was now a thing of the past. Quite simply, the train no longer had a *raison d'etre*. Before digging into their pockets, the British public were in need of an explanation.

Florence Preston drives home the last railway plate

Chapter 2

Birth of a Colony

Desperate to find a way to repay the enormous debt they had incurred, the Government began to look seriously at the country they had inadvertently acquired. Until now, they had considered it to be no more than a corridor through to Uganda. The great plains, stretching into the far distance, though sparsely populated, teemed with game of every kind. Unlike Rhodesia with its copper belt and South Africa with gold, there was nothing worth mining. Maybe agriculture was the answer? What troubled them was, they were not keen to extend the bounds of Empire any further. They had, quite simply, lost the zest for it. Uganda was never colonised. It became a Protectorate. And when, in 1918, after the First World War, Tanganyika (Tanzania) was wrested from the Germans, it became, not a colony, but a Mandated Territory under the League of Nations. The coastal strip was not colonised, but leased from the Sultan of Zanzibar, at his personal request. But, 'needs must when the devil drives', and in Kenya in 1903, the politics of expediency prevailed. What happened next provided the backdrop for the greater part of my parents' lives. The Government advertised for settlers; and in doing so, unwittingly fashioned a rod to beat their own backs with. They stipulated that the settlers must be men and women of courage and resource. They must come and farm the land and so help pay off the debt. Meanwhile a grant-in-aid would be arranged to keep the railway running. My father as a young magistrate from the West of Ireland answered the call of Empire and came in 1909 to help administer the rule of law in this, the last of Great Britain's territorial acquisitions.

If it seems strange to us to-day that people at that time had no qualms about choosing to settle in a country that was not their own, then perhaps an analogy might be drawn with the ethical position of the present American Space Programme. By the year 2030, they hope to have established a launch pad on the Moon in order to put people on Mars. If they discover primitive beings on the red planet, should they proceed with their plan to establish earthlings there? Or should they abandon the plan and leave Mars to the Martians? Central Africa, in the last half of the 19th century and the first decade of the 20th, was what Space is for us today: somewhere to be explored, researched and developed. Livingstone, Stanley, Speke and Burton were the 'astronauts' of their time. Nothing was going to halt the momentum they had generated. And so people did respond to the call to come and cultivate this newly discovered land in the Tropics. It was in this topsy-turvy fashion that the colony of Kenya was born: the settlers who came to give it life, came at the behest of an existing administration. Usually it had been the other way round.

All might have been well had the government had the same enthusiasm as the settlers; but sadly, Kenya was a dependency born out of time. Not only was the enthusiasm for Empire building on the wane, but the government at this time was more concerned with the politics of Europe than with the fate of a fledgling colony on the remote East African coast. Indeed, if it hadn't been for the railway debt, Britain would have been happy to have handed the territory over to anyone – bar the Germans – who would have it. In fact, between 1903-4, a large part of the country was offered to the Finns as a gift. They turned it down. Polish and Russian Jews were also approached, with a promise of self-government. This also came to nothing. Later on the Government thought they might placate the Indian Nationalists by handing the colony over to them as a sort of New World for Hindus. This might indeed have happened, had it not been for the intervention of Lord Delamere. 'Is it for this,' he protested, 'that this expensive railway has been built, and large sums of money spent on the country? Is the British taxpayer content that this beautiful and valuable country be handed over to aliens?' 'Its development' he promised, 'will mean the opening of a new world. Its destinies will influence a whole continent.' But for the towering figures of Lord Delamere and Ewart Grogan, it is doubtful if the colony would have survived as long as it did – a mere sixty years. Their dream for Africa was finally wrecked by an ugly tangle of politics. Churchill, who was for a time Under Secretary of State for the Colonies, took the view that 'the problems of East Africa' were 'the problems of the world'. In other words, it was man's flawed nature that prevented the realisation of what might have been a second Garden of Eden in this incredibly beautiful land.

Chapter 3

The Land Grab

'The British discriminated against [the Africans] at every level, making them outsiders in their own country; but the grievance that touched them most was the land. More than half of Kenya is barren steppe and desert. The British settlers reserved exclusively for themselves the best farmland, the cool green 'White Highlands' on the railway to Uganda.'

This accusation, made by Thomas Pakenham in his book *Scramble for Africa*, is a political untruth which is now accepted as historical fact. If Packenham had checked the facts, he would have discovered that a survey of the distribution of good farmland, made in 1960 by Kenya's Ministry of Agriculture, showed that Africans held approximately 32,3000 square miles of high potential farmland, while the Europeans held 8,460 square miles. In other words, the settlers farmed one fifth of the Highlands, leaving the Africans with four-fifths. The Kavirondo held the richest agricultural land in the country, with a better rainfall than any other part of Kenya. The Kavirondo and Kikuyu together held more fertile land than all of the White Highlands. In addition the grazing held by the Masai and the Nandi was superior to any held by Europeans.

It was not surprising that after nearly sixty years of careful husbandry, the yield from the White Highlands, though from a smaller area, was greater than that from the African sector. The figures for 1958 reveal that the European farms exported £26,300,000 worth of produce while the African exports totalled £5,900,000. It should be remembered that at this time the economy and stability of all races in the colony depended on these exports. They in turn depended on the country's infrastructure, in particular on the railway — the railway which Fenner Brockway, the Socialist M.P. and friend of the African Nationalist Party, scornfully described as 'that Capitalist Serpent in an African Garden of Eden.'

This picture of an African Garden of Eden, coupled with the concept of Africans being made to feel 'outsiders in their own country' presupposes a coherent sense of nationhood in a structured, if primitive society. This may have been the case with the Bushmen in South Africa: but here in Kenya, it was not so. The tribes, sparsely scattered throughout the country, hated, feared and despised each other in varying degrees (a fact which can still be detected in their politics to-day). In 1902 there were, roughly, forty tribes, each with several subdivisions. Unlike Uganda, there was no hierarchical structure, nor a system of hereditary chiefdoms, and the resultant internecine wars were so ferocious that they decimated – and in some cases annihilated – whole sections of neighbouring tribes. These tribes were nomadic. They originated from the north. The true, aboriginal Kenyans were the peace-loving Wa Dorobo people, who lived off roots, wild honey and elephant meat. These pygmy hunters were the sole possessors of the land for centuries until the time came when they were forced to take refuge in the forests from the marauding Masai and the Kikuyu. Eventually they were all but wiped out. Given the belligerent nature of the tribes, it is remarkable that the territory was settled by Europeans with so little bloodshed. Apart from a few skirmishes with the Nandi and Kikuyu (largely over theft of railway property), the Africans welcomed their arrival and expressed no dissatisfaction at the settlements. The resentment over stolen land arose twenty-two years later among a group of politically conscious young Africans. It was an urban concept, born in the beer halls of Nairobi, and nurtured in Moscow – with cataclysmic results.

The Land Commission of 1904 had clear instructions from the government to allow no settlement to 'encroach on native rights or native occupation'. The British had no ambition to dispossess Africans. Nor had they any need to, for large areas of this vast country were uninhabited. There were acres and acres of potentially good agricultural land that had never been cultivated. Famine, drought, disease and endless tribal wars were the causes of depopulation. A recent epidemic of smallpox had taken a further toll of the population, and left the survivors weakened and debilitated. Perhaps it was this that accounted for the lack of hostility toward the Europeans. Or maybe the prophecy made by Mbetian, the great Masai warrior, had something to do with it. As he lay dying, he predicted that 'an iron snake will one day cross the land, bringing prosperity to those who do not oppose it'. As he had also foretold the smallpox epidemic, Mbetian and his prophecies were taken seriously. It was believed that his spirit had found a resting place on one of the snowy peaks of Mt. Kenya – a good vantage point from which to observe how things turned out!

For their part, the British were anxious not to be seen as invaders intent upon conquest. By this date, they had perceived the wisdom of adopting a more liberal, patriarchal role in their colonies, than had previously been the case. Marxist propagandists, however, will not concede that any such policy shift ever took place. They have been intent on discrediting everything to do with the British Empire, by making it synonymous with 'colonial oppression'.

Kenya was perhaps fortunate in not having any mineral wealth. There was no temptation to recruit labour for the mines, as in the copper belt of Rhodesia, and the gold fields in South Africa. This made for a more friendly attitude towards the natives in this new Protectorate. The charming story of the Crawfurds' venture to set up an irrigation system, illustrates the point. Africans had no notion of irrigation; so when the Crawfurd family, who had settled at Molo, decided to dig a furrow to bring water from a nearby forest stream to their farm, the local Kikuyu were mystified. On the opening day, they came to watch. They made quite a ceremony of the occasion. Mr. Crawfurd had to wait while each old man came forward to invoke a blessing on the project. The Crawfurds later described the animated faces of their audience as they chattered and gesticulated with excitement throughout the proceedings. One of the men provided a translation of the speeches from Kikuyu into Swahili, a language the Crawfurds could understand: 'The mzei (the old man) is saying that he is happy to see water coming down from the mountain. He asks God to see that it is good and to help us'. Another asked for 'God to help the bwana, as the bwana helps the Kikuyu'. A third added that he "hoped the bwana will help the Kikuyu to get back their cattle that the Nandi stole; for it is a bad thing that thieves should come to this farm."

As the water started to trickle through, the group 'burst into smiling laughter and congratulations'. It was explained to the Crawfurds that had there been evil spirits around them 'the water would not have flowed'. From then on, Mr Crawfurd was looked upon by the locals in the same light as the Israelites looked on Moses.

Lord Delamere's dealings with the Masai are another example of the rapport that existed between the local tribes and the pioneer settlers. It was said that Delamere preferred the company of the Masai to that of his fellow Europeans. In the evenings, he would invite them in to his hut and sit them down on an old car seat placed by the fire. It was not long before the foetid smell from their bodies, liberally smeared with rancid fat, filled the room. It was no wonder he had few European visitors!

His first encounter with the tribe happened shortly after the arrival of his imported sheep. A group of Masai warriors walked up to his hut at Njoro, and asked to see him. "We have heard", they said, "that a white man has come, who is bringing many sheep and cattle, and that he claims to know better how to herd them than we do. We wish to see". After staying with Dalamere for some days, the spokesman addressed him again: 'Delamere' he said, (the Masai never used the prefix 'bwana'), 'How long will you stay here?'. 'I shall stay forever,' replied Delamere. 'Then we will look after your sheep. You do not understand the pastures. You do not understand the sheep. We will help you.' And so he bought them a hundred umbrellas, to protect them from the sun while minding his sheep.

This burgeoning friendship between the races owed nothing to conquest. It was, sadly, incomprehensible to politicians.

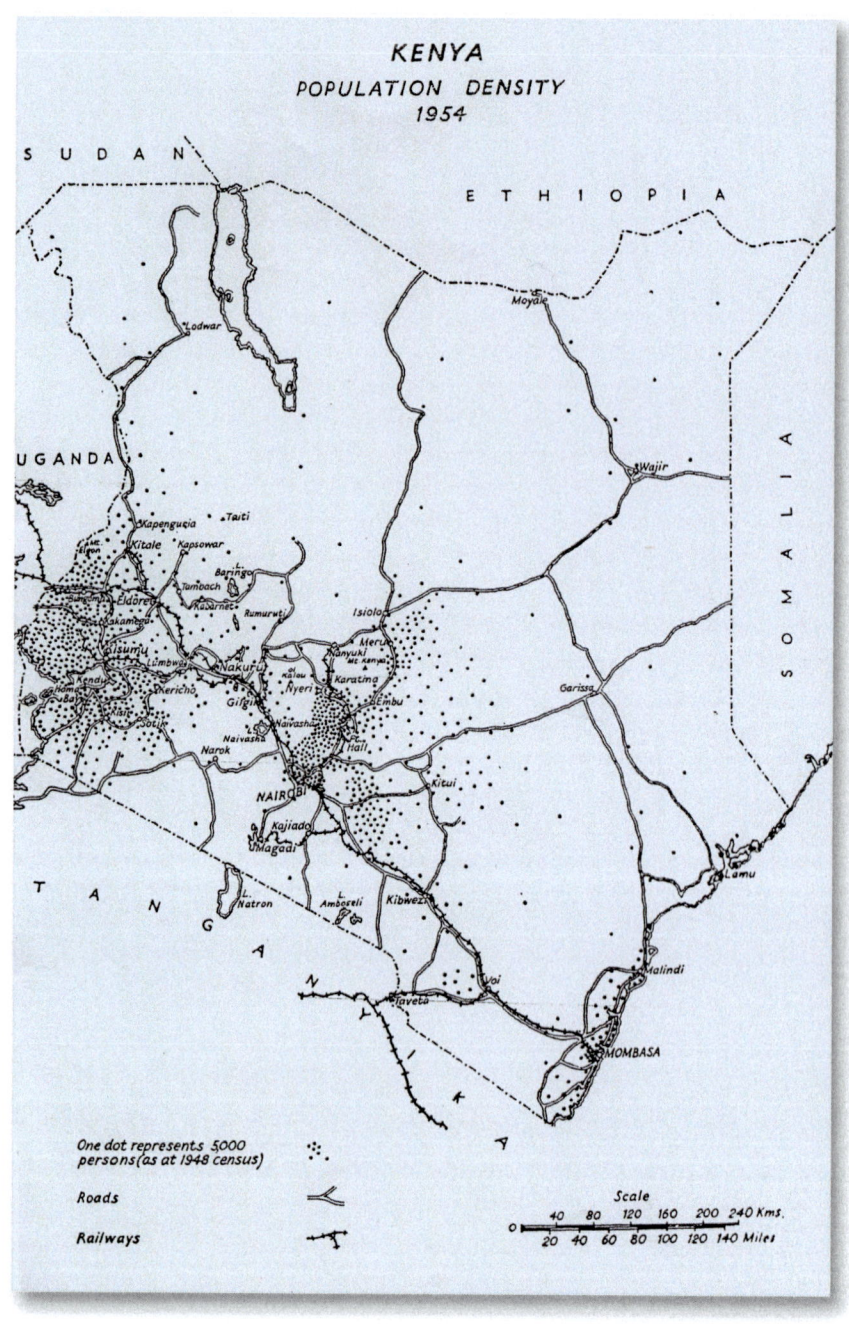

KENYA 1954

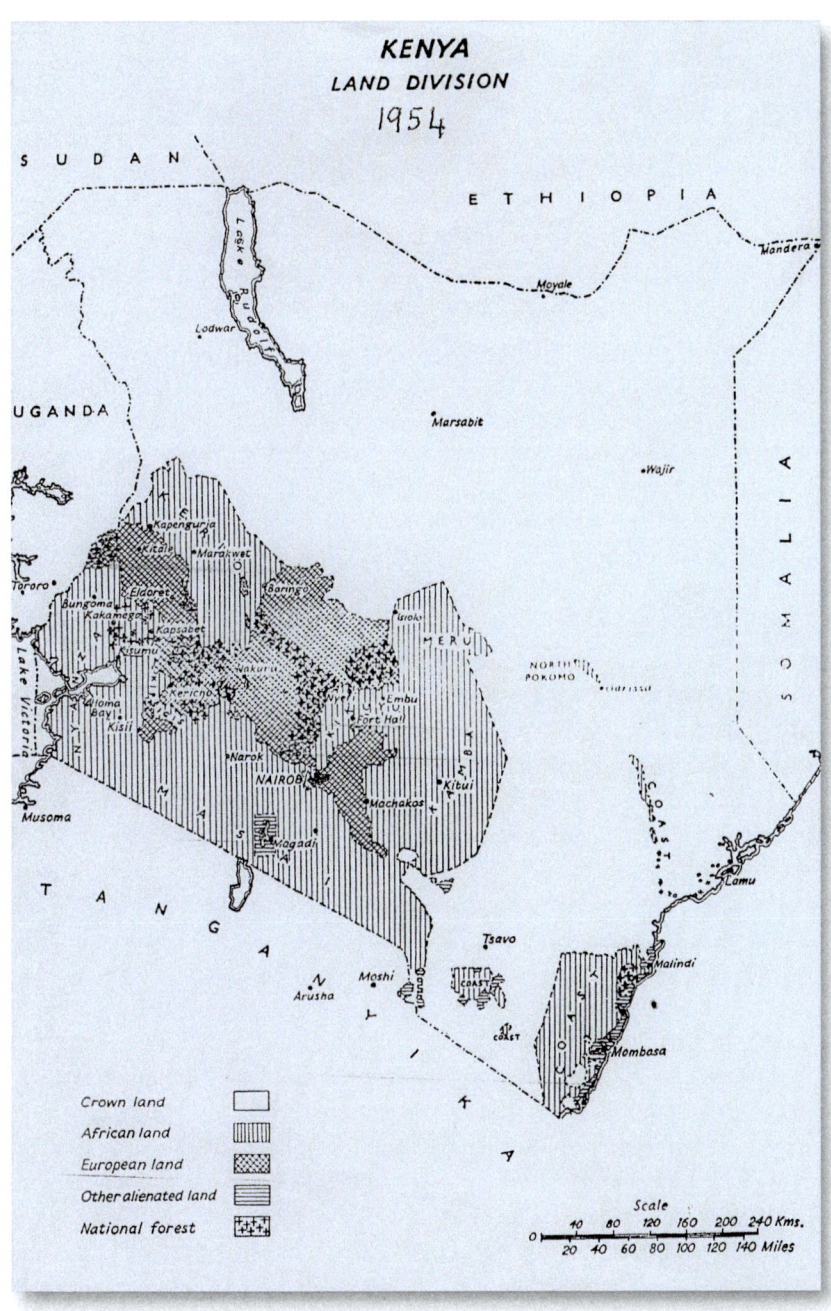

KENYA 1954

Chapter 4

Settling In

It was a wonder anyone answered the call of Empire in 1902, for scientists at that time were convinced that 'white labour under an equatorial sun, no matter how high the elevation, is impossible.' The sun's vertical rays, they declared, would have a damaging effect, not only on the brain, but also the stomach, the liver, the spleen, the heart and indeed the whole nervous system. Nevertheless, despite these dire warnings, a few Icarus-type people were prepared to swap the dank fogs of industrialised Britain for the hazards of equatorial sunshine. They brought yards of red flannel to line their clothes with for sun protection, pith helmets, spine-pads, cummerbunds and double-terai hats – made of two floppy layers of felt – and set sail from Tilbury Docks with little cash, a lot of courage, and only a hazy idea of where they were going. They had been reassured to learn from the Cranworth's manual, The Making of a Colony, that they would suffer no harm from the sun, if they were careful never to remove their hats while out of doors. Should they feel the need to 'adjust them', then they were advised to do this 'in the shade of a thick tree'. If their house was roofed with corrugated iron, - a British invention used extensively throughout the Empire – they were advised not to take off their hats even when they were indoors; for the metal sheets were thought to provide little protection from the ultra-violet rays of the sun. The manual, which was full of helpful hints, stresses the importance of 'keeping the spirits up; the bowels open and flannel next to the skin.'

And so, after a long, hot, sticky voyage, the first trickle of settlers disembarked at Mombasa. Like safari ants, they piled their packing cases onto the train – that political extravagance they had been summoned to subsidise. After twenty-four hours of being jolted along the newly laid track, they arrived at the shantytown of Nairobi. The place swarmed with retired Indian railway workers, who had chosen to remain as traders and shopkeepers, rather than return to India. There were so many tents that the South Africans referred to the place as Tentfontain. A few mud and grass huts on stilts, with wooden steps to the entrance, had been built. They were known as 'rondavels'; a construction the Africans approved of, because there were no corners for evil spirits to lurk in. The largest building, whose shiny, metal roof dominated the town, was the Stanley Hotel – named after the explorer. Although it had been completed, it was unable to open for business, because it had no mattresses. Abraham Block, a resourceful Jewish refugee from Lithuania, had noticed bundles of dry grass along the railway track. He gathered these up, and with some ticking from the Indian bazaar, and the help of a Goanese tailor, he was able to supply the hotel with as many of these grass-filled mattresses as they required. They used sharpened bicycle spokes for sewing-needles.

The profits from the sale of the mattresses, together with a small loan, enabled Abraham Block to buy a 600-acre farm. Without a plough, however, the farm was useless. Never daunted, he sold his pony, and walked a distance of eighty-five miles to purchase a homemade plough from a friend, together with six native oxen. Now he was able to set about breaking his patch of virgin soil in the Kenya Highlands. A few years later, by pawning his watch and gold chain, he was able to buy a plot of land in the centre of Nairobi. He kept it for twenty-three years, by which time it had become a valuable piece of real estate.

He decided to exchange it for the ownership of the colony's famous Norfolk Hotel. This was the foundation of his chain of internationally acclaimed hotels and game lodges. In 1941 I was a guest at his daughter's birthday party. I remember their house in Muthaiga being solemn and opulent with plenty of corners for evil spirits to lurk in. There were gilt mirrors, large pieces of dark furniture, and lots of richly patterned rugs. His daughter, Judith, was a biblical beauty with coils of lustrous, black hair. It was not only her looks that set her apart; her white dress edged with a keystone pattern in gold leather made the rest of us feel very frumpish and poor.

Having arrived in Nairobi, the pioneer settler was from this point on, enmeshed in red tape. Nothing could be done without government approval. No timber could be felled. No matter how much crop damage the animals might cause, they could not be shot. To obtain a gun licence was, for a settler, both expensive and difficult; whereas for a government official it was comparatively easy. No labour could be engaged except on government terms. The first seeds to be sown in this fledgling colony were the bitter seeds of resentment. Understandably, the settlers objected to being told what to do and how to do it by civil servants living over six thousand miles away, people, who, after all, had no notion of local conditions or of the hazards involved. From the outset the settlers found themselves on a collision course with the government.

It is said that politicians have short memories. This was certainly true in the case of Kenya. It was soon conveniently forgotten that there was any obligation owed to the settlers. The Foreign Office – which preceded the Colonial Office – chose not to remember that these people were there by invitation. As Charles Elliot, the first Commissioner, pointed out in his letter of resignation to the government: 'You don't invite people to dinner, and then lock the dining-room door.' They had been asked to come and risk their lives and sink their capital in the task of cultivating a dangerous, unknown land, in order to provide an economic base on which to run the railway. The settlers had been happy to accept the challenge.

What had been overlooked was the fact that the settlers, as their name implies, came to 'settle'. They came planning to live and die in their newly adopted country. They understood that their farms would be theirs for life, and their childrens' thereafter. The second generation would love the country as its own, for it would have known no other. These pioneers were not 'Planters'. Planters came to make their fortune and then retire to the country of their birth. They had little interest in the future of the place where they acquired their wealth. Officials, too, with the security of a salaried job and a pension for their old age, looked forward to retirement back in England. The government official was also alert to the possibility of promotion, which could entail serving in some other part of the Empire. His affiliation to the country he served in was, therefore, bound to be slight. Planters and officials could be described as the 'expats' of their day. Settlers, by contrast, arrived with packing cases that contained, not only tin mugs, camp beds, and kerosene lamps, but also silver vases, coalport coffee cups, walnut tables, family portraits and other treasured heirlooms. They had come to stay; to build a new country, where an offshoot of European culture would, given time, take root. If only Whitehall had shown some sensitivity in their dealings with these 'adventurers and dreamers', if only the Civil Service back in foggy London had trusted them more, then the friction which was to tear the colony apart, might have been avoided.

Chapter 5

Taming the Wilderness

By 1913 the settlers' dream of making Kenya prosperous was realised. The railway debt had been paid off and the country was self-supporting. Rows of glossy-leaved coffee bushes grew on what had been barren land; the rivers were stocked with trout from Loch Leven in Scotland; the Masai ewes had been crossed with Australian rams, resulting in flocks of sheep producing a fine, merino wool; dairy herds had been built up by crossing the native Boran cattle with English shorthorn bulls; there was a flour mill that exported flour to the other East African territories; and the verandas of the farmhouses overlooked lawns bordered with heavily scented flowers – roses, lilies, frangipani, bougainvillea and flame-coloured cannas all jostled with each other for a place in the equatorial sunshine.

The labour crises had been resolved. Africans came with their families and stayed on the farms for six months of the year. They worked under the direction of the Europeans, and were given in exchange free housing, food, blankets, a schoolhouse and money to pay their hut tax. They had a lively interest in, and a respect for, not only King George, but for all that the white man stood for: it was this respect that was the key to the settlers' authority. For the second part of the year, the labourer could, if he wished, return to his own 'shamba', where, it was hoped, he would put into practice some of the new farming methods he had learnt. It was not a bad life when compared with his English counterpart of that time. Why should it have been considered reprehensible to employ black labour, and yet praiseworthy to give employment to an Essex farmhand?

All this had been achieved in under ten years: a measure of the grit of these pioneer settlers and their determination to succeed, especially when one considers what they had to contend with back in those early days. They had set out from the swamps of Nairobi in 1904, in a spirit of hope and ambition; their open wagons loaded with the packing cases they had brought from England and the impedimenta they had bought from the Indian traders in Nairobi. Tin baths, tailor's dummies, rolls of barbed wire, lavatory seats and of course, boxes of provisions, all wobbled unsteadily on top of the rest of their luggage. The wagons were pulled by small native oxen. As they could not manage more than fifteen miles a day, there were frequent stops. The women must have suffered acutely in their stays and red flannel petticoats. There were no roads, only corrugated cart tracks. As they travelled they were tormented by flies, heat and the all-pervasive dust.

When at last they found their plot of land, the settlers' disappointment must have been profound. The roughly drawn maps, which had been issued by the Land Office in Nairobi, were wildly inaccurate. Most of the angle-irons used to mark the boundaries had been removed by wild animals. Where they had expected to find flowing streams, there were only dried-up watercourses. An expanse of brown spiky grass harbouring snakes and jiggas stretched as far as the eye could see. Pyramids of anthills peppered the ground between the knotted thorn trees. As they climbed stiffly down from their wagons and stood in the quivering heat, they must have been acutely aware of the thousands of miles that separated them from their friends and the civilisation of Europe. The 'da-tooo-ra' call of the Go Away Bird was all that broke the silence. At that point, the idea of creating a farm under the vastness of the African sky, a farm, moreover, on which their livelihoods would depend, must have seemed ludicrous. They were, after all, mere specks on this immense landscape.

The settlers' first problem had been labour. No matter what Kenyatta would later claim, it is a fact that Africans were never, at any time in the history of colonial East Africa, forced to work for private European employers. Imagination and ingenuity were the weapons used to entice labour on to the farm. Elspeth Huxley's parents, Robin and Nelly Grant, first tried music. On their old wind-up gramophone, they played 'The Bluebells of Scotland' over and over again, but to no avail. Another badly scratched record of 'The Lost Chord' was equally unsuccessful. It was the storm-lantern that eventually did the trick. One evening, there they were; just a handful of them, standing in the shadows, beyond the light thrown by the camp fire; their ochred ropes of hair just visible against the darkness of the forest. They carried spears, and wore short cloaks of animal skins.

On their arms and round their necks they wore amulets of coiled wire and beads. When they spoke, their voices were soft and mellifluous. Juma, the Grants' Swahili servant from the coast, acted as interpreter. 'They want to know', said Juma 'if this light is a piece of a star that has fallen from the sky.' On Robin's instructions, Juma took the lantern from its pole and carried it over for them to have a closer look. This caused panic. Like frightened antelope they bolted into the night. However, they returned the following evening in greater numbers. This time they were prepared to examine the lantern. Robin told Juma to tell them that he would give them a lantern like this one, if they would come and help him clear the bush. They weren't tempted. The lamp had a spirit in the glass; a spirit that would clearly obey only Europeans. 'Tell them', said an exasperated Robin, 'that the flame is not a spirit. Tell them it works on paraffin'. Poor Juma was now in some difficulty. There was no word in either Swahili or Kikuyu for 'paraffin'. The closest he could get to it was 'European fat'. Understandably, the Kikuyu now thought they were dealing with cannibals. In desperation, Robin told them they could take the lantern away. When its 'food' was finished they must bring it back and he would give it more. But it was no good. They left the lantern on the ground and retreated into the darkness.

The following morning, however, the Grants discovered that they had taken the lantern after all; and a few days later they were back, this time in daylight. Being hospitable, Robin and Nelly felt they should offer them a drink. Juma suggested beer; but there wasn't any. Nelly brought out the soda-water siphon, and filled some tin mugs with soda water. This caused a sensation. They studied the water carefully for some time, and then decided it was possessed by an angry spirit and the best course of action was to pour it slowly and reverently on to the ground. Again, Robin asked for their help in clearing the bush. This time, after lengthy negotiations, it was agreed that the village would receive one goat for every ten men who came and worked for a period of one month. The warriors then took their leave. To the Grant's dismay, they took the tin mugs with them, leaving Robin and Nelly nothing to drink from but their precious goblets of Waterford glass.

Having solved their labour problems, the pioneers then had to turn their attention to the business of ploughing. Ploughs were few and far between. Lord Delamere resorted to adapting an abandoned railway engine. Even after obtaining a plough, things were far from straightforward. The native oxen had to be introduced to the strangeness of the restrictive yoke. They bucked and cavorted and were wellnigh impossible to control.

The trick was to climb a tree holding on to the yoke, and then persuade a farm hand to drive the animal under the branch you were sitting on. At the right moment, you dropped the yoke over the beast's neck and, hey presto! – it was ready for the plough – you hoped!

The crops, once sown, were prey to a bewildering number of unfamiliar diseases. Wheat, in particular, succumbed to every kind of rust. Plagues of locusts could ravage a promising crop in a matter of hours. The rains proved fickle. They might fail altogether, or become torrential, sweeping away tender young seedlings in floodwaters. Karen Blixen felt at times that they were 'involved in a labour of fools'; and Mariella Ricardi, on discovering that their coffee crop had been wiped out after two months of incessant rain, concluded that it would be best if 'we bow our heads to Africa and gracefully retreat.' This is, indeed, what might have happened, had it not been for the inspiration and leadership of Hugh Delamere and Ewart Grogan.

Chapter 6

Grogan and Delamere

Hugh Delamere and Ewart Grogan, one an Etonian, the other a Wykhamist, were the founding fathers of the colony. With their patrician looks and passionate spirit of imperialism, they might have stepped out of the pages of a Rider Haggard novel. They should have been the best of friends, for they had a lot in common; but their colossal egos and fiercely competitive natures stood in the way. Their outlook on life was similar: all challenges must be overcome. The challenge of the day was, not as at present, to spread 'Democracy & Freedom' throughout the world, but 'Commerce & Civilisation'. As Kenya settlers, this is what they devoted their lives' energies to. Petty bureaucracy was their bete noir, exemplified by those civil servants described by Kipling as 'little men who feared to be great'.

As a Cambridge undergraduate, Grogan looked on his tutor as one of these 'little men'. He demonstrated his scorn by locking a sheep into the poor fellow's rooms, with disastrous results. Not surprisingly, he was subsequently sent down. Similarly, Delamere's academic career was brought to an abrupt end. During an argument with an Eton shopkeeper, his fiery temper got the better of him and he threw the contents of the shop into the high street.

These adolescent incidents of unacceptable behaviour were evidence of deeply embedded traits that marked them out as rebels and natural leaders of men. It was Delamere who, in 1908, led a settlers' revolt against the government's labour laws. He marched into Government House at the head of a group of disgruntled farmers and demanded the Governor's resignation unless their grievances were heard. Their grievances were heard, and the Governor, Sir Hayes Sadler, known as Old Flannelfoot, was posted to The Windward Isles.

One of Ewart Grogan's most spectacular brushes with authority was caused by a sloppily worded Mining Ordinance. 'Earth' was classified as a mineral, necessitating a licence before any digging operation could commence. Incensed, Grogan pegged out 400 acres in the centre of

Nairobi and then applied to the sub-commissioner's office for a licence to excavate for 'earth'. William Hobley, nicknamed Hobley Bobley for his habit of issuing confusing orders, was forced to re-word the offending clause.

Of the two, Grogan had the better grasp of finance. Delamere was inclined to regard economics as vulgar. He was a gambler by nature, once losing three thousand pounds on a single bet at Chester races. They were both profligate and came close to bankruptcy through the funding of their colonial enterprises. Coincidentally, they both acquired their knowledge of sheep farming in Australia, knowledge that was later to prove invaluable in Kenya. But it was their oratory, their wit and their astonishing powers of endurance which were to make them formidable adversaries of the Colonial Office. Their respective stories of how Africa entered their bloodstream make tales of high adventure, experiences that would bind them to Africa forever, but from which they would emerge physically scarred for life with chronic illnesses.

Delamere

Hugh Cholmondely was born in 1870. His father, the second Baron Delamere, was well into his sixties at the time. He was therefore still in his teens when he inherited the baronetcy. He was not rich, given the obligations of Vale Royal, the family estate in Cheshire. Hunting was his passion. As a boy, he dreamt of becoming a Big Game Hunter, but he had to wait until he reached his majority before realising his dream. Meanwhile, bored with county society, he left for Australia to study sheep farming. Once he reached the age of twenty-one, he lost no time in planning his first Big Game hunting expedition. He chose Somalia because it was less well known than South Africa, and therefore would be more exciting. Unfortunately, he discovered that the African sun made him ill. Undeterred, he ordered an unusually large topee. This oversized pith helmet, covering his long red hair, which he wore in a pigtail, became his distinguishing feature.

Protected by the giant topee, he returned to Somalia year after year, spending far more money than he could afford. On his third expedition, he was saved by his Somali gunbearer from being badly mauled by a lion. Abdullah, the gunbearer, managed to grasp the lion's mane, and then, unbelievably, he attempted to seize the animal's tongue, thus distracting the lion long enough for Delamere to reach for his gun and shoot it; but not before it had savaged one of his ankles. In order to prevent the poison from spreading up his leg, he lay motionless beside the dead lion. Twice he managed to lance the wound with his penknife to let the poison drain. They were rescued five days later by a caravan of Arabs and taken to a hospital in Berbera, where their wounds were dressed. For the rest of his life, Delamere walked with a limp and had to wear a built up boot.

On his last expedition in 1897, he strayed across the Abyssinian border into Kenya and saw the Highlands for the first time, their beauty made more intense after the months he had spent in the arid scrubland of Somalia. He was quick to recognise their potential for sheep farming and he vowed to return the following year to explore further. On the second visit in 1898, he trekked across the Laikipia plateau, down to Naivasha and over to the far side of the Leroki mountains without seeing any sign of life. At Njoro, he came across the Samburu tribe. They were so excited at seeing a white man, they named the spring near the place he had camped 'Delamere', They were not surprised when he indicated to them that one day he would return to stay, for they had a saying 'He who has tasted honey will return to the honey pot'!

Back in England, however, Fate intervened. He suffered a serious hunting accident and had to spend six long months on his back. His doctors warned him that a second fall would probably prove fatal and that he should give up hunting. While recovering, he studied and read a great deal and became an ardent admirer of Cecil Rhodes. His second fall when it came, was of a gentler nature. He fell in love with Frances Cole, the 21 year old daughter of the Earl of Enniskillen. After their marriage, anxious to share with her his vision of the Kenya Highlands, he arranged a trip out there to collect birds for The British Museum. Soon after they arrived, accident-prone as ever, he contracted malaria. It was four months before he was well enough for them to travel back to England. Nevertheless, despite his illness, they were determined to make their home in Kenya. With this in mind, they found an agent for Vale Royal, said goodbye to England and sailed from Tilbury docks for East Africa. The year was 1903.

Nemesis, however, struck once again. They had been back in Kenya no more than a few weeks when he had another fall while out hunting on the Athi plains. This time he spent a year in plaster, lying on his back in a grass hut in Nairobi, nursed by Frances. His health was so poor he was not expected to live for more than a few years. Consequently, when he applied for land, he was given preferential treatment. He was permitted to lease 10,000 acres on the Laikipia plateau. Before long he was buying yet more land from settlers who had lost heart and were returning home.

Delamere never lost heart. His powers of endurance over physical suffering were replicated in his farming, where he experienced catastrophic setbacks. Failure, was merely the spur to borrow more money; adopt new methods; try a new crop. He worked tirelessly, from dawn to dusk, never sparing himself. He came to realise that only through scientific research could he hope to win his battle with the soil and climate of Kenya. He therefore engaged a professor of botany from Cambridge University, and together they set up a mini field laboratory. Before long his crop experimentation began to yield positive results. He succeeded in breeding a strain of wheat resistant to all three types of rust fungus prevalent in East Africa. The methods he used are still considered to be noteworthy examples of successful plant cross-fertilisation. It is true to say that the wheat grown in Kenya today originates from Delamere's experimentation, hard work and determination to succeed. It was the same with livestock: he learnt the hard way, through trial and error. It was only after he lost 1.500 head of imported cattle and 500 merino ewes to East Coast fever that he realised he must inoculate the animals before importing them, rather than after. Among his many other achievements was the elaborate system of irrigation that he devised to run between his farms. It stretched for twenty miles and supplied 67,000 gallons of water per day.

All of this cost a great deal of money. To pay for it Vale Royal was mortgaged and eventually sold. He also borrowed heavily from the local banks who were notorious for their high rates of interest. In spite of all, he was a happy man, living a life of Spartan simplicity with Frances in their conglomeration of grass huts. The Masai were their friends, and the physical beauty of Africa their constant joy. They were content, too, in the knowledge that they were proving to the government and to their fellow settlers the agricultural potential of the country.

Grogan

Ewart Grogan, like Delamere, came from an influential family. His father had been Surveyor General to the Royal Household, and Gladstone was his godfather. Both of them used their privileged status to campaign tirelessly on behalf of the settlers. The Colonial Office had a particularly hard time in its dealings with Grogan. He has been described as 'a charmer, a cynic, a swashbuckler, a buccaneer born out of time'. He was also a realist. He distanced himself from Delamere's vision of white supremacy and dominion status. He envisaged, rather, the eventual creation of an African State, based on British institutions. The Government in Whitehall never understood his ideas for 'constructive colonialism'.

His impact on the country cannot be exaggerated. He constructed the first deep water port at Mombasa. He was the founder of the timber trade. He built the first childrens' hospital. He built an Agricultural Training College, which he offered to the Government, and for which he never even received a reply or acknowledgement. It was he who stocked the rivers with trout, and who built Torrs, the first luxury hotel. He was also instrumental in the building of Muthaiga, the exclusive settlers' club. But his greatest achievement was the creation of the Taveta Estate, on the border of Kenya with Tanzania.

In *Scramble for Africa*, Thomas Pakenham points out that 'more than half of Kenya is barren steppe and desert'. Taveta, between the Teita hills and the slopes of Mount Kilimanjoro, was just such a place. The Wataveta tribe, who lived there, were pathetically few in number, and so weak from disease and starvation that an official report in 1930 described them as being 'incapable of sustained labour because of their poor state of health and diet'. The report went on to say that 'it was doubtful if anything could be done to help them'. When Grogan applied for a lease of 30,000 acres of this dusty plain, he was considered to be out of his mind. Hydrology had always been a passion of his, and after studying the topography of the land, he was convinced that there was water beneath the volcanic dust bowl of the area. He was right. When they bored 20 feet below the surface the hydrologists discovered underground streams capable of yielding 100,000 gallons of water per day. The cost of the operation was enormous, but it was money well invested. Ignoring the gloom of the Great Depression, he planted hundreds of sisal plants. After coffee, sisal was Kenya's largest export. It was talked of as 'the White Gold' of the economy. In a short while, Taveta became the centre of the Colony's sisal industry. The effect on the local population was dramatic. He soon had two sisal factories in operation and 87,000 acres in production. He employed over two thousand Africans.

They were provided with stone built houses, canteens and a welfare centre. By comparison, his own house and the accommodation for the European managers was austere and basic. He let it be known that he did not want what he termed 'veranda farmers', but hard workers.

As well as sisal, the region produced cotton, beans, maize, grew bananas, sugar cane, citrus trees and potatoes for their own consumption. When the railway station was reopened, it was recognised by all that Colonel Ewart Grogan had really made the desert bloom. In the opinion of the present owner of the Taveta Estate, Grogan was never given full credit for this amazing development. He added 'What is our dream, was his reality in 1930'; which is a sad reflection on the state of affairs to-day, in post colonial Africa, and a tantalising reminder of what might have been in the rest of the barren steppes of Kenya, if the British Empire had not collapsed.

It is a strange thing, that in spite of all he achieved, Grogan's name, unlike Delamere's, has virtually dropped out of history. He was certainly a controversial figure. Elspeth Huxley loathed him. My mother, on the other hand, always spoke fondly of him. Like many women, she was, I suspect disarmed by his good looks, his intellect and his undoubted charm. My sister, Mary, lunched with him in Muthaiga Club, in the 1950s, when he was well into his old age. She found his penetrating blue eyes still held a twinkle.

His unpopularity was due in part to the scandals that surrounded his private life. He fathered three separate families, without any of them suspecting the existence of the others. Nevertheless, the love of his life was his beloved Gertrude. He was devastated when she died. They had met when, as a footloose young man, he had been visiting New Zealand with a friend. She was immensely rich: the heiress of a substantial fortune. His future father-in-law told him that he could not possibly think of marrying Gertrude, until he had proved himself to be 'a somebody'. This was the spur that led him to undertake his famed Cape to Cairo trek. No-one had attempted it before. It took him three years..

Throughout the arduous trip, he suffered, not only from recurrent bouts of malaria, but also from a painful liver abscess – a battlescar from his previous African adventures with Cecil Rhodes, which would plague him for the rest of his life. However, just as with Delamere, illness seemed to galvanize him into yet more activity and adventure. His defiance in the face of physical weakness enabled him to live to the grand old age of ninety-two.

After his celebrated walk, he claimed the hand of his bride and in 1904 they made their home in Kenya. Through a Canadian friend he had obtained a concession to export timber from the heavily forested Londiani area. And so began his long, passionate affair with the Empire's youngest colony.

Chapter 7

Law and Order

The economic success of the colony depended on the establishment of law and order. Without it, all the hard work and innovative farming methods of the settlers would have foundered. At that time, the British system of justice was respected throughout the world. It is what underpinned the Empire. To this day, the success of the City of London as one of the major financial centres of the world is due largely, to the fairness of its legal system.

The self-confidence of the empire builders in East Africa can be measured by the unhesitating manner in which they set about imposing the complexities of this system on a people accustomed to settling their disputes by consulting witch doctors whose judgement rested on the disposition of chicken bones. Their confidence was not misplaced. British law came to be held in high regard. It was seen to be fair, just and incorruptible. It took no account of race or colour. The father of a school friend of mine was, rightly, imprisoned for beating one of his farm labourers. Even the prestigious Ewart Grogan served a term of imprisonment for publicly whipping three rickshaw drivers, who, he maintained, had insulted his wife.

From 1934 to 1945, my father, as Chief Justice and President of the Court of Appeal, was responsible for seeing that the rule of law was upheld without fear or favour, throughout the territories of British East Africa. Before this, he had been, from 1929 to 1934, Chief Justice of Tanganyika, [Tanzania]: a territory mandated from the League of Nations, which had been in the possession of Germany before the First World War. The immensity of his task in this area is difficult to appreciate today. Tanganyika covered 365,000 square miles. Travel involved journeying over what were euphemistically described as 'dry weather roads'. The difficult terrain of the Northern Province was largely uncharted. Lake Tanganyika could be crossed only once a fortnight, in an unreliable boat; malaria and blackwater fever were rife; and the climate was hot, humid and prone to torrential rain. My father administered this enormous territory with just three judges.

Inevitably there were delays in cases being heard and brought to appeal. A commission of enquiry was sent out from London to see if things could be improved. The commissioners' solution was decentralisation. As a witness to the commission, my father robustly dismissed their proposal. Decentralisation would, he pointed out, weaken the authority of the High Court in the capital, Dar es Salaam. He insisted that the native African – who he was fond of referring to as 'the average person'– had the right to have his appeal heard by the highest court in the land, as near as possible to 'the scene of action'. In other words, in his opinion, the Appeal Court in Dar es Salaam must travel to the people. It must continue to circuit the country, and 'every effort, humanly speaking, should be made for the convenience of witnesses in regard to the journeys they would be required to make'. He spoke with sufficient authority for the Commission to abandon their plans for decentralisation, and instead to ease the workload of the Chief Justice by appointing two more judges.

And so five times a year, Tanganyika continued to be circuited. Silk robes, wigs and patent leather pumps were packed into tin trunks, along with a lavish sprinkling of mothballs against white ants. A cavalcade of stiffly upright Ford cars would set out from Dar es Salaam for strategically placed court houses where resident magistrates, district commissioners and tribal chiefs were stationed. At each place, on the opening day of the court, a guard of honour formed by the police would be drawn up for inspection by the Chief Justice. The precision of the drill of these proud African police would not have looked out of place on Horse Guards Parade. During the inspection, the police band added to the pomp and ceremony of the occasion. It was in this manner that His Majesty's Imperial Government kept the peace and administered the law in my father's time.

The importance of my father's role in Tanganyika was brought home to me by the present of a charming little parasol. Presents were generally reserved for birthdays. Seeing my astonished delight at receiving such an unexpected gift, my mother explained that there was to be a big ceremony when my father would become a 'Bwana Mcubwa' (an Important Person). As everyone wanted to see the new Chief Justice, the swearing in ceremony was to be held in the open and I would stand beside him on the platform. The parasol would not only look pretty, it would also protect me from the sun. However, my parents had reckoned without Nanny. My father might have jurisdiction over the Territory, but in the nursery, Nanny reigned supreme. Words were tossed to and fro between the adults. 'She is far too young. The heat will be too much for her. I won't hear of it.' And that was that. The parasol was put on the top shelf of the toy cupboard, along with other forbidden toys, 'out of harm's way'.

Preparations for the big day gathered momentum. Would my father's red silk robes arrive in time? Or, horror of horrors, would he have to make do with his judge's black silk? When they eventually arrived there was the exciting rustle of layers of tissue paper, as they were carefully unpacked from their black tin trunk. My father looked splendid in them; the very embodiment of British justice. My mother, however, was critical. She was convinced the robes were too short. On this occasion, she was overruled. The black silk hose and patent leather pumps had to be visible beneath the folds of scarlet. There was also – perish the thought – the hazard of His Lordship tripping over the silk. The full-bottomed wig had been packed separately in a circular tin box, which, when opened released a strong smell of camphor. My mother gently shook out the tight grey ripples of horsehair, and settled it comfortably on my father's head, arranging the long wide flaps over his shoulders. Under this awesome headgear, his black bushy eyebrows took on an air of stern authority, mercifully at odds with the laughter in his eyes. For once, Nanny was impressed. She stood in respectful silence before this tall, imposing representative of His Britannic Majesty's Rule of Law.

When they returned, flushed with excitement from the long ceremony, they explained that they would now be known as Sir Joseph and Lady Sheridan. I took this to mean that the plaster statues of St. Joseph and Our Lady in their bedroom were likenesses of them. Then there was the picture of St. Therese of the Little Flower of Jesus. Perhaps that was me? Could it be that we had been elevated to the rank of the Holy Family? I don't think I went as far as to consider that Helen might be the baby Jesus, despite the fact that she was referred to with some devotion as 'Baby'. It was disconcerting, though, the way people fell about with laughter when I tried to discuss these muddled matters.

Chapter 8

How the British came to colonise the East Coast of Africa

In contrast to the interior of Africa, the history of the coastal regions of East Africa stretches back in time over many centuries. Because of the monsoon winds the East African coast enjoyed a flourishing trade with the countries bordering the Eastern Mediterranean, a trade which was unknown to Europe for five thousand years. In Chapter 9 of the Book of Kings we read that King Solomon built ships 'on the shore of the Red Sea', and that his admiral, Hiram, 'sent his men, who knew the sea, to serve in the fleet. They sailed to Ophir (Mozambique) and brought back four hundred and twenty talents of gold, which they dedicated to Solomon'. And again in Chapter 10 we read that 'Hiram's ships brought gold from Ophir; and from there they brought great cargoes of almugwood and precious stones. The king used the almugwood to make supports for the temple of the Lord and for the royal palace and to make harps and lyres for the musicians. So much almugwood has never been imported or seen since that day'.

It was the Persians who became the first colonists of this African coast. They arrived from the Gulf in the 7th century, fleeing from the war that had broken out between the Shias and the Sunnis after the death of Mohammed in 623 AD. They sailed down the coast in their dhows, establishing settlements in Mogadishu, Kilwa, Mombasa, Pemba, Zanzibar, and Dar es Salaam. These places were well known to them. They had after all been trading along this coast since the time of Solomon. These settlers brought with them all the skill of the trader. They cultivated the land, harvested the sea and exported their produce at realistic prices. With their hard-earned wealth they built themselves magnificent mansions of coral and limestone. Arched porticos led into courtyards planted with jasmine and roses. Their rooms were panelled with rosewood and inlaid with ivory. They ate with silver cutlery and rinsed their hands in gold fingerbowls encrusted with emeralds. One gourmet traveller in the 14th century listed the number of mouth-watering dishes he was offered. He noted that these delicacies were eaten by everyone, not just the rich. As a result he observed, 'the people of Mogadishu were very fat and corpulent'. They covered their obesity with robes of embroidered silk. Silver daggers with jewelled hilts protruded from the sashes encircling their immense girth, and their heads were swathed in tall, complicated turbans of rich damask. Islam, the religion that they had introduced to the indigenous population, had spread not by coercion but through intermarriage. Intermarriage was also responsible for the birth of the polyglot language of Swahili – the language which would in time, become the lingua franca of East Africa.

The trade winds, responsible for bringing so much wealth to the east coast of Africa, were not discovered by the Europeans until the fifteenth century when Vasco da Gama made his voyage to the East. He was quick to realise their potential. These ports, he knew, would be of vital interest to Portuguese ships en route to India. He alerted the king of Portugal to their whereabouts. And so began the first European incursion into East Africa.

Not surprisingly, the comfort-loving inhabitants of these coastal states were a pushover for the conquering Portuguese. They surrendered with hardly a fight. Their luxurious life-style was brought to an end with shocking brutality. It is a measure of the hatred that the invaders engendered that barely a trace of the Portuguese occupation is to be found today, in either the language or the culture of the coast. The exception is the fortress that dominates the entrance to the old harbour in Mombasa. In the Arabs' struggle for independence it had changed hands like a baton in a relay race. Despite having witnessed many appalling acts of violence, it has kept its original name of Fort Jesus. Today I believe it is a museum. When I knew it in the 1940s it was an unloved ruin: its ochre walls, covered with Arabic graffiti, smelt of urine. Its nearest neighbour, on the rocky promontory overlooking Kilifi Creek, was the Mombasa Sports Club, where the British came to relax in the cool evening breeze and enjoy their 'sundowners' while exchanging news and gossip.

It was the Sultan of Oman who successfully ousted the Portuguese. He took control of the territories at the beginning of the eighteenth century. Before the century was out, a European presence would again make itself felt in the Indian Ocean. This was at the time of the Napoleonic Wars. In 1799 the French landed in Egypt, threatening India – the jewel in Great Britain's imperial crown. Napoleon planned to invade Oman with the idea of 'kicking down India's back door, and wresting India from the British'. But the British outmanoeuvred the French. Using diplomacy rather than force, they concluded a treaty with the Sultan. In exchange for British protection the Sultan agreed not to allow French troops on his soil, or their ships in the Gulf. He agreed also to a British garrison being built at Bandar Abbas – a port at the entrance to the Persian Gulf. Furthermore, a British agent was to be posted to Muscat. It was stipulated that he had to be 'an English gentleman of respectability'. Oman and its territories and coastal settlements, including Mombasa, Zanzibar and Kilwa, had now become British protectorates in all but name.

Soon there would be another reason for Britain to stage a presence in the Indian Ocean. After her conversion from being a slave-trading nation, she became dedicated to stamping out this practice throughout the world. No nation was better equipped for the task, for after Trafalgar Britain really did rule the oceans of the world. One of the busiest slave-trading routes was that used by the Arabs. Their dhows used the kusi and the kaskasi trade winds to sail up and down the East African coast. The British navy became fully engaged in hunting them down, arresting the crews and setting the slaves free. Empire building was not on the agenda. Whatever the sentiments of Elgar's 'Land of Hope and Glory', the Government at that time felt it had enough on its plate without setting the bounds of Empire any wider.

But in 1823 something happened which tested the British government's foreign policy of non-interference. It has been described as 'Britain's Awkward Moment' and it had all the makings of a Gilbert and Sullivan opera. Captain Fitzwilliam Wentworth Owen, who was as pompous as his name suggests, was the commanding officer of two naval frigates patrolling the Indian Ocean, HMS *Leven* and HMS *Barracouta*. While on a routine visit to present the Sultan of Oman with a Bible translated into Arabic, Captain Owen instructed his junior officer, Captain Vidal, to proceed to Mombasa in HMS *Barracouta* to take on provisions. On arrival Captain Vidal found the port under blockade.

This was not unusual, for it was the time of year when the Omani officials were due to collect the annual tax. The powerful Mazrui family, who dominated Mombasa, invariably refused to pay and the rest of the population took their cue from them. Eventually they would capitulate and order would be restored. On this occasion the blockade was lifted briefly to allow the British man-of-war to enter the harbour. Then the wily Mazrui sought, and were granted, permission to go on board HMS *Barracouta* and introduce themselves to the ship's officers. Resplendent in their Arabic robes, the Mazrui were welcomed on board by Captain Vidal and his fellow officers, equally resplendent in their gold braid and white uniforms.

This glittering group sat on deck, shaded from the sun by a large green awning, drinking bitter black coffee from little ornate cups. The naval officers listened patiently while the Mazrui complained at length about the hardships they suffered under their rulers, the Omani Arabs. Then, with breath-taking audacity, they offered the British the port of Mombasa, if they would free them from the tiresome demands of the Sultan. Captain Vidal remained courteous and sympathetic but explained that he would need time to consider such a proposal. He promised to give them his reply the following day.

Unfortunately the captain went down with a fever during the night, and his very young first lieutenant, Thomas Botiler, was sent ashore with orders to politely refuse the Mazrui offer. At the same time he was urged to keep uppermost in his mind the ferocity of the people he was dealing with. On stepping ashore, he was escorted into Fort Jesus. Here the Mazrui once again made an impassioned plea to be rescued from the tyranny of the Omani Arabs. They produced a crude handmade version of the Union Jack and asked the young lieutenant to be so kind as to hoist it over the Fort in order to demonstrate that their allegiance was now to the British. When he refused the mood became ugly. Botiler decided to make a run for it. He reached the safety of the ship, convinced he had been lucky to escape with his life. As the Mazrui watched the Barracouta sail full steam out of port, they set about hoisting the flag themselves. So ended Act I.

Act II was, if anything even more bizarre. The zealous Captain Fitzwilliam Wentworth Owen had been through a frustrating time with the Sultan. After presenting the Bible, he had chosen to lecture the

Sultan on the evils of the slave trade. The Sultan, however, regarded this as a lucrative business which he was not prepared to abandon. In a fit of pique, Owen threatened to give the people of Mombasa their freedom if the Sultan remained obdurate. The Sultan was unmoved. Then without consulting the Foreign Office, the Admiralty or even the directors of the East India Company, Owen sailed for Mombasa to carry out his threat.

On entering the port, his curiosity was aroused by the strange flag over Fort Jesus. After examining it through his telescope, he realised what it was meant to be. This would make his job much easier. He called a meeting with the sheiks and promised them a proper Union Jack, on condition they gave up their slave trading. The Mazrui were delighted. They promised to stop the illicit trade, and to show their good faith, they gave Captain Owen, not only Mombasa, but also two hundred miles of coastline belonging to the Omanis. Satisfied with the deal, Captain Owen sailed away, leaving his third lieutenant, John Reitz, in command. It could be said that he was the first Governor of British East Africa.

Not surprisingly, the moment HMS *Barrracouta* was over the horizon, the Mazrui resumed the business of slavery. Poor Lieutenant Reitz's protests fell on deaf ears. To pacify him they gave him a plot of land, which was named English Point. (In the 1950s, before independence, this was a fashionable part of Mombasa.) Feeling thoroughly dispirited, the young lieutenant decided to make an expedition into the interior and thus discover the source of slavery. Of course, the locals did their utmost to dissuade him, warning him of the prevalence of malaria and other fatal diseases, but he was determined to go. Sadly, their predictions were only too true. He contracted malaria and died. Command of the fledgling protectorate now fell to a sixteen-year-old midshipman, George Phillips. He distinguished himself by capturing a slave dhow, releasing the slaves and establishing the first of many settlements for freed slaves. This did not endear him to the Mazrui.

In the meantime, Captain Fitzwilliam Wentworth Owen had returned to Great Britain and found himself in water much hotter than he had experienced in the Indian Ocean. He was relieved of his command and the government were quick to repudiate his annexation of Mombasa. Midshipman Phillips was ordered back to sea, but not before hauling down the flag over the Fort. The delicate business of mending fences between the British Government and Oman took some time. The lesson had been learnt that diplomacy rather than 'bible bashing' was a better way to persuade Sultan Seyid to give up slavery. This policy was to pay dividends in the future, especially in the case of Zanzibar.

Chapter 9

The Sultans of Zanzibar

It is often said that history is fashioned by individuals rather than governments. This was certainly the case when it came to the story of the European struggle for power in East Africa during the latter half of the 19th century. The outcome of the struggle might have been quite different but for three major players: Sultan Barghash, Sir John Kirk, the British Consul, and Carl Peters, a German adventurer who, almost single-handedly, succeeded in grabbing the whole of East Africa for the Kaiser. The person who set the scene was Sultan Seyyid. It is possible that none of these people would have met, if Seyyid had not fallen in love with Zanzibar, the first time he set eyes on it.

From this moment on, he lost no time in moving his capital from Muscat to Zanzibar and changing his title from the Sultan of Oman to that of Sultan of Zanzibar. On discovering that the soil was particularly good for growing cloves, he ordered that every fallen palm tree must be replaced by three clove trees. He also lowered taxes, thus attracting those merchants from Europe and America who were looking for new outlets for their manufactured goods. By the 1840s Zanzibar's deep-water harbour was a forest of masts from the number of foreign ships at anchor there. Trade consuls were appointed, and the prosperity of the island grew. It became the hub of Seyyid's empire.

This empire was vast. It covered today's Tanzania, Malawi, Zambia, Congo, Uganda and Kenya. It used to be said 'When the flute plays in Zanzibar, they dance on the Lakes' (Lake Victoria, Lake Tanganyika, Lake Nyanza). But it was an empire in name only. It was not colonised. Its purpose was the harvesting of slaves and ivory. Understandably Britain was deeply concerned. Wilberforce's Anti-Slavery Act had been passed in 1833. Pressure was bought to bear on Seyyid to give up his slave-trading. Palmerston's foreign policy rested on the hope of achieving dominance in the region through moral force and free trade. His plan was to persuade Seyyid to become the Wilberforce of East Africa – a role that did not appeal to Seyyid. Eventually, in 1867, he did reluctantly sign a treaty to this effect, but one which was riddled with loopholes. It would take another twenty-six years of patient diplomacy before the Arabs could be properly brought to heel.

It was Britain's steely determination to eliminate slavery throughout the world, coupled with the awesome might of the Royal Navy, that contributed to her growing influence in the Indian Ocean. Empire building was not, at this time, on the agenda. Any Prime Minister who suggested it would have been considered crazy. The government was having a rough time in India after the Mutiny.

There was trouble, too, in Afghanistan and the Crimea. At home they were having to deal with the Chartists, the Corn Law Repeal, and there was the Reform Bill looming. It was no time to be thinking of setting the bounds of empire any wider. The Government was focused on two objectives in East Africa: first keeping the southern route to India safe; and second dealing with 'the war on slavery'. It was this last objective which would, in an unforeseen way, lead Great Britain ineluctably along the road to the annexation and the colonisation of the East African territories.

Seyyid died in 1856, leaving his kingdom, storybook fashion, to be divided between his two eldest sons. Thuwaini, the eldest, was given the Sultanate of Oman, and Majid that of Zanzibar. The third son, Barghash, received nothing. It was not long before Thuwaini began to cast covetous eyes on Zanzibar. The island had, after all, superseded Oman strategically and economically. His younger peace-loving brother, Majid, was not interested in keeping up the Island's defences. He was occupied constructing palaces for his harem in Dar es Salaam. Thuwaini therefore seized the moment to attack. On learning of the threatened invasion, Majid turned to the British navy for help. A warship was sent to intercept the Omani fleet. Thuwaini took fright the moment he was challenged and fled back to Muscat with his tail between his legs. Lord Canning, who was Governor-General of India at the time, took it upon himself to arbitrate between the warring brothers. His solution, which they accepted, was to recognise the independent sovereignties of the two kingdoms. This permanent division spelt the end of Oman's power.

It was now the turn of the third brother, Barghash, to make a bid to unseat Majid. By all accounts, Barghash was the most colourful character of the family. With the help of his two sisters, Princess Salme and Princess Chole, he instigated a palace revolution. Majid, however, discovered the plot and had Barghash's house surrounded. Dressed as a woman, Barghash escaped during the night to a nearby sugar factory, where his supporters rallied round. Once again, Majid appealed to the British. A Royal Navy cruiser was conveniently anchored in the harbour. A detachment of armed men was sent ashore to the scene of the riot. Bullets pinged and whined through the sugar canes until Barghash admitted defeat and gave himself up. He was arrested and exiled to Bombay, where he lived in some style under the watchful eye of the British.

In 1870, on the death of Majid, Barghash became the legitimate successor to the Sultanate. Like his father, Seyyid, he cared passionately for the island. He nurtured its prosperity by fostering development and trade. In this, he was greatly helped by his friendship with the British Consul, Sir John Kirk, who, over a period of sixteen years, provided him with invaluable advice, assistance and support.*. Sir John's devotion to the Sultan, together with his love of the island, at times tested his loyalties severely and made his job as Consul very difficult.

The treaty of 1847 was being openly flouted. Dhows packed with slaves could be seen leaving the harbour. The British Government was losing patience. It threatened to blockade all the coastal ports, including Zanzibar, unless Barghash signed another more forceful treaty promising to end the Slave Trade once and for all. Kirk patiently dealt with the Sultan's remonstrations, explaining that it was imperative for him to sign if he wanted to preserve the independence of Zanzibar. In 1873, Barghash finally gave way. He signed. The naval blockade was called off and the infamous Zanzibar Slave Market was closed forever. Today an Anglican Cathedral marks the site.

The effect on the traders was devastating. The situation became ugly. There were riots up and down the coast. When the Slave Market was closed, the population were already struggling with the after effects of a hurricane. Their livelihood was hit badly and they were angry. But for the support of John Kirk, it is doubtful if the Sultan would have been able to hold firm. Because of the diplomatic encouragement of this remarkable British Consul, the British Government were able to achieve their aim of using the Sultan of Zanzibar as their 'willing instrument of the British civilizing mission in East Africa' without taking on the burden of annexation.

All this would change, with the entrance of Carl Peters on the stage of East African affairs. He was a German merchant who has been described as a character who was 'short on ethics and long on cruelty'. He could also be said to be the person who lit the fuse for the Scramble for Africa. In 1884, he formed a private company called the Society for German Colonization. Resentful of the British 'sphere of influence' in the Indian Ocean, he and two companions travelled to Zanzibar disguised as mechanics. His intention was to grab as much of the Sultanate lands for Germany as possible. Bismark would have nothing to do with the plan and virtually disowned them. This did not worry Peters. He judged correctly that when this astute statesman was presented with a fait accompli he would change his tune. The three men hired a dhow and sailed from Zanzibar to Dar es Salaam. From there, they set off for the interior. The illiterate tribal chiefs that they met were persuaded to mark with a cross prepared written statements declaring that they were happy to hand over their territories to the representative of the Society for German Colonization.

Just as Peters had predicted, Bismark was delighted when presented with twenty-five of these documents of surrender. He hurried off to get the Kaiser to add his signature. Then at the Berlin Conference in 1885, he declared that this area of East Africa which included Witu, Kilimanjaro and Usangari were under German Imperial Protection. Barghash was outraged when he learnt of the trickery. 'These territories are under our protection from the time of our fathers' he protested. Kirk did his best to alert Great Britain to the Sultan's plight. But the Government was too busy with European affairs to pay attention. Besides they needed Germany as an ally at this time – against the Russians in Afghanistan, and the French who were being difficult over the Suez Canal. Lord Salisbury ignored Kirk's increasingly desperate cables. 'The Sultan cannot stand alone', drew no response. The Government deemed the Sultan's problems to be no more than a storm in a teacup. The politics of a small island in the backwaters of the Indian Ocean were of little interest in comparison to the weightier matters before Parliament at this time. Kirk warned that 'unless Great Britain took a less passive stance, the possession of a strong naval station in East Africa will have to be considered from a strategic point of view'. For Lord Salisbury, however, it was not worth alienating Germany over so trifling an issue as the Sultan's claims over East African territories.

So Barghash was deserted by the one European power he had come to trust. It had been Britain, after all, who had seen off Thuwaini in 1861; and in 1875 it had been the Royal Navy who had confronted the Khedive of Egypt when he invaded Benadir. On that occasion, John Kirk himself had sailed in one of the warships. The commander of the Egyptian forces had greeted him with the words 'God says in His Holy Book, "Do not enter another's house without his permission"'. Kirk replied that if he was not allowed ashore by a certain hour, his ship would open fire on the town. Whereupon the commander had thought it best to retreat.

It was after this episode that Barghash felt Zanzibar and its territories needed some form of protection. With this in mind, he planned a visit to Great Britain, with a view to interesting someone who might consider investing capital in developing his mainland territories. Lord Derby knew just the right man: Sir William Mackinnon, a philanthropic financier and passionate anti slave-trader. A deal was struck, but the Government refused to back it, and so it came to nought.

The rest of the visit, however, was a resounding success. The Queen gave a state banquet for him at Windsor Castle. He was also invited to a concert at the Crystal Palace, where on seeing the choir stand up to sing, his innate good manners dictated that he should also stand, whereupon the rest of the audience, to save him embarrassment, followed suit. In his farewell speech, he spoke of how overcome he had been by his reception: 'You all welcome me. You all tell me I have done something for the abolition of the slave trade…What can I say but thank you, thank you, thank you.' The British people had taken him to their hearts.

But that was all of ten years ago, in the summer of 1875. Now he could only watch helplessly as a squadron of five German warships steamed into Zanzibar harbour, their purpose, as Bismark put it, 'to bring the Sultan to a more correct bearing'. Kirk's instructions from London were explicit: 'Unless he yields, he will invite a conflict fatal to his independence'. Nothing must be done to upset the Germans. Kirk's loyalty to the Crown was being stretched to the limit, as he advised the Sultan to accept defeat and acknowledge German sovereignty.

As he stood beside the Prince, studying the scene in the harbour through his binoculars, frustrated at not being able to help his friend as he had so often in the past, he was struck by the amount of activity on one of the cruisers Intrigued, he thought it worthwhile investigating. He sent a boy selling crates of oranges out to the ship, with instructions to find out whatever he could. When the boy returned, he brought the dramatic news that the Sultan's disgraced sister, the Princess Salme, was on board.

In the 1860s, the princess had caused a scandal on the island by having an affair with a German merchant and becoming pregnant by him. To escape the death penalty – for it was a crime for a Muslim to have sex with an infidel – she eloped with her lover, Heinrich Reute, on a German warship. They married and settled in Hamburg. She converted to Christianity and became a respectable, German citizen, bearing him three children. Then tragedy struck. Her beloved Heinrich was killed stepping off a tram. Heartbroken, Frau Reute moved to Berlin, where she became a good friend of the Kaiser.

She kept up a correspondence over the years with her brother, Sultan Barghash, always urging him to befriend Germany rather than Great Britain. With Bismark's approval, she frequently enclosed fond messages and small gifts from the German Emperor. By this time she had been enrolled as a spy for the purpose of wooing the Sultan into the arms of Germany. Now it appeared that she was back.

The orange-seller discovered that the Germans were planning to put Frau Reute ashore. They had told her that she would be of more use to them on the island than back home in Germany. She needed little persuading; for after the death of her husband she had suffered acutely from homesickness and longed to return to Zanzibar. What they had not told her was that they would arrange for her cover to be blown. Once again, she would face the death penalty. The murder of a German national would give the Kaiser the reason he sought to invade Zanzibar, get rid of Barghash and install Frau Reute's son as Sultan. In this way, he would secure Zanzibar and its territories for the German 'sphere of influence'.

Kirk barely waited for the orange-seller to finish his report before cabling London. The news electrified the British Government. At last they realised the significance of Germany's colonial intentions. A Delimitation Conference was hastily convened between the European powers. Its purpose was to define the boundaries of the Sultanate.

Neither Barghash nor Kirk were consulted. The outcome was that the Sultan could keep 700 miles of coastline, 10 miles in width. He could also keep the islands of Zanzibar, Pemba, and Lamu, along with 5 towns on the Benadir coast. The British would lease the strip of coastline from the Sultan. The remainder of the interior, where the flute had once been heard, was divided between British and German 'spheres of influence'. Kirk was recalled. As for the Princess Salme/Frau Emily Reute: she found refuge first in Beirut, then the Lebanon and Jaffa. She died in Jena in 1914 aged seventy-nine, having written her memoirs, *The Story of an Arabian Princess*.

All that remained to be done was to plan for the administration of these 'spheres of influence'. As so often in her history of empire-building, Great Britain solved the problem by choosing to do this through a chartered company. William Mackinnon, the shipping magnate who had attracted Barghash's attention in 1875, was approached. This time he was able to form the Imperial British East Africa Company with backing from the Government for the development of the territories. He chose Mombasa for the headquarters of the Company, and it was from here that he embarked on the mammoth task of building the railway which gave birth to the Colony of Kenya.

Barghash died the following year in 1888. In 1890 Zanzibar was declared a British Protectorate. Five years later the Sultan's coastal domains followed suit. The British Government pledged that 'all affairs connected with the faith of Islam will be conducted to the honour and benefit of religion, and all ancient customs will be allowed to continue.' In essence, the coastal strip remained the property of the Sultan. The British Government paid the Sultan an annual rent of £11,000. The Sultan's red flag was the only one that was permitted to fly from a flagstaff in the ground. All other flags, including the Union Jack had to be flown from rooftops.

And so it was throughout the reign of nine more Sultans In 1963, however, the whole structure of the Sultanate was blown away by the Socialist Revolution.

These plaited strands of history are what helped form the bond of friendship between my father and one of the most powerful of the Arab sheikhs on the coast. My father's respect for all Ali bin Salaam stood for, and Ali's love of everything British, is an example of the concord that is possible between East and West. Something we should take heart from today.

★ In the 1950s, my brother Roderick and Clare's father-in-law, Julian Oxford, worked in the secretariat in Zanzibar. They found the bond of friendship established by Sir John Kirk between the Arab community and the British had remained unbroken.

Chapter 10

Sir Ali bin Salem

When the north-easterly monsoon known as the 'kaskasi' swings round to become the south-westerly 'kusi', Dar es Salaam becomes unbearably hot. It was thought advisable for women and children to leave the port at this time, and move to the more temperate climate of the Highlands of Kenya until the weather cooled. To escape the hot breath of the 'kusi', we took the little coastal steamer to Mombasa. The following day we travelled by train to Nairobi. I remember it as a hot bad-tempered trip. My mother complained about our cramped cabins; Nanny fussed over the lack of fresh milk; I sulked because the boat bore no resemblance to my beloved Union Castle ships; and Baby Helen roared with rage throughout the entire journey.

We travelled around staying with a succession of friends. Their newly-constructed houses were simple and unpretentious; roofed with either corrugated iron, or *mkuti* (a kind of thatch made from dried palm leaves). The gardens were glorious. As you stepped outside, the warm scented air made you dizzy. One, I remember, was set against the misty blue line of the Ngong Hills. It was a riot of colour, crammed with bougainvillea, petunias, roses and banks of nicotiana. Wherever we went, the jagged peaks and shadowy bulk of Mount Kenya dominated the horizon. In the afternoons we watched polo matches, with other children and their nannies. We would sit on the coarse, spiky grass, perilously close to the polo field. As the horses thundered past, we would feel the ground shake beneath us. I can only presume the nannies had thrown all caution to the wind, in their anxiety to get a close look at the celebrities who made up the teams: – the Big Game Hunters, the wealthy Americans and minor Royals. Their need to boast, pre-empted their customary discipline.

On our way home to Dar es Salaam, we would break our journey in Mombasa. This was a place steeped in the culture and history of the coastal Arabs. The sounds; the smells; the little, narrow streets, with the coffee vendors clicking their cups together, like castanets; the steam from the slender spouts of their brass coffee pots, exuding an aroma of Turkish coffee; the muezzin's call from the Baluchi Mosque to midday prayer; the clamour of the market place – all this spoke of Arabia. If the monsoon was right, there would be the early morning excitement of the arrival of the dhows from India and the Gulf, heralded by the eerie sound made by the crews blowing on conch shells and beating their brass trays. They were keen to let everyone know that they had a cargo of goods for sale. To watch these beautiful craft, with their great scimitar sails billowing in the breeze, sailing past Fort Jesus into the Old Harbour, was to be taken back in time to the days of King David. Now, though, their cargo was not gold 'from distant Ophir', but carpets, dried dates and brass-studded chests.

We would stay with my father's dear friend, Sir Ali bin Salem. He was a cousin of the Sultan of Zanzibar, and the leader, or 'luwali' of the East Coast Arab Community. But of all his titles, the one he was most proud of was that of Honorary Admiral of the Royal Navy. He liked to be addressed as Sir Ali bin Salem and chose to wear his Admiral's uniform on all possible occasions. He had earned his rank and knighthood in the First World War, when he had not only funded the British war effort with prodigious generosity, but had also persuaded his Arab subjects to enlist. It was said of Ali's forebear, Sultan Seyyid of Oman, that 'Justice he valued above all things'. People spoke of 'his honesty of purpose, kind feeling and decision of character' – epithets that could well have described Ali.

I remember him as a kindly old man: a person of authority and dignity. His voice was soft with an almost hypnotic lilt. I loved the way his eyes twinkled. I loved his robes; his jewelled dagger; his colourful turban. I loved his scent of musk and cigars. To my child's sense, he fitted perfectly into the ambience of his tropical garden. As he walked in the generous shade of his mango trees, beside the glittering sea, he seemed to me to have stepped straight out of a story book. He was the first person I loved outside my family.

We crossed to the other side of the harbour in Ali's launch. The discipline, grace and athleticism of the crew would have impressed the most critical of naval commanders. They would settle us on the white cushions before taking up their positions. The frills of the blue and white canopy fluttered in the breeze as we chugged our way over the sunlit sea towards the green lawns and white arches of Ali's palace.

This tribute to my father, written on an illuminated parchment scroll, that still holds a faint scent of musk, explains why we were such welcome guests.

TO HIS HONOUR JOSEPH SHERIDAN

First Puisne Judge of the Colony & Protectorate of Kenya
Chief Justice of the Colony and Protectorate of Kenya
Chief Justice Designate of the Supreme Court of the Mandated Territory of Tanganyika

Sir,

We, the Arabs of Muscat and Handramaut, the Twelve Tribes and Baluchis of Mombasa and the Protectorate of Kenya, tender you our heartiest congratulations on your appointment to the highest judicial post in the Mandated Territory of Tanganyika.

During the stay of your period in Kenya you have at all times been mindful of your solemn oath to dispense justice without fear or favour, affection or ill will; in short you have most worthily upheld both as Magistrate and Judge the highest and noblest traditions of the Bench.

It is inevitable that being so patently true to your oath you would gain respect of all but there has been in addition an indefinable something which has won our regard and affection.

Your promotion is a loss to us but we rejoice with you nevertheless on your promotion and wish you many many years of successful endeavour in your new appointment and we pray that there will be still further and greater promotion for you. We rejoice that your local experience will not be lost entirely for from time to time your judicial duties will bring you here and no other member of the Court of Appeal for Eastern Africa will be more warmly welcomed.

In bidding you then God Speed we should like to express our thanks also to Mrs Sheridan for all the good & good works which she has done during her stay.

Signed by the Sheiks of the Sheikdoms of the Red Sea.

As far as I was concerned, Ali was no one else's friend but mine. He suffered this childish conceit with gentle humour. I was invited to sit beside him at the head of his dining-room table. He would pour limejuice into a green crystal goblet for me. We ate off plates patterned with the deep blue, crimson and gold of Crown Derby. He held my hand as we walked in his gardens. Through a gap in a tall hedge we watched a party of sheikhs moving over the lawn, their long silk robes trailing over the grass behind them. This was a 'baraza', a political meeting. Had they spied us, Ali said they would chop off my head. Barazas are forbidden to women. From his smile, I guessed he was joking. He told me stories about his lion cubs. One was in disgrace for biting the hand of his keeper. I was relieved they were behind bars! When I became restless, he would produce from the folds of his robes, a gold fob watch. He would dangle it on its golden chain close to my ear and watch with amusement for my reaction when it chimed. I was enchanted, believing it to be magic. And in a way, it was.

Goodbyes between friends are painful affairs. As we boarded the launch to return to Mombasa Island, I found it hard to hold back the tears. The sting of parting on this occasion, however, was lessened by Ali's decision to accompany us. I settled myself on the cushions beside him and watched with sadness the sight of the mango trees casting pools of shade over familiar lawns, recede into the distance. Ali took out his gold watch to distract me, and held it to my ear. Once again, I listened to its bell-like chime. With a smile, he said softly , 'You can have it.' Astonished, I said 'But it isn't my birthday!' 'No,' he replied, 'That doesn't matter. This is a present from Me to You.'

I never saw Ali or his enchanted palace again. Had I known that in a matter of months, all the sunshine of my African childhood was to be exchanged for the grey, London fogs, then, I don't think even Ali's gold watch would have consoled me.

My parents were quick to take custody of my treasure. The first thing they did was to open the back. There, traced out in diamonds, rubies and pearls, was the German Kaiser's coat of arms, together with the date: 1873. Is it too much to suppose that this was, maybe, one of the baubles Princess Salme was asked to send to her brother Sultan Barghash by the German Emperor? Could it have been passed on to Ali by his cousin, Barghash, when the Royal Navy came to the rescue of Zanzibar? And could Ali, by 1930 have felt it was time he, too, got rid of such a compromising jewel? We shall never know.

Once in England, my parents sold the watch. It barely reached its reserve of £30.00. The Kaiser's coat of arms detracted from its value.

Chapter 11

Conclusion

There was no aggression involved in Great Britain's acquisition of the East African territories. In no sense could she be described as a conqueror. She came to occupy this corner of Africa with some reluctance. Kenya was the only one to be colonised. Uganda and Zanzibar became Protectorates, retaining their sovereignty and national identity under British rule. After the First World War, the German colony of Tanganyika (Tanzania), was added to the list, as a Mandated Territory to be administered by Great Britain on behalf of the League of Nations.

By the 1960s all these territories were able to play their part on the international stage, politically and economically, as independent, self-governing nations. Would this, I wonder, have been possible without the intervention of the British Empire in the 19th century?

Unfortunately, the closing years of British Rule in Kenya were cloaked in scandals, so that the benefits of the Empire have been eclipsed by them. The high ideals and noble aspirations that had fired the imagination of people like my father and the early settlers were blown away by the aftermath of the two World Wars and the notoriety of the Erroll murder trial. But above all else it was the Government's handling of the Mau Mau rebellion that destroyed forever Britain's right to rule.

Mau Mau was a secret society mainly confined to the politically astute Kikuyu tribe. It was formed by a group of extremists from the African nationalist party, KAU (Kenya African Union) whose president was Jomo Kenyatta, a flamboyant figure, revered by the Kikuyu. Many of the members of Mau Mau were disaffected ex-servicemen from the British army. Its aim was to kill every European living in the Colony and to claim back the land they said had been stolen from them. In fact, over the four years of conflict, they killed nearly two thousand of those fellow Africans who chose to stay loyal to the British, and only thirty-two Europeans, (among them, the Davis family, whose daughters had been at school with Helen and me). Their method of killing was particularly gruesome. They hacked their victims to death with pangas, and then proceeded to disembowel them. One of the reasons the movement failed to spread was because of the bestiality of its secret oath-taking ceremonies. Unlike the Kikuyu, who specialised in oaths, using them to ensure unity, the other tribes found them repugnant and refused to have anything to do with Mau Mau. There were, too, a number of Africans who had converted to Christianity who would not take the oaths. They went to their deaths with impressive courage.

The Europeans panicked. To them it seemed as though the primitive forces they had always suspected of being just below the surface of this dark continent had now erupted. Keenly aware that their white population of just thirty thousand was attempting to control five million Africans, they lost their nerve. The extremists among the settlers screamed for action.

They marched on Government House. The Governor, the patrician Sir Evelyn Baring, vacillated, then finally, in October 1952, declared a state of emergency. Kenyatta was arrested.

From the start, Kenyatta had been suspected by the government of being the instigator of the rebellion. Even though he publicly disowned Mau Mau, government spies reported that in private he was seen to give encouragement to the rebels, advising them, for instance, where to set up their guerrilla camps.

What fuelled their suspicion was the fact that for seventeen years he had been a guest of the Communist Party in the Soviet Union and Britain. It was obvious, too, from the rapturous welcome he received from his followers on his return home in 1946, that he was accepted as the natural leader of the African community.

On 24th November, Kenyatta and his colleagues on the executive committee of KAU were brought to trial, not in Nairobi, but in Kapenguria, a remote, deserted area close to the Uganda border. There they were charged with the management of Mau Mau a proscribed society. The offence carried a maximum penalty of seven years' imprisonment. The trial was a disgrace. It was a travesty of British justice. It had more in common with one of the show trials of the Soviet Union than with anything resembling the rule of law as practised by my father in the law courts of Nairobi. (Mercifully, my father knew nothing of it. My parents had long since left the country and the frailties of old age prevented him from comprehending any information that might have filtered through to their retirement flat in Hove). The verdict was never in any doubt. Kenyatta and his colleagues were found guilty and duly sentenced.

The atrocities, meanwhile, accelerated on both sides. At Lari, in the Aberdares, the Mau Mau hacked to death ninety-seven Kikuyu men, women and children, set fire to their huts and nailed the bodies to trees, as a penalty for remaining loyal to their tribal chiefs. The British rounded up some seventy thousand Kikuyu suspects, and caged them in camps (no-one agrees on the exact number). One of these camps was at Hola, in the northern area of Kenya. It was for hard-core Mau Mau detainees who had been sentenced to hard labour.

The camp proved difficult to control and the warders had been instructed to 'step up' the punishments if they faced further trouble. When eighty-eight inmates refused to work and became threatening, the African warders, acting on instructions, set about beating them with clubs and whips while the British warders looked on. Eleven were killed and the rest were severely injured. The report on the incident, later exposed as an implausible cover-up, was accepted by the District Officer, the Governor, Sir Evelyn Baring and the Westminster Government. According to the District Officer, it had been a hot day, there had been a fight among the prisoners; water from nearby water butts had been thrown and some of them had 'accidentally drowned'. It took three inquiries to uncover the truth. As Enoch Powell, then a young backbencher in the House of Commons, said, 'Britain had no right to an Empire if it could not show leadership of a higher order.'

By 1956, with the capture of their leader Dedan Kimathi, Mau Mau was finished. The country was restored to stability and the transfer to independence took place peacefully in 1963. But gone were those days of bright promise when the Masai had asked Hugh Delamere 'Delamere, how long will you stay here?' and he had replied, 'I shall stay forever', and bought them a hundred umbrellas when they offered to show him how to look after his sheep.

To those who would point the finger of blame after reading this sorry tale, I would urge them to think on Guantanamo Bay, and to think too of the 'collatoral damage' inflicted on the civilian population of Afghanistan by American drones. Think and weep, and ask, 'When will we ever learn'?

Building the Railway

Nairobi Station

A Railhead: the beginnings of Nairobi

Hugh Delamere *Ewart Grogan*

The first settlers

A barazi in Ali bin Salem's garden;
my father 2nd from left, Ali bin Salem 3rd from right

My father inspecting the police guard of honour, Mombasa

Our house in Dar es Salaam

Part Two

Orphans of Empire

Chapter 12

I meet my sister Helen

Against a backdrop of tall white marguerites, a podgy three-year-old faces the camera. This is August in England and the year is 1931: the year and the moment when my conscious memory begins. My mother and I were staying with friends in a house in West Sussex, in a village called Three Bridges. The name is etched on my mind, because I can recall asking several people where the bridges were, and never getting a satisfactory reply. I imagine we were there because it was conveniently close to Worth – the Edwardian mansion recently bought by the Benedictines from the Cowdray family as a Preparatory School for Downside. My brother Roderick was one of its first pupils, and indeed the first head boy. The extended school complex and the great Abbey Church had not yet been built. In the years to come, they would be designed by my husband, Francis Pollen, the father of our five children. The oak-panelled banqueting halls which at this time served as dormitories would, seventy years later, be the venue for the wedding reception of our youngest daughter, Louise. Worth has, in many ways, been part of the warp and the weft of my life.

This year of 1931, unaware of all that was before me, and with only three years behind me, I was conscious of being happy and pleased with myself, as I stood facing the photographers who were urging me to smile. I was aware from their remarks that I made a pretty picture. The sun was shining, and if there was a cloud on the horizon I was unaware of it.

Was it the same day or sometime later that I was introduced to a thin, crabby old lady dressed in grey? 'Therese', my mother said, 'This is Nanny Heytus. She is going to look after you.' Now I had heard talk of nannies. I was led to believe that they were cosy people who cuddled you. This one did not look inclined to be that way. However, I was prepared to giver her the benefit of the doubt. In a voice that managed to be both quavery and commanding, she was saying 'We're going to be friends, aren't we?' 'Yes', I replied hesitantly. 'And you are going to be a good girl?' I could not confirm this. Until now, I could not recall anyone complicating my life by asking me such a question. It was suggested that I went for a walk with her before bedtime.

Across the road there was a wood planted with larch trees. Their needles were slippery underfoot. 'Shall we play hide and seek?' she ordered, rather than suggested. Her reaction when she realised I had no idea of what I was meant to do confirmed my worst suspicions; we were not going to be friends. Dutifully, I stood behind a tree and waited to be found. The sun had gone in; the wood was dark. Time passed. I became frightened. I was lost but I did not want to be found by Nanny Heytus. When we eventually sighted each other, open war was declared between us.

Tearfully I was put to bed. For the first time, I noticed how small and dark the room was. I waited for my mother to come and kiss me goodnight. The minutes ticked past. She did not come and I cried loudly. A pretty young woman came to console me. She sat on my bed and explained that my mother had had to go to somewhere called the Welbeck Clinic and she would be back in a few days with a surprise for me. This all sounded very grand. Perhaps the Welbeck Clinic was a kind of palace, I thought sleepily. As she shut the door gently behind her, a shaft of late evening sunlight played on the blue glass of the Milk of Magnesia bottle standing on the dressing table. Possibly the colour reminded me of African skies, or maybe the bottle evoked memories of maternal love and concern; whatever it was, I felt impelled to steal out of bed, reach up for it, and return to bed with this hard cold object to cuddle until I fell asleep. I was fully aware that, in Nanny Heytus' eyes, I had done something very naughty.

The following morning I stood by the window while Nanny brushed my hair with her accustomed verve. A Morris Cowley Saloon car was crunching its way over the gravel drive below us, with a curious uncertainty. Our host was giving his wife a driving lesson. The vehicle bucked and lurched round the oval flowerbed before coming to halt with its snout in the shrubbery. I laughed and laughed, as did Nanny; but Nanny's laughter was short lived. As the car doors flew open, two angry people confronted each other. I was ordered away from the window and reprimanded. You must not laugh at grown-ups. It was very naughty. It must not happen again. So a moment of shared fun, once again, turned to tears and recriminations.

Some days later, when Nanny and I were in the barn that had been converted into a playroom, the belligerent silence between us was broken by the sound of excited voices. Suddenly the door flew open, flooding the room with sunlight, and there was my mother surrounded by friends. In her arms, she held a billowing foam of white fluffy shawls. 'Here is something for you, Nanny' she said with laughter, as she handed the bundle over. Everyone seemed to be talking at once, and Nanny was making the most extraordinary noises – cooing like an elderly pigeon recovering from an attack of laryngitis. The shawls were removed with infinite care, to reveal furbelows of fine muslin, trimmed with yards of pink ribbon. As Nanny gently put this bundle of finery in a wicker cradle, it became astonishingly animated. A tiny foot pushed its way through the layers of muslin, and a lusty howl of protest cut through the sound of merry chatter. My mother turned to me and asked 'How do you like your baby sister Helen?' I paused before replying and considered for a moment how Nanny was transformed. She was pink and shiny and wreathed in smiles. This baby must be good news. Surely, life with Nanny must now take a turn for the better. The future looked bright. 'I am very excited' I replied.

Chapter 13

I am part of a large family

Saint Jacût de la Mer: the words sounded beautiful wherever you put the emphasis. I would repeat them over and over again without being sure of what they referred to. It was here, in this seaside town of southern Brittany, that I discovered I was part of a large, boisterous family. We were staying in a small hotel, whose shuttered windows rambled round a courtyard. It was the summer holidays of 1931, Nanny Heytus and her bundle of joy were safely out of reach, back in England. Wrapped as I was in the noisy affection of older brothers and sisters, and doted on by my parents, I hoped this was a permanent arrangement – such is the optimism of innocence!

It was while we were staying here that, one day, we saw a group of people in the hotel courtyard, grouped around a performing bear. The bear was held by a chain attached to his collar. Standing on his hind legs, with a muzzle over his head, his enormous height dwarfed the keeper. In response to a peremptory shout from the man, and a couple of sharp jangles on his chain, the bear began to shuffle about, nodding his head up and down and lifting his big black paws in a rather appealing manner. 'Voila!' shouted the man excitedly, 'Il danse, il danse. C'est incroyable, n'est pas?' My family moved off as the man came round with his upturned cap with a few sous in it. Yes! The sight had been 'incroyable' and not a little frightening. What I shall never forget was the sadness of the bear's eyes behind his muzzle.

Each morning of this holiday was marked by a sense of urgency, to get down to the beach before anyone else, in order to claim possession of 'our' rock. This was a sprawling and accommodating rock with a perfect niche for each one of us. Then there was the serious business of the sandcastle, which was enormous: the largest ever seen by the local inhabitants, and all the work of the Sheridans. It got bigger day by day. Ramparts were added, also keeps and complicated tunnels. Inevitably, we arrived one morning to discover there had been an act of sabotage. The French were suspected although it could equally as well have been an unexpected high tide. The outrage was greeted with noisy accusations and protestations. Schoolroom French was shouted across the beach at a party of Breton children, who, in turn, returned a fusillade of abuse in the local patois. 'C'est la guerre!' I was too small to take part. The sound of the tumult was on the periphery of my consciousness. My recollection of the battle was of being quietly content just to belong to the 'right' side.

Dermot, the hero of our family, was my companion. He was seventeen years old at this time and was the eldest. He had a glittering career ahead of him. He would win a scholarship to read Law at Cambridge, and go on to win the Harmsworth scholarship; practise as a barrister of the Middle Temple during the London Blitz; survive an ambush in Africa (the rebels had been digging his grave at the side of the road when he was rescued.) As Chief Justice of Uganda, he would fearlessly stand up to the bullying tactics of the President, Idi Amin. Like his father before him, he would in 1970 receive a knighthood. All these triumphs were made more remarkable by the fact that he was the victim of polio. He had contracted the illness when he was only three years old and it had left him severely disabled. At this time, his legs were encased in heavy metal splints. He walked with the aid of two sticks. I was always so proud to accompany him. I loved his rhythmic panting as he struggled along the stony path to the beach. You could never be sure he would get there without falling. It was a performance of amazing courage, grit and determination. Some years later his walking was made easier through a series of operations performed by a Professor Nicco in his clinic in Lausanne. While his left leg was made rigid, his right leg was able to swing almost normally from the knee. He could never abandon his sticks, but at least he was released from the hated splints. We all adored him for his humour, his wit and merry company and also for his wisdom. He would listen patiently to my childish prattling as I sat on the rocks beside him. Even if he was engrossed in his studies for his final year at Downside, he would still find time to answer my endless questions.

Then there was Peggy, aged fifteen, who held my hand when I was frightened of the bear. She came to my rescue again when an ominous spider threatened me from the wall beside my bed. I yelled in terror, and in a moment she was in my room. Tall, with a graceful athleticism, her presence alone was enough to reassure me. In one movement she removed her shoe, and dealt the spider a mortal blow. 'You goose,' she scolded in a voice where laughter always lurked, 'Sure the spider was more afraid of you!' I am indebted to her to this day, for spiders have never bothered me since.

Roderick and Mary completed my circle of siblings. They were chiefly responsible for the groundswell of noise that seemed to accompany us wherever we went. Binding us together into this family were our parents, Joe and Muriel. Joe was a Colonial Judge in Kenya. Because of his job, it was rare for us to be together on a holiday like this one at Saint Jacût de la Mer.

The next time, Peggy would not be with us. She would be in a sanatorium in Sussex. In 1934 she became ill with tuberculosis. Without the cocktail of antibiotics available today there was little hope of a cure. She died in a clinic in Germany in 1937 after a disastrous operation. She was just twenty-one years old. Dermot was the only member of the family present at her funeral. The snow was unusually deep that February, which would have made it particularly difficult for him. My mother had been at her bedside throughout those last harrowing days. She was overwhelmed by grief and could not bring herself to follow her beloved daughter's coffin to the grave. She was buried in the cemetray in St Blasien in the Black Forest. My sister Mary and her husband tried to find the grave when they were travelling in Germany in 1978. Sadly, after the devastation of World War II, they could find no trace of it. Many years later, I came across a letter my mother had sent my father, describing the agony of Peggy's last days. One can only speculate on my father's anguish as he read this letter, alone in Africa, tied to his work. He adored Peggy. Such was her personality, many, many hearts were broken the day she died.

Chapter 14

Kenya

Before the advent of air travel, there were two ways of travelling to East Africa: by Union Castle ships or the British India Line. Although the B.I. ships were smaller and slower, people preferred them for their comfort and elegance. The Company had been formed after the Napoleonic Wars to carry mail out to India, and life on board had the semblance of life under the British Raj. The sahibs and their memsahibs were waited on by Goanese stewards and Lascar sailors. They were purposeful little ships with black hulls, buff-coloured upper works and slender, upright funnels.

As a child, I preferred the Union Castle ships. They had lavender-blue hulls and chunky, pink funnels, tilted backwards in order to give the impression of speed. They also had a regimental band that used to thrill me as it played us out of harbour. Gilbert and Sullivan melodies would compete with the excited, staccato toots from the tugs and the deep-throated blasts from the pink funnels. Each ship was named after a British castle: a reminder to port authorities of the presence and might of Empire. For those with children, this was the Line to choose. Not only was there a nursery on board, but also a nursery maid. There were organised games, a swimming pool, and children's mealtimes. But for all that, my parents disliked the formality of the Union Castle Line. They found the multitude of petty regulations irritating: the dinner gong had to be obeyed; certain sections of the ship were out of bounds to children; First and Second Class passengers could not mix, and, in contrast to the B.I. ships, the stewards were white and could not be summoned with the peremptory call of 'Boy'.

The voyage from Tilbury to Mombasa would take from three to four weeks, depending on which Line you chose. Either way, the passenger lists were drawn from that section of society engaged in the task of sustaining Pax Britannica in the newly acquired East African territories, recently opened up by the great explorers of the late 19th century. Although one or two of the passengers could be described as 'shady people seeking a place in the sun', the majority had a serious purpose to their voyage. In their various capacities, they were embarked on a crusade to civilise the primitive people of East Africa.

Today this might sound like blatant colonial arrogance, but as Elspeth Huxley warned, when writing on this subject 'it is an injustice to judge men of yesterday by the standards of to-day'. In my father's day, there was no doubt about what constituted civilisation. It was built on Christianity and the rule of law. It carried with it the fruits of the artistic and scientific knowledge demonstrated in the Great Exhibition of 1851. My father, despite being Irish by birth, was proud to be part of the British Colonial Service. He believed Britain had earned the title 'Great'. Her Empire, after all, was 400 years old, and to quote from the American author, Charles Miller, 'brought with it the traditions of Magna Carta and a 600-year-old Parliament.' In those days there was no such thing as racial equality. Racial distinction was, as Miller points out 'obvious: the forebears of the British were Shakespeare, Pitt, Swift, Wren, Newton and Hogarth…'. How could they treat as equals Africans who slept with their goats, settled their business matters by consulting sheeps' entrails, covered their bodies with ochre and animal fat and considered it right to beat their wives? In the eyes of the First Commissioner for the Territories, Sir Charles Eliot, the British 'were not destroying any old or interesting system, but simply introducing order into blank barbarism'.

Unlike the Belgians and the French, or indeed the British in South Africa, government policy for East Africa in the early part of the 20th century was essentially paternalistic. These were the last colonies to be added to the Empire. Great Britain had learnt some hard lessons after the Indian Mutiny and the disasters of the Boer War. 'Responsible Imperialism' was the name of the game now. These primitive tribesmen would be taught to clothe their nakedness, so that, in time, they too would acquire the dignity of the European. They must be taught to sing the praises of the Lord. Their devastating intertribal wars must cease; and the cycles of famine and disease would be brought to an end if their witch doctors could be persuaded to jettison their bags of chicken bones and adopt instead the methods and benefits of modern medicine. The Africans, in short were children with a lot to learn, and the British were there to teach them. With this in mind, Great Britain had made a pledge to the League of Nations to govern her Protectorates as 'a sacred trust of civilisation until such time as they were able to stand on their own feet in the strenuous conditions of the modern world'.

What the government had not taken into account were the sentiments of the Kenya settlers. Out of necessity, certain pledges had been made regarding their position in the country. They were given to understand that the land they were asked to farm would be theirs in perpetuity. Unlike the Colonial officials, who had half an eye to their career prospects elsewhere, the settlers dug themselves in; and with each forkful of earth they turned, their hearts became more deeply wedded to Africa. It was the beauty of the place that captivated them. Kenya had no gold or mineral wealth for them to grow rich on – just a primal, heart-stopping beauty that enveloped the mind and soul. Winston Churchill, in his book *My African Journey* written in 1907, describes the profound effect the landscape had on him: 'As one rides or marches through the valleys, across the wide plateaux of these uplands, braced by their delicious air, listening to the music of their streams and feasting the eye upon their natural beauty, a sense of bewilderment overcomes the mind. How is it they have never become the home of some superior race, prosperous, healthy and free.' Another lovely word picture can be found in Elspeth Huxley's biography of Lord Delamere, where she describes the view from one of the grass huts he built on the slopes of the Mau Escarpment in 1904: 'You could see how the forest rose and fell in ridges. From the summit of one ridge you could look down on to the tree tops from above and see two shades of colour, sea-deep of cedars and spring-green of olives, splashed with the racing shadows of clouds merging into the restless pattern like a leafy ocean...The windows looked out onto a long grass-covered slope merging into the flat plains below. You could see from these apertures, slow-moving and compact herds of zebras, gazelles and hartebeests mingling with awkward, striding ostriches and occasionally a placid rhino, ruminating beneath a thorn tree. Everywhere colours were vivid and deep, always changing: distant escarpments sharply defined the sky, rich with moving clouds, the atmosphere clear with the rarity of mountain air, and charged with a sense of space and freedom blown on cool, crisp breezes from the hills.'

This was the world my parents moved in. It was the backdrop to my father's work. As a servant of the Crown and a member of the Colony's judiciary, he had to be seen to be impartial in the increasingly acrimonious disputes between the settlers and the Whitehall Government. He could not take sides. It was a difficult position to hold in such a small community. A measure of his success could be seen in the deep affection everyone in the Colony had for him. Because of his lovely voice, he was known by some as the Singing Judge; by others who were impressed by his faith, as Holy Joe. Quite simply, he was loved by all, Africans and British alike.

In 1929, when I was two years old, he was appointed to the post of Chief Justice of one of the newly mandated territories of the League of Nations, the former German colony of Tanganyika (Tanzania). It was here, in Dar es Salaam, that my earliest recollections of Africa begin.

Chapter 15

Dar es Salaam Remembered

Many years later, when she was well into her eighties, Nanny Haytus travelled up to London from St. Leonards-on-Sea to visit me. She had seen the announcement of Clare's birth in the papers. Noting the address, she found her way to my parents-in-laws' house at 57, Onslow Square, and rang the bell. I opened the door to a little old lady with rosy cheeks and a sweet smile. Over a cup of tea, she started hesitantly to explain why she had felt impelled to come. Of course, she had wanted to see our beautiful baby, but she also wanted to apologise for having been beastly to me all those years ago. She confided how ill she had felt at the time. The climate had not suited her. She had hated the heat and the sun. As she spoke, a well of sympathy rose up within me. Those knobbly hands, which had caused me so much amusement, were indications of the cruel pain of arthritis. I recalled her grey, lisle stockings; her black, lace-up shoes; her uniform – all so unsuitable for life in the tropics. Her only friend had been the young nanny from Government House. They would sit side by side on our exclusive stretch of pumice-strewn beach, and discuss their employers – always referred to as 'my people' – while we children collected cowrie shells and built sand castles in the fine white sand that smelled of copra. She embraced me with affection, and before she left, handed me a pair of beautifully crotcheted bootees for the baby before stepping into a taxi. I did not see her again. She died that winter in her retirement home in St Leonards-on-Sea.

Unlike Nanny, I remember Dar es Salaam as a place of enchantment. This is where I first experienced the intoxicating impact of colour upon my senses. Because Nanny refused to speak Swahili, it fell to me to call down to the kitchen for hot water to be brought upstairs for our baths. As I leant over the veranda that overlooked the kitchen quarters and called for 'mahji moto', I would thrill to the way the scarlet plumes of the flame tree, growing in the yard, tangled with the yellow blossom of the African laburnum. Running up the wide, shallow steps at the front of the house, the torch of orange petals bursting from the bronze leaves of the canna lilies, planted in tubs on either side, made me tingle with delight. The red wheels of my beloved tricycle, flashing past the blue agapanthus and purple bougainvillea, filled me with a sense of power. I would pause for breath in the lavender-misted shade of the jacaranda tree, inhaling the heavy scent of the frangipani bushes and listen to the lazy call of an African dove and the gentle rattle of the leaves of the coconut palms. Many centuries ago, the Sultans of Oman chose this inlet of the Indian Ocean to build palaces and pleasure gardens for their concubines. I can well understand why.

From the house, we could glimpse the estuary through the trees, as it wound its way round a headland towards the arc of the harbour. The sun broke the surface of the water into myriads of sun-stars. Midstream, the rusty-red of a half-submerged wreck introduced an air of menace into this otherwise tranquil scene of tropical bliss. I believe its purpose was to divert a sand bank from blocking the shipping channel. The pink funnels of a Union Castle passenger ship, gliding slowly round the headland, out towards the open sea, would send me into paroxysms of joy. I would clap my hands and jump up and down as I heard the strains of a Gilbert and Sullivan melody drifting over the water from the band on deck. These memories of Dar es Salaam - its scents, its sounds, its vibrant colours - would sustain me in the dreadfully dark days that lay ahead.

The house also contributed to the enchantment. It had been newly built by the Germans, and its architect, I suspect, had a sympathy for the geometric symmetry of Walter Gropius. It still stands today on high ground overlooking the estuary, partially hidden from the road by a grove of coconut palms. One of our delights was to watch the nuts being harvested. Using no more than their bare hands and feet, the men would grip the smooth, straight trunks of the trees, and with astonishing speed, shin up to the top. There, they would lean perilously far out and cut free the heavy bunches of nuts. As with any African activity, the operation was conducted with a lot of noisy comment from on-lookers and passers-by.

Much of our day was spent on the wide, stone verandas – a notable feature of the house. The lower one was where my parents liked to relax. It was approached from the garden by a double flight of steps. The upper one was, strictly speaking, a balcony. It was cut flush into the six rectangular columns that supported the roof and divided the façade into bays. The overhang of the two layers of roof, their long horizontal lines of red tiles contrasting with the white colonnaded facade, provided generous canopies of shade over the verandas. Alain de Botton, the architectural critic, would recognise it as the architecture of happiness.

Cool black and white marble tiles covered the floor of the entrance hall, and a wide stone staircase led up to the first floor. Here, all was jollity and light: shimmering sun-light made patterns on white walls; floors of red and white tiles danced beneath one's feet; a breeze off the sea kept the rooms cool and gently rattled the palm leaves outside. To the left of the stairs, a door opened onto the two nurseries. These were big airy rooms running the width of the house, the day nursery leading into the night nursery. This was Nanny's fiefdom. She liked to sit on the veranda, working her treadle sewing-machine, and listening to the wind-up gramophone while I played with my toys on a large, circular, grass mat in the middle of the room behind her. Her favourite record was 'Will You Walk Into My Parlour Said The Spider To The Fly'. 'There's a moral lesson to be learnt there' she would comment, while putting it carefully back into its brown, paper cover.

The night nursery could have been described as our Green Room. This is where Helen and I were groomed. There was a great deal of hairbrushing and washing to be done throughout the day. My protests were invariably greeted with 'Come along child. Cleanliness is next to Godliness'. I stood very still though, while having my hair brushed, for I understood that the poor woman was having to deal with – oh horror of all horrors – Rat's Tails. We were dressed and undressed several times a day. Nanny was determined that we should be the best-dressed children in Dar. There were dresses for the morning; dresses for the afternoon; dresses for going to Government House; dresses for parties; dresses for tea time – all with matching knickers and sun hats, of course. The cost of our wardrobe was an ongoing bone of contention between her and my mother. The night nursery also doubled as a stadium for Nanny to chase me with a hairbrush when I had been naughty – rather in the manner of the farmer's wife in Three Blind Mice. As we slept on the veranda, there was little furniture to impede us. I was, therefore, able to get up quite a head of steam, outrunning her poor, stiff, legs and so evading capture.

Twice a week I escaped from the nursery. Thursday was Nanny's day off, and Sunday was the day my parents kept for me. Sunday was a day of liturgy and ritual. It began with Mass, celebrated in the Catholic Church near the harbour. Its silvered spire could be seen from some distance, piercing the skyline of the buildings that huddled round the bay. A newly arrived naval vessel riding at anchor might compete for our attention, but the insistent ringing of the bell demanded that we turn off the sandy road, turn our backs on the sunshine and enter the quiet, calm of the church. *Et intriobo ad altare Deum: ad Deum qui laetificat juventutum meam'*. ('I will go unto the altar of God: to God who brings joy to my youth'), were the opening words of the Mass. My mother caressed my hand, as the priest murmured the Latin prayers. My father's head remained bowed throughout. This was my cradling into Catholicism. Few of my parents' friends shared or understood their faith, yet they were highly respected for it.

We returned home for the ritual of Sunday lunch, which was served in the dining room. We were waited on by two houseboys with all the decorum of acolytes. They were dressed in freshly-laundered white 'kanzus', coloured cummerbunds and gold embroidered waistcoats. Their little Arabic hats or 'kofias' were embroidered to match the waistcoats. With a gracefulness no English butler could emulate, they moved barefoot round the table presenting the dishes. Simba, our kitchen 'toto', who served in the nursery and was the bane of Nanny's life, had a lot to learn. The meal over, we would rinse our fingers in glass bowls, disturbing the frangipani blossoms floating in the water.

Now it was time to settle into the large wicker chairs on the veranda just above the garden where the air was filled with the scent of jasmine. My father would sing my favourite songs and twiddle his black bushy eyebrows into funny shapes to make me laugh. My mother chattered away in her lilting, Irish brogue, giving my father the latest news and gossip, while puffing on a de Reszke cigarette. I was dimly aware that I had siblings other than Baby Helen. They were at school, I was told – overseas – and one day I would join them, and it would be a lot of fun.

Later, in the cool of the evening, we would drive along the deserted coastal road to Leopard's Cove. We passed the sinister column of smoke that rose from behind the bamboo screen that hid the Indian crematorium: 'Don't look, Tays! Don't look!' But I always did, and was always frustrated by how little I saw.

Thursday, by contrast, was a day of Misrule. It was a day for picnicking at Oyster Bay. Picnics, in those days, were not for children. They were grown-up affairs. Nevertheless, even grown-ups occasionally need toys. And so, in Nanny's absence, my mother's friends would storm the day nursery, raid the toy cupboard and carry off my inflatable red rubber duck – and me, their real, live dolly. In the car, I was jostled from one lap to another, amidst gales of laughter and general *bonhomie*. Once there, I would make a dash for the little pink crabs that formed a frilly line at the edge of the surf. I never managed to catch one. The moment they sensed me coming, they scuttled away.

During the rest of the afternoon, I was hoisted on to shoulders, toppled by waves, rescued spluttering with salt water and rage, only to be hoisted up again on to another pair of shoulders. And now I could see my precious inflatable duck being swept out to sea. My rage and the plight of my duck went unnoticed. The party was going well. Everyone, bar me, was having a wonderful time. On the drive back, I snuggled, animal-like, up to my mother, a sulky heap of exhaustion.

But the day was not over. Bath-time had to be endured. I was lathered, soaped and sponged by several pairs of elegantly manicured hands. I have been told that on one occasion, one of the pairs of hands belonged to the Duchess of Gloucester. How, I wonder, could I have recognised the royal poke and tickle? After they had all had a go at Rub-a-dub-dub, I was carried to bed, limp as a rag doll, safe at last under my mosquito net. I refused to ask God to bless them, and they gradually drifted away, leaving behind a mixed scent of powder, perfume and cigarette smoke. I fell asleep, secure in the knowledge that Nanny would be there in the morning, once again ready to take charge of the day with Truby King professionalism.

Chapter 16

Nursery Life in Dar es Salaam: two true stories

Cleanliness next to Godliness

'What is that?' the woman asked, not daring to believe her eyes. The child followed the line of the quivering index finger as it stretched from the polished bumps of the arthritic hand. It seemed to be pointing out towards the horizon, far beyond the line of white foam where the Indian Ocean crashed angrily onto the coral reef. The child was embarrassed. Nanny never asked a question to which she did not know the answer, but this time there was an urgency in her voice – a note of genuine enquiry for information. Sophie knew she would earn a reprimand for stupidity, but she could not see anything unusual, not even the shadowy outline of a ship.

'I think it is a seagull,' she said in an effort to provide some kind of answer. 'It does look a funny shape' she added, offering the nurse an excuse for having been puzzled by something quite ordinary.

The woman choked on her irritation. Why was the child so obtuse? She did it on purpose, of course.

'Out there, child! Out there! Your eyes are sharper than mine.'

Filled with a sense of importance, Sophie put her bucket full of shells down with care, and shielding her eyes in nautical fashion, once more looked out to sea. With her feet neatly together, she concentrated on her task with all her might, the jolly bands of colour that circled her swimsuit quite at odds with her seriousness. The lapping of the water in the lagoon, the occasional chuckle of a gull and the distant roar of the ocean were the only sounds that broke the silence. Even Baby was still; her attention caught, she sat Buddha-like under a green-fringed canopy, her podgy fists gripping the leather sides of the pram, as she tried to follow her sister's gaze.

'I can't see anything, Nanny.'

The child, feeling puzzled and inadequate, turned to look at the woman beside her. Nanny's legs had always held a fascination for her. It had crossed her mind more than once that they might be stuffed with kapock like those of her gollywog. They certainly had nothing in common with the silken elegance of her mother's slender legs, or with the straight mahogany limbs of the Africans. Now in their rigid immobility, they looked odder than ever, as though they might not give her support for very much longer. Standing on the white sand, one black-laced shoe in front of the other, she resembled an awkward runner, frozen at the first step by the sound of the starting pistol. Her face was shaded against the sun by the brim of her double terai hat. Beneath its shadow her eyes puckered into slits in an attempt to focus on an object beyond their range of vision. Her lean, taut body in its grey dress emanated an urgency that had nothing to do with its customary crackle of irritation.

'Make haste, child. Put on your sandals and give me a hand with the pram. Don't dawdle. We must go for help'.

Sophie brushed the sand off her ankles. She noticed that if you looked closely, you could see that each grain was a tiny fragment of a shell. As she knelt over her task, she was aware of the sharp smells of the beach. Nanny was fond of pointing out the heaps of pumice that lay around. 'That shows it's a clean beach,' she would say, adding 'and cleanliness comes next to godliness, you know.' They never went to the more frequented harbour beach, for there, Nanny maintained, they would 'pick up disease'. The nanny from Government House was of like mind, and occasionally she and her charges would join them on this lonely stretch of the shore. When this happened, Sophie had a muddled notion that the beach then became 'godly'. She struggled with the buttons on her canvas shoes. They were rounded, like beads, and slipped several times between her sandy thumb and forefinger before she finally coaxed them through the narrow slits on the straps. She rose quickly from her crouching position and ran to join her nurse.

With the persistence of an ant, the elderly woman was pushing the heavy barouche over the soft sand towards the road, taking care to avoid the tussocks of sea grass. At last the big wheels stopped spinning and moved smoothly over the tarmac. She stood, panting with exhaustion at the side of the dusty road. The afternoon sun still held a great deal of heat, and there were small beads of sweat on her upper lip. The convulsive twitching of her hands on the chromium bar of the pram indicated the troubled theme of her thoughts. What could have persuaded her to come to this godforsaken country! She should have known better. If only she had had the good sense to retire when she finished her last job; but she had been too proud.

Her previous employers had been White Russians; she liked to emphasise the word 'White'. She had been with them for a number of years, and when the children were ready for their boarding schools, the family would have liked her to stay on. She could help in so many ways, they pointed out; there was the household linen to be repaired, and the children would need supervision in the holidays; she would be so useful too, when they had house guests. But she knew her rule was at an end; her kingdom gone; so when she saw the advertisement in *The Lady*, 'Titled people require fully trained Children's Nurse. Must be willing to travel', she applied for the post. To her delight, she discovered at the interview that a second child was expected shortly. The prospect of a new babe was irresistible, and when she was offered the job, she accepted without hesitation. With hindsight, she realised her foolishness. She had not considered that life in the colonies could be appreciably different from the one she had been accustomed to. She should have paid more heed when her friend referred to Africa as 'the dark continent'. As it was, she found herself totally unprepared for what lay ahead.

The heat was one thing. She found it very hard to bear. But what repelled her was the dirt. The dirt, and the jaunty insolence of the Africans. How could you maintain Truby King standards of cleanliness and order in the nursery, when the boy who served at table wore no shoes and was unable to keep his thumb out of the food? Time and again she had sent the food back to the kitchen, only to have it served a second time in exactly the same fashion. No reprimand would dim the brilliance of the boy's wide, toothy smile; and his ability to release from Sophie a spasm of uncontrollable giggling infuriated her. As for her employers, they hardly paused in their merry-go-round of parties and picnics to even listen to her complaints, much less take any action on her behalf. And so, debilitated by the climate and devoured by homesickness, she struggled on from day to day. And now this final horror, this insult to everything she stood for, must be contended with.

She calmed herself and addressed the child. 'We must watch out for a car, Sophie. When you see one coming, wave your hand.'

'Why must I wave my hand, Nanny?' she asked

'You know very well why,' came the terse reply. 'We want it to stop.'

'But nanny,' the child persisted, 'I often wave to people in cars, and they never stop.'

The argument was brought to a premature close by the distant drone of an engine.

'Wave, child, wave!'

Sophie waved in the only way she knew how. Her small hand fluttered from side to side in a merry gesture of 'farewell and Godspeed'. Nevertheless, the car did slow down, and a bevy of dark, jewelled faces peered out at them curiously.

'Oh dear! They're Indians! They won't do!' the nurse shouted above the noise of the motor, 'Shake your head, Sophie!'

In a welter of embarrassment, Sophie's hand sunk slowly to her side, and casting her eyes firmly on the ground she shook her head. The driver let in the clutch and drove off in a plume of dust. Through the small rear window the swaying heads of the passengers were visible, as they engaged in an animated discussion on the strange ways of Europeans.

And it was not only the Indians who were puzzled. Sophie, too, wondered what could have caused her nurse to behave so strangely. Standing dutifully beside the pram, she stole a glance over her shoulder at the deserted beach. Perhaps there was something strange out there. The tide was coming in quite fast, and she watched with fascination the eager way the waves spread themselves over the dry sand. She noticed a quantity of seaweed floating behind the waves, rolling and turning on the gentle swell. It was being eyed with interest by some noisy gulls. But by now her attention was called back to the road. A speck of dust in the distance, accompanied by the noise of a steady hum heralded a second car. It was the District Commissioner on his way to the Club for a sundowner. Frowning against the low light of the sun, he recognised trouble in the little group at the roadside. Withdrawing his elbow from its relaxed position at the window, he gripped the wheel more firmly, and drew in beside them.

The old lady did not wait for the car to stop, but ran alongside it and then giving the young officer no time to alight, she thrust her head in the offside window and told her story in gasps, pointing every now and then toward the shore.

Sophie was out of earshot, but once again, she turned to follow the direction of the pointing finger. And this time she saw it.

The tangled vegetation she had noticed before was quite close now, for the tide was fully in. It remained sluggishly behind the curve of each new wave, as if ashamed to reveal its gruesome burden, but Sophie could see, quite plainly, that cocooned within its slippery mass was the bloated body of a human corpse.

It must have been in the water for a number of days, for it was covered in barnacles. Its colour and texture was similar to that of the dugout canoes the Africans used for fishing and from which the poor man must have fallen. Although good fishermen, few Africans could swim, and death by drowning was not an uncommon event. Sophie stared and stared, taking in every detail, for she knew that it was only a question of time before she would be forbidden to look on such a dreadful sight.

The District Commissioner drove off in the direction of the town and officialdom, promising the nurse, before he left, that the matter would be dealt with as speedily as possible. The man's word was as good as his deed in Nanny's estimation, and now that her panic was spent, she was determined to see the business through properly. Guiding the pram towards the shade of a nearby casuarina tree, she beckoned to Sophie to come over without disturbing the now sleeping baby. They sat down on the mat of dark pine needles and waited.

'Keep your eyes straight ahead,' the nurse admonished quietly 'and don't you dare look to your left.'

'But Nanny,' the child whispered back, as she peeped between her fingers at the men carrying the tarpaulin bundle to the dark green van. 'I thought you said we must never sit here, because you said the natives used this tree for their lavatory'. And as she said this, she was joyfully aware that nanny would never again be deceived by pumice stone or anything else, into believing that any part of Africa could be clean. She knew, too, that it would not be long before she would be waving her small hand in that merry gesture of farewell as Nanny boarded the ship for home.

Diamonds in the Sky

The nurse was a dour, colourless presence in the cool, Arabic architecture of her employer's house. She was not in the habit of allowing her nursery routine to be interrupted. Every line of her thin, straight body demonstrated to those who crossed her path that here was a force to be reckoned with. The rigid folds of her linen dress, the grey lisle stockings disappearing into the sensible, black lace-up shoes, the knobbly hands twitching at her side, were in strong contrast to the graceful figure of the Chief Justice's wife. This time, however, Lady S knew she had no need to press her case, for Nanny H, like so many of her breed, was a snob, and the mere mention of the governor's name was enough to gain her grudging consent. HMS *Amethyst*, a battle cruiser, was in port, and a dance was to be held on board. The children from Government House, accompanied by their nanny and an askari were going to walk the short distance to the harbour after their supper to see the ship lit overall. His Excellency had asked if Sophie and her nurse would like to join them. 'I can't say I approve of the idea,' the nurse remarked in her flat authoritative tones. 'But, be that as it may, the decision and the consequences are yours, m'lady'.

The small child heard the news with astonishment. In all her four years, she could not remember nanny allowing such a thing. Her mother said the ship would be lit 'from stem to stern' with fairy lights. Would the fairy lights be made of amethysts, like her mother's ring, she wondered. Perhaps amethysts glowed in the dark, like the flying fish she had once seen. But what had fairies and jewelled lights to do with the steely grey ship she had seen sail down the estuary – so different to the jolly passenger liners she was accustomed to? Nanny's terse replies to her enquires made her none the wiser. And now the unbelievable was happening: Nanny was leading her out of the house, down the broad, shallow steps, past the tubs of ghostly canna lilies into the enveloping black of an African night. The little girl could sense that even Nanny felt fear.

At the gate, they were met by the small group from Government House. The nurses exchanged polite greetings. The children, who were not Sophie's friends and had no intention of becoming so, stood apart and stared at her in a way that would denote hostility in an adult, but in a child meant little more than curiosity tempered with a fear of the unknown. They set out along the harbour road, following the lithe figure of the askari. Clad in his immaculate khaki uniform with its scarlet cummerbund and glistening clasp, the tassle swinging jauntily at the side of his tall fez, the African bodyguard provided a proud symbol of security of British rule in the Colony. The carefully cultured voices of the English women broke on the night air with an alien sound. When they paused in their conversation, other sounds of the night could be heard: the gentle rattle of the palm leaves, water lapping against the sides of canoes; Swahili greetings from a shadowy passer-by, and the ceaseless croaking of frogs. The smell of rotting copra was more pungent than by day. Through the thin soles of her best shoes, Sophie could feel the warmth of the road dust. The flame trees, robbed of their colour by the night, cast intriguing shadows on the ground. She became used to the dark, and no longer feeling the need to make out familiar landmarks, she turned her gaze upwards.

In an instant, she was transported with dynamic suddenness, into a state of near ecstasy. The quick intake of her breath, the suspension of that breath and the slow exhalation, failed to attract anyone's attention. Stunned and unable to move, she let go her nurse's hand and abandoned her whole being to the contemplation of the myriad of stars displayed in all their iridescent glory. Their diamond patterns twinkled, throbbed and vibrated with a palpable force. It seemed as though they held all beauty, all laughter, all happiness, all energy, that had ever been. She could not be separated from these dancing jewels. They were part of her very being. 'Oh Nanny, stop!' she cried. 'Look up at the stars!' she shouted. 'Oh do look up. Please...' she entreated with all the urgency her small person could command. 'Will you cease being such a nuisance', the nurse replied. 'Now walk up and stop dallying. When will you learn to behave', she added irritably.

They reached the jetty. 'Ah, there she is!' exclaimed the women, as they pointed out HMS *Amethyst* to each other. 'Oh, she is a fine sight.' Their proprietary tones betrayed the vicarious pleasure they were enjoying in the knowledge that their 'people' were on board dancing the night away in the company of, not only His Majesty's Representative for the Colony, but also with other titled folk and certain high-ranking officers of His Majesty's Royal Navy. The askari, too, was murmuring appreciatively. Only the children were silent. Perhaps they, like Sophie, felt that a row of naked electric light bulbs shedding their harsh, yellow light from a ship's cable was hardly worth applauding. True, the battleship did have more lights than other ships in the port; but how much more mysterious and exciting were the small lights of the fishing boats and the soft glow that radiated from the carpeted interiors of the dhows. The frenetic notes of a saxophone echoed over the water. It sounded sad, in its desperation to be happy, quite out of key with the beauty of the harbour, whose Arabic name, Dar es Salaam, means 'Haven of Peace'.

'And did you see the lights?' her mother asked the next day, while dandling Baby on her knee during her morning visit to the nursery. 'Oh yes', interposed Nanny, unusually enthusiastic. She had certainly enjoyed the spectacle, and enjoyed even more the loquacious company of the indiscreet nanny from Government House. 'But I fear it was a waste of time taking Sophie. As I have always said, that child has little or no imagination. 'What a pity', commented the Chief Justice's wife. 'Perhaps it was rather late for her', she added wistfully.

Chapter 17

The Voyage

My separation from home came earlier than I expected and without warning. I knew my brothers and sisters were away at school in England, and that one day I would join them, but I had been led to believe that would not be for another three years, when I would be seven years old. In 1933, my eldest sister, Peggy, was diagnosed with tuberculosis. This meant my sunlit childhood had to end sooner than anticipated. Even if I had been forewarned, children lack the experience to apprehend the future. They tend to live in the immediate present, and my immediate present was one of overwhelming bliss.

We were passengers on one of my beloved Union Castle ships about to sail for England. I had no troublesome thoughts about leaving Africa. I fully expected to be returning with my parents in three months' time. As Chief Justice of Tanganyika, my father was entitled by the Colonial Office to take three months' home leave every two and a half years. If this seems generous, consideration needs to be given to the length of the journey. He seldom managed to spend more than six weeks in England. My mother would generally stay longer if she possibly could.

Several people, many of them officials, had come to see us off. Close friends, carrying bouquets of flowers and baskets of fruit, made their way to my parent's cabin for a farewell drink. Our luggage had been sorted in the stifling heat of the tin-roofed Customs Shed. Each piece had been labelled with a large, purple 'S' for Sheridan. The tin trunks, with their 'NOT WANTED ON VOYAGE' stickers had been jumbled into big, rope nets and lifted high in the air by the cranes, before being carefully lowered into the holds of the ship. Smaller cases were carried on board by dockers, then brought to the cabins by white-coated stewards. The confusion and hubbub added to the excitement. Passengers making their way up the gangways were looking forward to spending time with families and friends they had not seen for many months. After four weeks at sea they would be greeted by those faithful correspondents who, over the years, kept them abreast of events at home in England.

Our imminent departure was heralded by the sound of a gong cutting through the buzz of voices, together with the repeated command 'All visitors ashore please'. This was our cue to hurry on deck, being careful, on the way, not to trip on the big, brass bulkheads. Held up by my father, I watched the land slip slowly away, and along with everyone else, I waved and waved at the diminishing figures left on the quay. Two tugboats, like the handmaids of some stately duchess, led us out into the estuary. And now came the moment I had been waiting for: the band, positioned on the forward deck, began to play. The sun glinted on their brass instruments and twinkled on the silver badges of their white topees. What were they playing? Was it the overture to HMS *Pinafore*, or tunes from *The Merry Widow*? It didn't matter. It was thrilling. To my annoyance, this jolly music kept being interrupted by deep-throated blasts from our funnels, that reverberated right through me. The answer was to block my ears and concentrate on the conductor's baton.

Finally, it was time for bed: time to be introduced to the strangeness of a bunk, and the sound of the sea splashing past outside the porthole. After my bath in an enormous tub with giant taps that released a flow of hot salt water – a smaller tap had fresh water, to be used sparingly – I was lulled to sleep by the steady rhythm of the ship's engines. In a few days' time this would be normality, but on this first night it was a little frightening.

Aden was our first port of call. We were now at the entrance of the Red Sea and the temperature soared. Several passengers fell victim to a debilitating skin complaint known as 'prickly heat'. My mother dreaded it and managed to keep it at bay with a daily dose of Epsom salts. The decks were lined with limp figures on chaises longues, too exhausted to speak much less go ashore. For me, the Red Sea was a disappointment. I had expected it to be red; but it wasn't even pink. It was greenish-blue, like any other sea. True, there were swirls of reddish sand in the water, but that, in my opinion, hardly justified calling it red.

Leaving Aden and the Yemen behind, we sailed on past Ethiopia, to reach Port Sudan, on the edge of the Nubian Desert. It was here that the 'gilly-gilly' men came on board. They were magicians. Instead of rabbits coming out of top hats, their trick was to make baby chicks appear out of the clothing of someone in their audience by calling out "gilly-gilly-gilly-gilly". To my horror, one came chirping out of the sleeve of my dress. Screaming with fright, I ran to my mother and refused to stay for the rest of the show. Then there were the Sudanese dockers with their thickets of fuzzy hair and wild, menacing eyes who worked in the holds of the ship. I called them 'Fuzzy Wuzzies', but this endearing appellation did little to allay my terror when one afternoon I encountered one of them on the deck.

Suez, at the northern end of the Red Sea, was our next port. There is a magical moment on board a ship, when someone says 'I can see land'. You strain your eyes in the direction of their pointing finger. Is that cloud on the horizon, more solid than you had at first thought? Others join you at the deck rail clutching their binoculars. The misty blob starts to take shape. Cliffs and coves appear; then trees and buildings. Land birds fly overhead. The pilot boat speeds out to meet you, and the pilot climbs up the awkwardly swaying rope ladder. Slowly you steam towards all the busyness of a harbour. The scenery of a new country spreads out before you, like the opening set for a play. The ship, once anchored, takes on a different role. It is no longer an ocean-going vessel; it has become a floating island, a curiosity for the inhabitants of the mainland.

We didn't berth at Suez, but rode at anchor. This meant lots of little boats coming out to fuss around us. Water-taxis ferried passengers ashore for shopping trips. Launches carrying police and customs officials came alongside. Fresh water and victuals had to be loaded off bigger boats. And then there were the traders who rowed out in their skiffs: some would choose to come on board and spread their wares on oriental carpets on the deck; others did business from their boats. Customers would lean over the rail and point to whatever took their fancy. Some traders were happy to accept barter in lieu of money, and the items would be put into a basket and lowered into the boat bobbing in the water far below. Shell necklaces, carved figurines and beaded bangles would be exchanged for cigarette lighters, wristwatches and powder compacts. I am ashamed to say that my delight was to throw coins overboard and watch young boys dive like dolphins through the clear, green water to retrieve them. When we travelled back to England in 1947, we found this death-defying stunt had been banned. Too many boys had either drowned or suffered permanent damage to their lungs.

After leaving Suez we entered the Canal. Here my excitement knew no bounds. I raced between the decks, explaining to an exasperated passenger who stood in my way that I wanted to be on both sides of the ship at once. There was so much to see. Apart from where it opens into the Bitter Lakes, the Canal is narrow, and shipping has to pass through it very slowly, giving one plenty of time to study the scenes on both banks. Fortunately, Nanny liked to spend as much time as possible on deck. She distrusted the ship's nursery, believing it to be a breeding ground for germs. In fact she was of the firm opinion that other children were carriers of every kind of dread disease, and therefore should be avoided at all costs. She even persuaded the stewards to serve our meals on deck. So while Baby Helen sat happily in her playpen, I was free to chat to everyone and to observe everything. I watched scenes unchanged since Biblical times: men in white robes rode on donkeys, their head dresses held in place by colourful bands; goats sheltered from the sun under date palms; children waved, and women emerged from the doorways of flat-roofed, mud-baked houses, gracefully balancing water jars on their heads. In the distance, ships' masts, apparently sailing through the desert, proclaimed the hidden presence of the Nile.

On the starboard side, ships with strange names and foreign flags passed slowly by. Curious passengers stared across at us. We, in turn, stared back at them. My eyes couldn't open wide enough when I spied a Chinaman with a pigtail, wearing a beautiful blue silk coat and black baggy trousers. Every day there were new surprises. I watched the grownups playing deck quoits and swimming in the square, canvas pool. I saw flying fish and dolphins, and the evening sun light up the desert sky. As the sun set and the distant mountains became stained with deep purple shadow, the Southern Cross could still be seen in the sky, though now it was very low on the horizon. Soon it would disappear altogether, as we continued our journey northwards.

Every day, at four o'clock, we would join our parents for afternoon tea in the saloon. This was an ordeal. I had to drink cupfuls of tinned milk and eat horrible biscuits with NICE traced on them in gritty sugar. No fuss was allowed. It was a time for best behaviour. The occasional concert was another formal affair that had to be endured with good grace. Baritones with twirly moustaches and sopranos of uncertain pitch, sang Edwardian love duets. Sitting in the front row, it was hard to control one's giggles.

When my father sang, accompanied, as always, by my mother on the piano, it was a different matter. The rich tones of his lovely baritone voice, moved his audience to tears. He had been tempted, as an undergraduate of Trinity College, Dublin, to abandon his law studies, and accept a contract with The Carl Rosa Opera Company. It is interesting to speculate on how successful he might have been. He would stand with his right hand cupped over his ear and his left on his heart. He sang with conviction. No one doubted his true love for his Snowy Breasted Pearl, or the sincerity of his plea for the Lord to Bless This House, and when he had finished singing her praises, everyone was prepared to toast The Star of The County Down.

Our passage through the Suez Canal on this occasion took longer than usual. We hit a sandbank during the night. There was a tremendous jolt. The force of the impact threw me out of my bunk. Fortunately, there was no structural damage, and nobody seemed to have been hurt. In the morning there was much discussion on how it had happened and on how long it would be before a tugboat could come to our rescue and help re-float us. People tramped impatiently round the deck, hoping to glimpse some activity. They were not happy about the delay to their journey. To their dismay, the view ahead of the wide, glittering expanse of The Bitter Lakes remained unchanged for several days. Eventually, two fussy little tugs tut-tutted their way towards us. Hawsers were attached and after a great deal of pulling and straining and shouting, we were once more underway.

Port Said is the gateway into the Mediterranean. This is where the Canal ends. It is also the place where everyone left the ship to go shopping. It used to be said that 'you could pick anything up at Port Said'. Simon Artz, for instance, was an emporium of international acclaim. I remember how my brothers used to enjoy watching me dissolve into a pool of outraged tears when they pointed out that my black hair was evidence I had been 'picked up at Port Said'! The narrow streets of the port were lined with shops, whose merchandise spilled onto the pavements in a riot of colour. The shopkeepers stood outside their emporiums, sharp-eyed and ready to pounce on the hapless traveller. The men selling 'feelthy' postcards were a feature of the place. They would display their wares by opening their jackets and calling out, seductively "Look, I show you. Very naughty. Very nice. Very cheap."

Their heyday would come with the troop ships in the war. Nanny, of course, saw to it that we stayed on board, protected from such sights. The port was no place for children.

After the confines of the Red Sea and the Suez Canal, the cool breezes of the open sea were wonderfully refreshing. The pencil-grey lines of warships were everywhere, for the Mediterranean at that time was virtually the home of the British Navy. Everyone on deck had binoculars trained on the flags, and people were busy distinguishing battleships from cruisers. The spirit of Nelson was in the air. Dolphins played merrily round the prow of the ship and large islands appeared unexpectedly out of a lavender-blue mist. It was early April and as we headed north, the weather turned chilly. The deck stewards brought round mugs of Bovril instead of the mid-morning ice creams. Marseilles would be our first European port followed by the triangular bulk of the Rock of Gibraltar. Then it was out into the Atlantic and the stormy seas of the Bay of Biscay before reaching journey's end: the waste lands of London's Tilbury Docks.

This time, however, I would not see the Barbary apes of Gibraltar, or feel the ship pitch and roll in the Bay of Biscay. It had been decided that my father and I would leave the ship when we got to Marseilles and travel by train to Calais, where we would board the ferry for Dover. The cause of these hasty rearrangements was, apparently, Nanny. The general consensus was that it was in my best interests that we should be parted from each other as soon as possible.

This drastic course of action was due, in part, to an incident at the outset of the voyage, when everyone was preparing for the fancy dress party which traditionally marked the celebrations for Crossing the Line. The highlight of this occasion was when one of the ship's officers dressed as Neptune stepped out of the swimming pool clutching his trident, and with noisy ceremony was led to a makeshift throne. From here, after a light-hearted speech, he presented prizes for the best fancy-dress costumes. Now while other children's parents were busy assembling gossamer wings, wands, sailor-suits and gold crowns, my mother's circle of fun-loving friends had taken it upon themselves to devise a costume for me they felt sure would catch Neptune's eye, and secure me the First Prize. I was to be dressed as a Beach Belle from the South of France. There is a photograph of me, clearly very unhappy, scowling from underneath a large sun-hat, wearing multi-coloured beach pyjamas and a heavy application of scarlet lipstick. Nanny was furious. The friends had to retreat before her rage. To my relief, I went to the party dressed as myself.

From then on, Nanny was a marked woman. Our days on deck gave them plenty of opportunity to observe her strict Truby King methods of childcare. My table manners were in constant need of correction. Then there was the time, in the merciless heat of Port Sudan, when I refused to eat the pink blancmange pudding wobbling unattractively on my plate. Conscious of the fact that I had a sympathetic audience, I managed to be triumphantly sick. Little Helen, on the other hand, could do no wrong: she was 'Nanny's Baby', the apple of her eye. And so it appeared to those well-meaning friends that I was the target of Nanny's bad temper. They concluded that something needed to be done; and so the plan was hatched. My mother, who had crossed swords with Nanny many times, was easily persuaded. So it was, when we docked the following day, I left the ship with my father. There were no 'good-byes'. Poor Nanny! She should have retired years ago and should never have taken on such a demanding job. I did not see her again until I was a married woman with a baby of my own.

The train journey through France was cold, and frightening. We had no tickets for the wagon lit, so we sat up all night. Nor had we brought any provisions, and as I was too frightened to walk along the narrow, swaying corridors to the dining car, we went hungry. I cannot say who was furthest from their 'comfort zone', my father or me.

Throughout my life, however, I have noticed God never fails to send a helpful angel when things become difficult. The woman sitting in a corner of our compartment was not wearing dazzling, white robes, but she had every other angelic attribute. As the train screamed its smoky way through the tunnels of the Massif, she drew me close. From her handbag, she produced a notebook and pencil and throughout that long, tedious journey, she entertained me by illustrating her charming stories. She shared her homemade buns with us. She calmed my fears when the lights went out, and reassured me when the compartment became lit with an eerie blue night-light. She covered me with her coat, and cradled my sleepy head in the crook of her arm until I eventually fell asleep.

My mother joined us in London. Our hotel, the Savoy Court, off Portman Square, belied its grand name. It was, in fact, intimate and cosy. As you entered the lobby through the revolving doors, you were greeted by the smell of furniture-polish and hot buttered toast. The low-ceilinged rooms were dark, so the electric light was on all day. The other guests were quiet and genteel. Some were permanent residents. There was one old lady, weighted down by her string of amber beads, who delighted in dropping pennies into the small pink purse I liked to carry. This treasured possession was tied round my wrist with a ribbon that matched my coat and bonnet perfectly. I was surely the picture of a happy, pampered four-year-old. In the lounge of the hotel my father would struggle to modulate his voice to the same hushed tones of the other residents. The result was a dramatic stage whisper which embarrassed my mother as much as it startled everyone else. This was the hotel where Dermot, as a barrister of the Middle Temple, lived throughout the war. Regardless of the dangers and the chaos of the Blitz, he would make his way from Portman Square to his chambers in the city. He found this daily struggle helped him to come to terms with the bravery of so many of his friends fighting in France.

Everything appeared dark and dingy and threatening after the brilliant colours of Africa. It wasn't only the daytime electric light I found strange. There was, for instance, the oddity of gas fires, with their clay candles, curious popping noises and greedy meters. As for the vacuum cleaner, surely it was a product of the devil. Half snake, half monster, with its terrible groaning and moaning, it was obviously intent on consuming its nearest victim; and, if I had anything to do with it, that was not going to be me! It rained a lot, so we hired taxis. These had hardly changed from the days of horse-drawn hansom cabs. Their cavernous interiors, smelling of old, damp leather, invariably made me feel sick. But the strangest sight of all was seeing white people do the work I associated with African servants.

I was too young and too preoccupied with all that was new and different to notice my parent's distress. For them it had been a miserable homecoming. The news from the Convent where my sisters were at school was that Peggy was seriously ill. She was barely sixteen. In those days tuberculosis was almost invariably fatal. At the same time, they were concerned for Dermot, who had been a polio victim from the age of three. He had been through public school at Downside, and was about to go to Cambridge to read Law, but before going to University, he was in Switzerland undergoing a series of operations under Professor Nico, to improve his walking. On top of all, there was the trouble with Nanny and the problem of what to do about Helen and me.

Before anything else, they had to decide what would be the best thing for Peggy. Dar es Salaam was not a good climate for her. The Highlands of Kenya on the other hand were ideal. My father decided he would apply to the Colonial Office for a posting to the High Court in Nairobi. Meanwhile they would set about finding a good sanatorium for her. To complicate matters still further, the doctors were adamant that, as young children we were particularly vulnerable to the TB bacillus, we must be kept away. It was decided I would join my sister Mary at the Convent immediately, while Helen, who was too young to accompany me, would, for the time being go with my mother to my grandmother's house in the West of Ireland. My father would first visit Dermot in Switzerland and then see my brother Roderick at Downside, before returning to East Africa on his own. It must have been an agonising time for them, having to wrestle with all these divided loyalties.

Peggy's illness impinged on all our lives. Roderick remembered her being 'full of fun, tall, slim, athletic and lovely to look at.' She was also, he recalled, 'so motherly'.

Mary must have felt the shock waves of her illness more acutely than any of us. Peggy, after all, had been her surrogate mother at the convent. Dermot adored her. Mother Aquinas, my mother's formidable sister and the headmistress of the convent was so devastated by her death she refused to leave her room for several days afterwards. But it was my father who loved her the most. I found some letters she had written him from school. They were full of fond, teasing affection. The year before she became ill, Peggy, together with Dermot, Roderick and Mary spent the summer holidays in a rented cottage at the seaside village of Enniscrone, not far from Ballina. Peggy, aged fifteen, had been in sole charge. It was a time full of laughter and light-hearted fun. Peggy's death created a void in our family circle that could never be filled.

Chapter 18

The Convent

The Convent of Jesus and Mary, LSJM, Crownhill Road, Willesden, NW10 was the first address I learnt to write. The LSJM stood for Laus Semper Jesu Maria. If you omitted these four initials, you were deemed to be a mean-spirited heathen. The school is still there, though the nuns have long since departed. I understand that now it is a high-achieving comprehensive school, and bears no resemblance whatsoever to the establishment my sisters and I knew and which was so accurately portrayed by Mary McCarthy in her play *Once A Catholic*.

The Order of Jesus and Mary was founded in Northern France towards the end of the 18th century for the purpose of teaching young girls embroidery. In 1886, they moved to London. A chapel, which had been built a few years earlier on the site of the medieval shrine of Our Lady of Willesden, was up for sale. It had been used as the parish church and had proved to be too small. The nuns bought it and engaged the architect William Goldie to build their convent adjoining it in the Gothic style.

A high wall bordering the road marked the property. The entrance was through what appeared to me, on my arrival at the age of four in May 1933 to be enormous sheet-metal gates. These opened on to a gravel driveway, which circled past a bed of tired evergreen shrubs to the steps that led up to the front door. Another flight of steps at the side of the building plunged down to the basement. This was the entrance used by the children, with which I would become all too familiar.

An unsmiling lay sister answered the bell. We followed her into a dark interior of polished floorboards, curtainless windows and lofty ceilings. There was a strong smell, not unlike the inside of a musty wardrobe, of old clothes, incense and tea. This, I learnt later, emanated from the damp tea-leaves the lay sisters threw on the floors to absorb the dust before sweeping, the sweat from their exertions with the heavy floor-polishers, and the proximity of the Chapel. We were shown into the parlour. The

Turkish carpets and Italianate furniture, while giving the room a sense of importance, did little to make it either comfortable or welcoming. A portrait of Pius XI had pride of place on the wall between the windows. But it was the photograph of the austere-looking foundress that dominated the room. She managed to make even the image of the Shroud of Turin on the opposite wall appear insignificant.

The chairs did not look inviting, so we stood waiting for the arrival of Mother Aquinas, my mother's sister, and Headmistress of the Convent. She blew into the room on such a wave of overpowering energy that I took fright, and retreated behind my mother. I simply could not look at this large, dominant woman whose face was squashed by starched frills and whose black habit was decked with rosary-beads, holy medals and a large silver cross. 'She's shy', they explained, as I refused to lift my eyes from studying the carpet. 'What on earth is she shy about?' Mother Aquinas asked brusquely.

Forced to face the company, I noticed that a thin, gawky girl in a gymslip had joined us. This, I learnt, was my sister Mary. She was ordered to take me to play in the Box Room. It had been some years since she had seen our parents, and she did not take kindly to being dismissed so soon after greeting them.

The Box Room was in the undercroft of the chapel. It was where the school trunks were stored. We wandered aimlessly between the alleyways of luggage piled high above us, like blocks of flats. We had little to say to each other and when a nun eventually came to fetch us she expressed surprise at our gloomy silence. She had expected to find us squealing with merriment. It was a rare privilege to be allowed in to the Box Room. 'And isn't it a great place to play hide and seek!' she enthused.

We joined the grown-ups who, by contrast, were chattering like magpies (my parents were exceptionally noisy people!) Mother Aquinas, known to my mother as 'Kitty', and to her favourite nieces as 'Quin', suggested we all visit the dormitories. She took us to the main staircase and we climbed and climbed up the wide stone steps to the top floor. We were shown the Babies' Dormitory and introduced to a dear little nun, barely taller than me, with rosy cheeks and twinkly eyes, called Sister Josephine. She had one oddity – a silky moustache on her upper lip. Two rows of twelve beds were separated into cubicles by white curtains. It was all very neat. A picture of my favourite cartoon character, Mickey Mouse, hung on the wall. Sister Josephine took me over to have a closer look. When I turned round, my parents had gone – vanished! I ran screaming into the corridor, but there was no sign of them, or of Mother Aquinas, or even of Mary. I was alone with Sister Josephine, and Sister Josephine had 'morphed' into a demon. Her rosy cheeks were red with rage. Her twinkly blue eyes were now slits of steel and her silky moustache was bristling. She caught me and held me in an iron grip. There was no escape. The portcullis was down, the drawbridge was up and I was a captive of the Jesus and Mary nuns.

For the next seven years, the Jesus and Mary nuns were our guardians. It was not a happy arrangement. They were psychologically ill-equipped for the task. We, on the other hand, after the freedom of Africa, were particularly resentful of the constraints of institutional living. Above all, we missed our parents. To add to our woes, the headmistress was our aunt. This meant that, unlike other children whose parents lived abroad, we did not spend our holidays with kindly relatives in country cottages or old rectories, but remained in the school. For us the end-of-term excitement was that of sleeping in a room rather than a dormitory.

Over the years the greyness of convent life seeped into every fibre of our being. This greyness became normality. We were too young to recognise its abnormality. The loneliness and the uncontrollable rages were all, had we known it, manifestations of our deprivation. Happily, on the rare occasions when we enjoyed a family holiday, we slotted together as easily as pieces of a jigsaw puzzle. In retrospect, those precious holidays, so full of laughter, outweighed the misery of the intervening years.

On behalf of the nuns, I suspect few of them had true vocations for the religious life. The dearth of young men after the carnage of the First World War left many young girls facing spinsterhood. Several Catholic families resolved the problem by making endowments to those religious orders who would relieve them of their unmarriageable daughters. Girls from families who could not afford such payments entered as unpaid domestics under the guise of lay sisters. Communities composed of these embittered spinsters were not the places to find either sanctity or joy.

Mother Aquinas was the exception. She was, after all, a Macaulay like my mother. Macaulays deal with adversity by turning their backs on it. Their exuberant self-confidence is rarely dented. They have no time for those who linger in the slough of despond. Their gregariousness leads them to seek out other ebullient characters. Mother Aquinas had gathered round her a jolly entourage of Irish nieces: Biddy Newman, Sheila Macaulay, Sheila Fitzgerald, my sister Mary and Peggy, who had been queen of them all until her illness. I longed to be part of this glittering circle of cousins, but alas, I was too young and possibly too woebegone. On one occasion, I was found in a pool of tears on the big stone staircase by an irritable nun in a hurry. 'Go and see Mother Aquinas' she said impatiently, pointing towards the door; adding 'After all she's your aunt.' I stopped crying and studied the door. The word 'Headmistress' was spelt across it in large gold capitals. I decided, first, the door was too big and secondly, that whatever fright I was suffering from on this side of it, it was nothing compared to the terror of Mother Aquinas on the other. In that instant I realised that I was going to have to fend for myself. No amount of sobbing and sighing was going to change my situation. Children are remarkably adaptable. Like so many others, I did just that. I adapted.

Although the nuns were never physically cruel, they nevertheless used every opportunity to make their hostility plain. Throughout those long dreary years I do not remember receiving a single word of encouragement or any gesture of endearment from any one of them. Today such treatment would be classed as 'emotional abuse', defined in a Department of Health manual as 'persistent emotional ill-treatment that may involve conveying to children that they are worthless or inadequate.' As far as I am concerned, that is an accurate description of their attitude. I believe I did once succeed in pricking the conscience of at least one nun. I had been chosen to sing *The Miller of Dee* at a school concert. When it came to the line 'I care for nobody, no not I, for nobody cares for me!' I sang the words with all the molto espressivo I could muster. It was too much for the visiting Mother Provincial. 'Take that child off' she was heard to say. 'She upsets me'.

It was Nancy McGuinness who helped me to adapt. Lying in bed at night, when even the terror of Sister Josephine's barked order to "Stop that noise, Traizesherdon" failed to silence my sobs, I would spy Nancy's face with its fringe of lank hair peep round the curtain that divided our cubicles. After a whispered exchange, I would climb stealthily into her bed and be warmed by her sympathy. After the lady in the overnight train to Calais, Nancy was the second angel to appear in my life. In time her plain features must surely have been transfigured by the goodness of her soul. Perhaps she became a great beauty. I do hope so. She came to my rescue again in the morning by helping me to dress. There were so many buttons to do up, and knots to tie, and knickers and vests – known as 'liberty bodices' – to sort out. It was a relief when the navy-blue serge gym tunic slipped over my head and fell into place. Now all that remained was to secure the blue and yellow girdle with one more fiendish knot, arrange my mantilla, and I was ready to join the line of girls waiting to go down to the chapel.

The Convent Chapel was sweetly scented and full of light. Like the church in Dar es salaam, it had an air of prayerful, tranquillity. Maybe this had something to do with it having been built on the site of the medieval Shrine of Our Lady of Willesden. As one of the younger children I knelt in the front row, and so had an unrestricted view of the Sanctuary and the soaring, sweep of the Chancel arch. Two miniature altars of white marble stood on either side of it; one dedicated to Our Lady, the other to St. Joseph. Little Gothic arches, richly crocketted, formed protective canopies over their statues. In the evening, during Benediction, the high altar twinkled with light from the tiers of branched candlesticks; their pool of light deepening the darkness above. This was the Chapel where I made my First Holy Communion.

Before Mass began, there was the ritual vesting of the priest; a ceremony full of symbolism, performed with a quiet reverence. The vestments were laid out on the right hand side of the altar. The priest would kiss each garment before putting it on. While clothing himself, the priest would recite a prayer, relevant to the symbolism of each particular vestment. The Amice came first. This cloth, worn over the shoulders, signified protection against evil. The long white robe, known as the Alb, symbolising purity came next; then the Girdle, representing chastity, followed by the Maniple, the Stole and the Chasuble; each with its own significance. I could not understand the Latin prayers, but I was impressed by the orderliness of the ceremony. It was in stark contrast to my own chaotic method of dressing.

After breakfast, beds had to be made, washstands scrubbed and lockers tidied. If a counterpane had so much as a single crease, the bed would be stripped and the owner called back to remake it. The school bell would have rung and the first lesson of the day be well under way by the time my bed-making skills had satisfied Sister Josephine. Breathless from running down the many flights of stairs to the Kindergarten classroom in the basement, I made my entrance. As I opened the door, the chanting of the multiplication tables stopped while everyone studied my discomfiture with smug satisfaction. The class mistress would deliver her customary reprimand before directing me to the back of the class. Under her baton, the chant would then resume. It was not a promising start to my academic career. Being at the back of the class was tantamount to being dismissed, for the lesson appeared to be solely for the benefit of those seated in the front rows.

No day girl could sit in the front row. You had to be a boarder to be one of the elite. Day girls were considered to be inferior beings, whose weekend activities were suspect. Who knew what they got up to outside the Convent walls! They might – God forbid – even go to cinemas! They also had a defiant way of coming to school wearing white knickers instead of the regulation navy-blue. These rebels were my companions at the back of the class. We lived with the fearful possibility of being shaken out of our state of detached boredom without warning, by the class mistress demanding an answer to an impossibly difficult question. Failure to give the right reply meant standing in front of the class for the rest of the lesson, wearing the dunce's hat. I ran into trouble during a Handicraft lesson. I severed the arm of a paper doll while struggling with a pair of scissors, At the sight of the dismembered limb the nun exploded with anger. I shivered with fear. This must be a mortal sin! We were due to make our First Confessions soon. Would I have the courage to confess my crime?

Most of the time, I dreamt my way through the lessons. Gazing out of the window at the bank opposite, I would wonder what the world was like up above. In my imagination I filled it with 'All things bright and beautiful'; but instead of 'The tall trees in the greenwood, the meadows for our play', my mind's eye saw the white beaches of Dar es salaam, and, if I thought hard enough, I could hear the rattle of the 'kukuzi' breeze in the palm trees. No wonder I was considered backward. I overheard a nun referring to me as 'stupid'. Her companion's reply was more understanding: 'I don't think she is stupid. She just spends her time wool-gathering'. No one took into account the fact that I had arrived in the middle of the last term of the school year; and that, at the age of five, I was a good deal younger than the others in my class.

It was not surprising that before long, I became ill. The doctor was called. After he left, several nuns grouped themselves round my bed in a scene reminiscent of Rembrandt's 'Anatomy Lesson'. 'She's white as a sheet', remarked the Infirmarian. Mother Aquinas was concerned about the sores on my face. 'I expect that is her wickedness coming out', suggested Sister Josephine. The doctor had diagnosed bronchial pneumonia. Before the discovery of antibiotics, recovery depended on skilled nursing. He suggested, therefore, that I should be admitted to hospital. Thankfully, my mother had not yet left for Africa. She had rented a house in Hampshire for the summer holidays. Built in the 1920's in a style described by Osbert Lancaster as 'Wimbledon Transitional', it went by the cosy name of Blue Gables. I was driven down there, cocooned in blankets and tucked into a bed, soft as thistledown. My room was flooded with sunshine and filled with the scent of the yellow roses that bobbed over the windowsill. With the love and attention of my mother and the ministrations of a trained nurse, I made a quick recovery. By the time Helen arrived from Ireland with my grandmother, I was ready to join the family downstairs.

Chapter 19

August in Grayshott

The summer of 1933 was slow to arrive. By the time we were settled in Grayshott, it finally made itself felt with a heat wave. We spent all day playing outside. Mary and Roderick busied themselves making camps in the spinney at the end of the garden. They gave me permission to watch, provided I didn't get in their way. Under instruction from Roderick, Mary raided the garden shed for tools. With a hammer and a saw tucked under her skirt, and her pockets bulging with nails, she would walk nonchalantly past the grown-ups sitting on the terrace. When the gardener became suspicious, we all three happily denied any knowledge of the whereabouts of his missing tools. The same unity, however, was not evident, when Roderick, in his new found fervour for all things Benedictine, decided to construct an altar. He of course, was the priest; Mary was his acolyte. I was allowed to have a walk on part as the congregation, provided I did not let the grown-ups know what we were doing. I questioned this. It seemed to me to be an excellent game, worth boasting about. Roderick, who was proud of his Church Latin, agreed – after all, it nearly resembled the real thing. Mary rebelled. She was tired of being an acolyte and said it wasn't a bit like the real thing, and it was wicked to pretend it was. The novelty of the game evaporated in the heat of the argument. The campsite was abandoned in favour of cricket.

Roderick was keen to practice his skill as a fast bowler. He claimed there was no need for a batsman, which was just as well, as we did not have a bat. Instead, Mary was the Wicket. I begged to be allowed to join in. To my great joy, I was told I could be the Fielder. After being stumped rather painfully a couple of times, Mary was given permission to protect her legs with a coat, but found it impossible to prevent the coat from slipping while at the same time attempting to catch the ball. It was not long before her bruises were noticed and the game was stopped. They spent the rest of the holidays riding their bikes through the deserted country lanes of Hampshire, and climbing trees – an activity that

Dermot, with his powerful arms, was good at, provided he had assistance coming down.

Meanwhile, my mother had arranged for me to be prepared for my First Communion at the nearby Cenacle Convent. I had missed making it with the rest of my class at the end of the summer term because of illness. Mother Aquinas was happy for me to make it on my own when I returned to school, provided I received instruction during the holidays. I have no doubt this plan was hatched in heaven; for it was in this way that the corner stone of my faith was securely laid.

Up to this point, my preparation had taken the form of learning the penny catechism by heart. As usual, I had turned to Nancy McGuinness for further information. She told me there was one thing above all others that I must remember. I must not drink or eat *anything at all* before I received communion. If I swallowed so much as a sip of water while washing my teeth, demons would come and drag me down to hell. Under the circumstances, I felt that I had had a lucky escape and was not at all pleased to discover that First Communion was still on the agenda. But I was in for a surprise. The difference between the Jesus and Mary nuns at Willesden and those of the Cenacle Convent was stark. The Cenacle nuns, far from being embittered spinsters, were true contemplatives, with a vocation to spread the Gospel message of love.

'Cenacle', derives from the Latin word *coenaculum* meaning 'upper room'. The inspiration for their Community came from the description in the Gospels of the disciples gathering in an upper room to 'devote themselves to prayer' while awaiting the coming of the Holy Spirit. The Order had been founded in 1826 in France by St Therese Couderc, for pilgrims who came to her village to pray at the shrine of a Jesuit priest, St John Francis Regis. Today, the Cenacle Retreat Houses are spread throughout the world. They have a threefold purpose: to help people who are searching for God, to provide a sanctuary for those who want to deepen their spirituality, and to enable people to discover their own individual gifts. I was in good hands.

I don't remember seeing the face of the nun who instructed me, for she sat, swathed in layers of black shawls, in a big chair by a window. I can't even recollect the sound of her voice. She was very old and very small. I sat on a footstool beside her. Time appeared to stand still as she spoke to me of Perfect Love. Christ was to be my visitor, and I would show him the garden of my soul. As we gazed out of the window onto the sunlit lawn, she described the kind of garden He liked, filled not only with lilies and roses, but also with a host of small flowers, like daisies and violets and buttercups. Each flower would mark some deed I had performed for love of Christ. She invited me to imagine my shame, when, as I showed my important Visitor round, there were only weeds to be seen; or perhaps I had let what flowers that had been there become strangled by brambles. When my mother came to collect me, I didn't want to leave. I should have been eager to tell her all that I had learnt, but I was silent. I didn't have the vocabulary to describe my momentous experience. I should have been bouncing with joy; but I was as big a cry baby as ever – prickling with sensitivity, and ready to be hurt by the slightest thing. What I had gained was a refuge for my tears. I can still experience the sense of calm the Angel of the Cenacle gave me. My life had a purpose and a goal.

The house at Grayshott was not far from Midhurst and the sanatorium where Peggy was a patient. My parents would often drive over to see her. One day, towards the end of the holidays, when the temperatures were still up in the 80s, it was proposed that we should all visit her. We packed a picnic lunch and squeezed into the Ford V8. But the sombre shade of the pinewood where we picnicked dampened our high spirits, and as we approached the sanatorium we fell silent, lost in our own thoughts. The sight of Mother Aquinas in the driveway cheered my mother, but did nothing to lighten my spirits. I sank into an even deeper gloom when I learnt that I would not be allowed in, for fear of infection. The same rule, of course, applied to Helen; but, as the force of her protest was in danger of shattering the tranquillity of the sanatorium, the Matron relented in her case, and I was left to sit on the steps of the terrace to contemplate the unfairness of life. I did manage to catch a glimpse of Peggy through an open door. She was laughing while being reprimanded by a nurse for pulling a jersey on over her head, while still having a thermometer in her mouth. This precious vignette, illustrating her courageous spirit, is my last memory of her.

And so August drew to a close. In retrospect, despite the golden days filled with laughter, a pall hung over these holidays. It was the first time I had heard my mother complain of headaches. There is a photograph of her taken at Grayshott, before attending a Buckingham Palace Garden

Party. She is wearing a beautiful lace dress. It was the colour of *eau de nil*, which suited her well. But underneath the wide brim of her hat, she does not look happy. She was smoking too much. The doctor she consulted told her every cigarette she smoked was a nail in her coffin. Her nerves were badly frayed. The past four months had been unbearably stressful, and now she was going to have to say goodbye to us all. My father had already had to return to Africa without her. He was still Chief Justice in Dar es Salaam. It would be six months before he could take up his new appointment in Kenya, where Peggy would be able to join them. Meanwhile my mother had to decide what to do about Helen. She could not be at home with Peggy and was too young for Willesden. Heart-breaking decisions had to be made.

We saw each other again for a week at Christmas in a Hampstead hotel, before the waters closed over our heads, and we drowned in a sea of misery.

Chapter 20

Back to School

The clank of metal gates; the crunch of gravel beneath our feet; stony-faced nuns hurrying to the sound of a bell; tearful farewells in the parlour: we were back at Willesden.

This was the Autumn Term with lengthening evenings and foggy days. During the morning break, we bowled hoops on the smooth surface of the tarmac playground. This was great fun. I had my own sturdy little hoop, painted with jolly stripes of red and green, and a stick to match. Everyone else had large bendy affairs, which were difficult to control. Skill was needed, especially on foggy days, to bowl the hoop at speed round the playground without colliding into somebody else and ending in a tangled heap on the unforgiving ground. My knees were permanently grazed and I became hardened to the sharp sting of iodine.

Sunday, the longest day of the week, was Visitors' Day. The dormitories were transformed by patterned bedcovers and matching tiebacks for the cubicle curtains. We wore clean underclothes, and put on blue rayon dresses. For High Mass, we covered our heads with white mantillas and were commanded to be on our best behaviour. The Liturgy of the Sunday Mass was interminable. The high, lonely voices of the nun's choir only increased the tedium. Like guardsmen on parade, some of us were given to fainting. The bundled exit of the fallen was looked on with envy by the rest of us. It was not unknown for some girls to attempt to induce the vapours by putting blotting paper in their shoes.

More tedium awaited us after breakfast. Those of us who had not been invited out for the day – a treat only dreamt of by the Sheridan girls – gathered in one of the classrooms to hear the Reverend Mother's weekly address. It is difficult to say who suffered most from boredom, the speaker or her audience. Her voice wavered and sank and rose hesitantly, swamping us with a great empty nothingness.

In the afternoon we formed up in pairs, and walked the windy streets of Harlesden in crocodile. We passed the hospital where the patients were pushed out onto the balconies in their beds in all weathers. We crossed the road at the new Belisha beacon (named after Hoare Belisha, the Minister for Home Affairs), entered the Cemetery, and returned by the long straight road bordered by a park on one side, and a chain-link fence on the other enclosing the Municipal Sports Ground. On wet days we promenaded in the school hall to the accompaniment of a piano played by a nun whose repertoire extended no further than the *Blue Danube* and the *Skaters' Waltz*.

The high point of the day came after tea. We queued outside a lobby at the end of a corridor, and waited for Mother Aquinas to come and unlock the sweet cupboard. I had 3 pence a week pocket money. This would buy me a handful of liquorice allsorts, or peppermint humbugs, in a three-cornered paper bag. A stick of sherbet cost 4 pence, while Mars Bars and Milky Ways cost 6 pence and were well worth saving up for.

After making our purchases, we would scurry back to our classrooms and either squirrel our booty into our desks, or engage in complicated negotiations for 'swops'. 'You can have some of my sherbet, if you give me one humbug and half a liquorice bootlace.' These exchanges were interrupted by the bell for tea, after which it was time for composing the weekly letter home.

Home. I tried to conjure up in my mind what the word meant to me. While I carefully copied the words from the blackboard, I considered how different Dar es Salaam was from the picture of 'Home' in my Radiant Reading Book. My Daddy did not sit by a fire smoking a pipe. My Mummy did not wear an apron and bake cakes for tea. In Africa cats did not sit on mats, but roared at night in the bush; and we certainly did not own a dog called Rover who chased balls. My picture of home was so different, and experienced such a long time ago, that perhaps it didn't qualify as 'Home'. Nevertheless I stepped up to the nun's desk and gave her my letter, written in pencil on blue lined paper – DEAR MUMMY AND DADDY, I HOPE YOU ARE WELL. I AM WELL AND HAPPY. IT RAINED TODAY. LOVE FROM THERESE. It was too much to believe it would ever be seen by my parents. The tedium of Sunday eventually closed with supper and Benediction.

And so the days dragged by. I made my First Communion solo. I had been well prepared and felt calm and happy. It was a strange day. The nuns did not know what to do with me. I wandered up and down the corridors, clutching my curious presents. The stone holy water stoup was difficult to carry, and the certificate, in its cardboard cylinder, was also awkward. Mother Aquinas took a photograph of Mary and me with her Box Brownie camera, standing on the front steps of the Convent. Frankly it was a relief for everyone when the time came for me to change out of my white dress, back into the anonymity of my school uniform and could rejoin the rest of my class.

It wasn't only my spirits that were dampened by the cheerless regime of Willesden; my health suffered too. I fell victim to every cold and bout of influenza that came my way. Mother Aquinas' nervousness about my possible susceptibility to TB meant that instead of being put in the school infirmary when I was ill, I was isolated in a guest room kept for visiting Mother Provincials. I spent many a long day and night in this forbidding room, filled with heavy pieces of Victorian furniture. The tall windows looked out onto a neighbouring school. This was Keble, a Church of England Charity School for the poor of the parish. Its pupils were held in such low esteem by the nuns that we felt entitled to stick out our tongues if we should catch a glimpse of them through a window. Needless to say, they had no hesitation in returning the insult.

A grumpy lay sister would bring me my meals; otherwise the only sounds to break the silence were my coughs and sneezes. Copies of the *Illustrated London News* lay on a table beside my bed. With horrified fascination, I studied the photographs of the soldiers engaged in the Sino/Japanese War. Nobody seemed to be worried about the unsuitability of such literature for a six-year old. What did worry them was how apparent it had become that damp, foggy London was no place for a child brought up in the tropics. The decision was taken to move us to Ipswich. I was just seven, and Mary was ten.

The move had everything to recommend it. The Convent at Ipswich was smaller than Willesden, and the clean, Suffolk air would be much healthier for me. Conveniently, my mother had another sister in the Ipswich Community, who, because she was not involved in the school, would be able to devote more time to looking after us. With this in mind, we were packed off to Suffolk, to the Jesus and Mary Convent in Ipswich. Here we were allocated a bedroom in the nun's domain, rather than being put in one of the school dormitories. This part of the Convent was known as Homewood. It had previously been a private house. Its wisteria-clad façade and domestic interior were in contrast to the plain, penitentiary style of the main building. The two were connected by a newly-constructed brick passageway, used solely by us and the community of nuns. For the rest of the school, it was out of bounds.

So what went wrong? We all agree that while our days at Willesden were purgatorial, the years at Ipswich were hell. Was the arrival of Helen the catalyst, or was it our aunt, Mother St Brendan's inability to understand us? Perhaps it was caused by Mary's fury at being uprooted from her coterie of friends, and finding herself closeted with her younger sisters. The frosty, Reverend Mother and her headmistress certainly contributed to our discomfort. Their resentment at having had their hands forced by Mother Aquinas into granting us privileged status was all too evident. I was miserably aware that my health was the reason for the move; but for me, Ipswich would not have happened. Being set apart meant that we were neither fish, nor flesh, nor fowl. We made few friends. A swirl of hatred enveloped us. Vicious words and cruel comments punctuated the air. And all the while, our hearts ached for the presence of our mother.

What made her absence even harder to bear was her lovable personality. She was jolly. She was fun. She was warm and glamorous. She was everything the nuns were not. Above all, she loved us. I used to stand on a bank that overlooked the railway, hoping to catch a glimpse of her in one of the LNER trains that sped past. On one occasion, I was certain I had seen her. The woman moving along the corridor, in a navy check suit, with a silver fox fur over her shoulder, was surely her. I imagined I could even smell her perfume – and wasn't that her ruby and diamond shamrock brooch in the lapel of her coat? That night I did not wet my bed.

When Helen arrived, things lurched from bad to worse. For poor Mother St Brendan (no one ever referred to Mother St Brendan, without the prefix 'poor') Helen was the straw that broke the camel's back. Unlike her sisters, Mother St Brendan had little or no Macaulay spirit. She was, by contrast, one of those characters bullies find irresistible. She spoke with an apologetic whine, and acted with tired exasperation. As a baby, she had been dropped by her nurse. The accident had left her with a limp. Realising how slim her chances would be of finding a husband, my grandfather arranged for her to follow her elder sister, and enter the Jesus and Mary Order of nuns. She was terrified of her Reverend Mother and ill at ease with the Community. How she must have dreaded the responsibility my mother was asking of her! She had had no experience of how to deal with young children. Her duties up till then had had to do with the Community, not the school. She must have known that our presence would put her on collision course with the Reverend Mother.

Neither Mary nor I had been forewarned of Helen's arrival. One afternoon, I became aware of a commotion at the top of the staircase outside our bedroom. An excited group of nuns was clustered around Mother St Brendan. They were attempting to snatch a golden-haired toddler from her arms. The child was bellowing with rage. Undeterred, they laughed and chortled and cooed. "Its tea-time, Henny Penny – lovely tea, with bread and strawberry jam!" They tumbled down the stairs in a noisy heap, their black veils flying like crows wings across the child's face. How strange! I thought. It was sometime later that someone mentioned that the child was my baby sister Helen. I had not recognised her. It had been a while since I had seen her. She was now three years old and had grown a lot. Also, the name 'Henny Penny' meant nothing to me. I was aghast. My first reaction was – she is too young for all this. She can't possibly stay here.

Although I had not recognised her, Helen certainly knew me – her sister 'Tays'. I must have seemed like a beacon of light to the poor, confused child. For me, however, I felt more like the rock that she vented her stormy rages on. Mother St Brendan found her unmanageable. I would be summoned from wherever I was, to come and appease her anger. I became her whipping boy. I was the focus for all her unhappiness. It was me who had pushed her over; taken her teddy; made her lose at Snakes and Ladders. I asked her recently what her memories of Ipswich were. She replied. 'It was horrible'! And maybe that is all that need be said of it. After enduring four and a half years of misery, we rebelled, and were sent back to the cut and thrust of Willesden.

In 1983, my youngest daughter Louise was taking part in a Junior Athletic Meeting at Ipswich. I left her at the stadium and drawn like a magnet, I set out to find the Convent. I had heard that it had been taken over by a lay education authority. I parked the car in Woodbridge Road. It was not hard to find. A new school board stood conspicuously on the verge. Timidly, I walked up the drive to Homewood. The house was in the hands of builders and was obviously undergoing a major reconstruction. Expecting to be challenged at any moment, I entered the building with trepidation. Heaps of rubble, planks of timber and rooms stripped bare, made the place unrecognisable. I climbed the stairs and located our bedroom; the place where we had fought and quarrelled, like ferrets in a sack. I opened the door and gasped. It had been turned into a washroom. Like a memorial by Duchamp, a row of partially demolished lavatory pans marked the site of my enuresis. Feeling slightly ill, I closed the door. Before I left, I felt impelled to find the brick passageway linking the house to the main school. It was still there. I opened one of the classroom doors, and - oh horror of all horrors – surely more solid than any figment of the imagination – there were the nuns! They stared at me from chairs that lined the walls. The silence was broken by a voice asking 'Isn't that Traizesherdon, the naughty one?' With difficulty, I extricated myself and ran back down the drive. Fumbling for the ignition key, I nestled into the safety of my car. It did not surprise me that there was a sudden freak drop in the summer temperature that afternoon. When I reached the stadium, the spectators were shivering under rugs, sipping hot drinks from their thermos flasks. I was so pleased to join them, and applauded with gusto as I watched Louise hurl her javelin further through the air than anyone else. Oh the relief of no longer being a child!

Chapter 21

Willesden Again

After our anomolous years at Ipswich, it was a relief to be back at Willesden, and to once more be accepted members of mainstream school life. It was 1937 and I was now ten years old. My health improved as a result of a number of measures prescribed by Dr Twistington Higgins, a Harley Street paediatrician. After breakfast I joined a queue of other pallid-faced children for a dose of Virol Malt. At midday, the infirmarian ruined any hope there may have been of my ever liking oysters, by forcing me to gulp down a raw egg, floating in a glass of milk. My tonsils were removed in Guys Hospital. I was right not to share the enthusiasm of a lively child in the bed next to mine, who was beside herself with excitement at the thought of being sedated with chloroform. It was not a pleasant experience. After the operation we were fed a diet of bread and dripping. Poor little Helen underwent the same painful experience the following year. There were visits too, to a health clinic for sunray treatment. Mother Aquinas accompanied me. Her partiality for barley sugar on the bus, taken for travel sickness, precluded any conversation. On one occasion, she forgot to give me my bus fare. I was much too frightened to ask for it, so I raided my 'Mission Box'. This was tantamount to killing a black baby. My conscience is still troubled.

Whiskery Sister Anne replaced Sister Josephine as my tormentor. I was unable to master the intricacies of arithmetic. The graph paper of our exercise books confused me. The crossings out and messy hieroglyphics I presented her with were taken as personal insults. I took to cheating. I copied the neat figures, the division, equal, plus and minus signs and the confident QEDs from Monica Dowling's book. Of course I was found out, and my wickedness was confirmed.

Miss Williams, on the other hand, was altogether different. A Welsh woman with a deep lilting voice and a halo of black, frizzy hair, she mesmerised us with her love of language. She taught us to recite 'Hiawatha', using our voices to caress the mellifluous lines of

Longfellow's verse. She taught us the beauty of storytelling and the limitless power of imagination. Her lessons were full of enchantment.

Dermot was at this time in London. After getting a First Class Honours in the Law Tripos at Cambridge, he had won the Harmsworth Scholarship to the Middle Temple, where he was doing his pupilage. He persuaded Mother Aquinas to let us have lunch with him now and then. He liked to take us to the Lyons Corner House at Marble Arch. I could talk of nothing else for days after. The orchestra, the mirrored walls, the waitresses in their lace caps and aprons, the manicured nails and scarlet lipstick of Dermot's current girlfriend, were for me the epitome of glamour. I do hope we thanked him adequately, for it must have not only cost him money he could ill afford, but also precious time and energy; and, we cannot, by any stretch of the imagination, have been scintillating company.

And so the years passed. George V and Queen Mary celebrated their Silver Jubilee and the streets of Harlesden fluttered with red, white and blue bunting. Kings and Popes died and we stitched black armbands on to our blazers. The abdication of Edward VIII rocked the nation, but was not mentioned by the nuns. The day girls, nevertheless, taught us rude songs on the subject of how 'Mrs Simpson's Pinched Our King'.

Terrible things were happening in Germany of which we knew nothing. Being now in robust health, I no longer had access to the Illustrated London News in the Mother Provincial's guest room. It came as a shock to be told one morning that we must pack a suitcase, because that very evening we would be leaving for Ireland to stay with my grandmother 'in case there was a war'. This was September 1938; the time of the Munich Crisis and the German occupation of Czechoslovakia. We were bundled into an overcrowded train at Willesden Junction. Mary left a box of chocolates to reserve our seats while we said goodbye to Mother Aquinas. When we re-boarded the train, the chocolates and our seats were gone. We had to split up to find what space we could in different coaches. As I attempted to curl into a sleeping position in my cramped space, a woman covered me over with sheets of *The Evening Standard* to keep out the cold. I squinted up at the newsprint and saw my first picture of Hitler addressing one of his massed rallies.

We spent two nights in Ballina, before being ricocheted back over the

Irish Sea, arriving at Willesden Junction at four in the morning. From then on, worried knots of nuns were to be found in dark corners, whispering to each other things they dared not think, and recounting tales of 1914 they had thought best forgotten. For those who could not sleep, the sound of a bi-plane droning across the night sky was unsettling. What we Sheridans could not have known then was that Hitler's swastika would be the key to our liberation.

I cannot leave Willesden, without a mention of Gilbert and Sullivan. If there was any doubt about where Mother Aquinas' true vocation lay, it was to be found in her bi-annual production of these operas. She oversaw every detail. She engaged a professional orchestra: she hired, not only costumes from the D'Oyley Carte Opera Company but also soloists for the patter song roles. Rehearsals for *The Gondoliers* dominated the summer term of 1939. As the performance dates drew near, the excitement intensified. While storm clouds gathered over Europe, the Convent in Crownhill Road rocked to the music of 'Dance a Cachucha, Fandango, Bolero', and 'Take a Pair of Sparkling Eyes'. Mary strutted the stage with her fellow peers, her coronet slightly awry and her faux ermine robes billowing behind her, singing 'Bow, Bow Ye Lower Middle Classes, Bow, Bow Ye Tradesmen and Ye Masses, Tan Tan Tara, Tzing Boom', with lusty conviction. The applause was deafening, and Mother Aquinas beamed with delight.

It was on this note of euphoria that our days in the Convent drew to a close. The day after the concert, we left for France on 21st July 1939 for the summer holiday we had spent two years looking forward to.

Chapter 22

Holidays

*'No more Latin: no more French
No more sitting on a hard old bench
This time next week I shall be
Having lots of fun with my family'.*

I hated this ridiculous ditty. As the term drew to a close, girls would link arms and strut round the playground giving vent to their mounting excitement. It rarely applied to us. Although Mary was old enough to stay with friends of our parents such as General Northey and his family in their castle on the west coast of Scotland, Helen and I remained captive in the Convent. For us, the end of term was marked by pushing desks back against the wall in order to clear a space for games. We were joined by a beautiful girl, who was considerably older than us. Her name was Lal. She was half Indian with dark, deep-set eyes and an air of permanent melancholy.

We played Draughts and Snakes and Ladders, and learnt how to knit. At Christmas, we pasted together pieces of coloured paper to make paper chains and wrapped small presents in crepe paper to give to the poor of the parish. Mostly, however, we hung about like limpets on the rocks, waiting for the tide to come back in.

The summer holidays were more enjoyable. The nuns spent them in either Felixstowe or Southwold. Southwold holds many happy memories for me. Felixstowe, on the other hand, with its pebble beach segmented by ominous breakwaters and its dreary promenade, was a place of little charm. The convent where we stayed was an ugly red brick building near the centre of, what was, even then, a busy commercial town. Southwold, on the Suffolk coast, was, by contrast, a pretty little town, with an air of light-hearted fun. For instance there was the surprise of finding a lighthouse close to the market place, seemingly dropped there by someone who wasn't too sure what to do with a spare lighthouse. Then there was the row of gaily-painted bathing booths lining the edge of the beach. In those days, it was possible to hire one for the day for little more than the cost of a municipal deck chair. Today, I am told, they cost in the region of six figures.

The nuns rented a terraced house bordering the Common. This is where the Prince of Wales used to hold his Boy Scout Camp. In the evening, we could hear them singing jolly songs round their campfire. One day I saw one of the boys peeing into the hedges with a mighty arc of water. Not believing my eyes, I called another girl over to witness this amazing feat. We had no idea boys possessed such enviable equipment.

It was at Southwold, under the watchful eye of Sam the boatman, that I learnt to swim. I would fall asleep at night, dreaming of being able to swim out to the raft moored a hundred feet or so from the shore, and wake in the morning determined to improve on my three strokes of the day before without cheating, by keeping one foot on the ground. I discovered Just William and his Outlaws in Southwold Library. With the aid of a torch under the bedclothes, Ginger, Henry, Douglas and William stepped from the maroon covers of the book and involved me in their escapades.

By day, nuns dozing in deck chairs on the beach made a surprisingly benign sight. Caressed by the sea air, they lost their accustomed severity. On one occasion, it was not only their severity that they lost, but also one of their charges. It was a glorious, blustery day. The sea was capped with spray and the sun dodged in and out of the clouds. It was too rough to bathe, but it was perfect for flying kites. I watched with envy a group of children coaxing a multi-coloured dragon kite into the wind. They invited me to join them. Taking it in turns, we held onto the spool. It required all my strength to keep control of the wilful, bucking, soaring creature high in the air above me. I stumbled over the sand dunes, light-headed with joy. The afternoon had melted into early evening before I became aware of the search party combing the beach for a dark haired girl in a red spotted dress. Reluctantly, I said goodbye to my new-found friends and headed for the posse of nuns, battling against the wind which whipped through the folds of their black gabardine habits. Their relief at finding me was touching. Mother St Brendan was commended for having had the foresight to give me a red dress to wear that morning, and I was only mildly reprimanded for talking to strangers.

It was important to be friends with Mary on these seaside holidays, for she was in charge of our pocket money. Payment for comics, sticks of rock, donkey rides and other delights, came from the little circular purse that swung jauntily from her belt. At the end of the holiday, she counted out the remaining pennies, and divided them between us. Our hope was that we would have enough for each of us to buy a cornet of homemade humbugs sold from a stall close to the bus station. On this particular occasion, as I clambered onto the coach, clutching my precious humbugs, I learned that after my kite-flying escapade, it had been decided that I should be wedged into a seat next to the Mother Provincial in case I made another bid for freedom. This meant that I would have to wait for her to doze off before I could surreptitiously slip a humbug into my mouth. Eventually the moment came. With careful anticipation, I selected one. There was nothing in its appearance to prepare me for the shock of the explosion of peppermint oil it released as I popped it into my mouth. It produced a simultaneous sensation of burning and freezing. After a sharp intake of breath, I blew it out. Earning its name of 'bull's eye', it shot, like a rocket, into the recess of the Mother Provincial's enormous cuff. I froze with horror. Had I really spat a humbug at a Mother Provincial! Should I wake her up and apologize? Had I the courage? I studied the rise and fall of her large bosom. A faint smile played on her sun-kissed features. Surely it would be cruel to upset such serenity! It had, after all, been a good holiday. I did wonder, though, what her reaction would be, when the strong smell of peppermint led her to discover the sticky mess inside her big black sleeve. Hopefully, by that time, it would be too late for the discovery to lead her to the culprit.

Despite the pleasures of Southwold, nothing could dispel the ever-present ache of not belonging to anyone or to anywhere. Letters from my mother, written on blue airmail paper, would arrive sporadically. She wrote to us as adults, recounting the safaris they had been on; the people they had met; the parties at Government House. Mary would read as fast as she possibly could, aware that the litany of social engagements meant nothing to any of us. The stamps were of more interest, with their beautifully engraved pictures of Mount. Kenya, a dhow in full sail, or a charging elephant, each with the head of George V superimposed on the top right hand corner. Printed round the edge, the exotic trio of names – Kenya, Uganda and Tanganyika – spelt out the far-flung bounds of Empire. As Mary tossed the letter casually aside, I would find myself yet again wondering what 'home' would be like. What would it be like to sleep in a bedroom, not a dormitory; to eat in a dining room, not a refectory; to use a bathroom, rather than a row of wash basins with cubicled bath tubs, and most of all, to sit in a cushioned chair by an open fire, rather than huddle up to a lukewarm radiator on a wooden stool. The answer would come in 1937. In the summer of that year, we would experience family life as it might have been, had our parents not been caught up in the business of Empire.

Their visit back to England in 1935 had been overshadowed by Peggy's recent death. That year we spent a miserable family holiday in rented rooms in a lodging house in Littlehampton. Throughout the holiday, my mother was sad and withdrawn, battling to hold back her tears. Both Helen and I went down with chickenpox and a nurse was engaged to look after us. She was a clumsy creature christened Flannel Foot by Roderick and Dermot. The only cheery sound in that dismal place was the hollow p'link – p'lonk of a ping pong ball being hit back and forth by the older members of the family. Helen and I sat out of harm's way, underneath the table, studying people's feet.

The holiday of 1937 held no such shadows. There were the usual tantrums before our parents arrived. Jealousy was rampant. Who would our mother love the best? Surely not Mary. She was my number one enemy. And as for Helen, well she was too cross to be loveable. Please God, may it be me! Not if I can help it, was Mary's instinctive response. After the first emotional embrace, we would fight and jostle for a position close to her. I was determined to hold her hand forever: never, ever to let it go. The tension eased once Roderick and Dermot arrived. On reflection, it was Dermot who was the dominant force at these family reunions. With wit, humour and quiet authority, he never failed to defuse potentially explosive situations.

But in that magical Irish summer, harmony prevailed and time stood still. It was at Massbrook, the house my parents rented on the shores of Loch Conn, where we discovered our identity as a family. There was a popular Irish song at that time, whose opening words 'Sure a little bit of heaven fell from out the sky one day...' summed up how we felt when we first saw the place.

   Through a white-painted iron gate, past a gate-house, a long winding drive wandered through beech woods until it arrived at a balustraded terrace spread generously in front of a house whose large windows gazed serenely out at the lake and the hills beyond. Behind the gables and chimney pots, the reassuring bulk of Mount Nephin could be glimpsed. The central arc of the terrace was broken by a flight of steps which had originally led down to the water's edge. Over time, however, nature's disregard for such formality had won the day. Plantains and vetches, willow herb and meadowsweet had re-established themselves over the stonework. To the side of the house, a steep, path fringed by native ferns led through the woods to a clearing. It was an unlikely place to come across a tennis court. Each day, before play could begin, the surface had to be cleared of twigs, leaves and other pieces of woodland debris. Once play was underway, overhead branches presented a problem. There was also the disconcerting way the moss turned white tennis balls green, rendering them almost invisible. None of these hazards, however, deterred us from playing many an exciting game, in this most unusual sylvan setting.

   The path continued round the court and emerged beside a small jetty on the shores of the lake. Here we would abandon our racquets and change into swimsuits. As the cold water lapped round our heated bodies, our cries of shock and noisy laughter reverberated over the surface of the lake, so that ducks and herons took to the air in alarm. They weren't the only ones to be disturbed. My mother, like many Irish people, distrusted the lake. She would stand at the water's edge, begging us to come back before we were pulled under by 'drowning weeds'. Of course we ignored her pleas. This after all was heaven.

   We discovered a boathouse with two sturdy old rowing boats. Dermot, with his powerful arms, proved to be an impressive oarsman, and could manage one boat on his own. Mary and Roderick took an oar each in the other boat. As they seldom managed to pull together, they steered an erratic course. Helen and I, meanwhile, trailed our hands in the water. We would spend long days picnicking on islands and exploring concealed inlets. We would return late in the evening in the opalescent light of a slowly setting sun. The lake mirrored the colours spreading across the sky, reflecting them back across the little stony fields clinging to the sides of the surrounding hills. The rhythmic sound of the oars turning in their rowlocks, followed by the gentle splash of the blades, was all that broke the silence. We were bathed in a celestial beauty.

It wasn't always so peaceful. Storms could spring up unexpectedly, as Roderick, Helen and I discovered. It was a beautiful, calm, sunny, afternoon when Roderick took Helen and me out for a row on the lake. He was managing the cumbersome old craft splendidly on his own, when suddenly we were hit by a vicious squall. The force of the wind made him lose his grip on one of the oars. In a trice it slipped its rowlock and was gobbled up by the now alarmingly choppy waters. Helen and I responded as best we could to his urgent command to start baling. It was also up to me to navigate, while Roderick struggled to make progress against the wind and the rain with his remaining oar. My navigation skills however, were hampered by the fact that the boathouse, indeed the whole wooded shoreline that was Massbrook was shrouded in mist. The thought of 'drowning weeds' was never far from our minds as Roderick battled over the angry waters of Loch Conn to reach at last, the safety of the boathouse and the woods.

Back at the house a billiard room kept the men entertained on rainy days. My father loved the game and was particularly good at it. Mary took enough interest to master the intricacies of the scoreboard. As for Helen and I, we asked for nothing more than to be closeted in the big, warm, linen cupboard, where we would spend many happy hours playing imaginary games. She was Ginger Rogers and I was Jessie Matthews. We liked the names but weren't too sure whether they applied to people or horses. (I had recently read *Black Beauty*). In the kitchen, Mary Boffenaun, from the Gate House, prepared the kind of meals every family looks forward to. She was painfully shy. When she did speak, her Mayo brogue was incomprehensible, even for my mother. However, this didn't seem to hinder the smooth running of the household. Once a week, Moylett's van came out from Ballina with meat and groceries. The kitchen garden, another of Helen's and my favourite haunts, provided all the vegetables and fruit we needed. The raspberries were especially memorable. We liked to eat them straight from the canes with the scent of the rain still on them.

There was a small drawing room off the billiard room, filled with rosewood cabinets, chintz-covered chairs and precious *objets* displayed on delicate little occasional tables. Understandably, my mother declared this room to be out of bounds. But standing in the bay of the window was a boudoir grand waiting to be played, and Dermot, as a pianist was not going to let the opportunity pass him by. He was never without his leather-bound copy of the Beethoven sonatas. It had been given to him as a prize at Downside, and was a treasured possession to the end of his life. With his large, strong hands, he would play with verve and vigour, causing the Dresden china to rattle alarmingly in the glass-fronted cupboard beside the piano. He would respond to my mother's nervous pleas for something less turbulent by turning to Chopin. To this day, I have only to hear the *presto agitato* of a Beethoven sonata or Chopin's lovely Nocturne in B, opus 9, to be transported back to those halcyon days at Massbrook. This was where my love of music began.

The house was seldom without visitors. Jolly relatives came to swap stories and reminisce with their tales from long ago. My father's eldest sister, Aunty Peg, came over from New York, where she worked as a hospital almoner. She was enormous fun and would entertain us with her colourful descriptions of life in America. Sir Jack Shute, the MP for Liverpool, and an old friend of my parents, arrived in his Rolls Royce, which caused a stir in Ballina. He took my grandmother for a drive. She wore her best hat, and gave the royal wave to the tradesmen of Ballina as they drove at a stately pace down Pearse Sreet. As a Catholic MP, he was involved at that time with Sir Edwin Lutyens' design for Liverpool Cathedral. I could not have foreseen what a significant subject this would become for me, when I married my architect husband, Francis.

There were expeditions to Achill Island, Enniscrone and the family shrine on the slopes of Croagh Patrick. Here we had to remove our shoes, and while negotiating sharp stones and nettles, circle the very white statue of Our Lady reciting the Rosary, trying not to be distracted by the beaches of Clew Bay glinting in the sun far below. We never did climb Mount Nephin, though every morning we talked of doing so. When there was no room for Helen and me in the car, we were happy to be left behind. We would spend hours in the kitchen garden with a string bag stuffed with lettuce leaves, hoping to catch a rabbit as we lay beside their holes. Oh the bliss of it all!

Then the sword of Damocles fell, as we knew it would, but this knowledge was, until now, carefully buried in our subconscious. I came down one morning to find my parents poring over a plan spread out on the billiard table. It was the plan of a ship. They were selecting their cabin for their return to Africa. I ran upstairs to the warmth of the linen room and cried. As I cried, I could feel the pain of my heart being shattered.

Many years later, I heard a recording of Nina Milkina playing a Chopin Mazurka in A Minor, Op17. In its sweet poignancy, it evoked for me all the might-have-been of Massbrook.

Chapter 23

Return to Brittany

Our last family holiday was spent in Paramé, a small seaside town on the coast of Brittany, not far from Saint.-Malo. It was in August 1939, a few weeks before the outbreak of World War II. During the months of June and July of that beautiful summer, sandbags had started to appear in the streets of London. Gas masks were distributed, and plans drawn up for the evacuation of children out of the city into the countryside. Volunteers visited the schools to show the staff and pupils how to put the gas masks on. The sight of familiar faces being transformed into the bug-eyed monsters of sci-fi was terrifying. When it came to the business of fitting the contraption over one's own face, the sense of nightmare and claustrophobia was unbearable. I decided I would rather be gassed than wear one. Mercifully, the need to use them never arose. These grim preparations coupled with the ominous rumours were, however, only of secondary importance to me. I was eleven years old, and nothing, not even the threat of war could dim my excitement at the thought of our family summer holiday. This time, we would be going abroad. Now that really was something to boast about.

My mother had been given the name of the Bastide family by Downside. They took in school leavers as paying guests over the long summer vacation. This year they had had an annex to their house converted into a family apartment, which suited us perfectly. It even had a pingpong table. Apart from the grandmother, they were a delightful family. Professor Bastide was a distinguished looking man, whose family had lived in the Manoir de Rivesleau for many generations. He was cultured and charming, and enjoyed discussing topics of interest with his guests. Madame, his voluble wife, was brimful of energy and in command of every situation. They had two sons, Jean and Roger. Jean, the eldest, liked to imitate the portentous orations of Charles de Gaulle, the French politician, who, after the fall of France, would seek refuge in England where he became the Leader of the Free

French and a thorn in Churchill's side. Roger, the younger boy, was full of mischief. He showed Helen and me a field where we picked sun-ripened tomatoes without being caught. Monique, their daughter, was my age. With her tumble of dark hair, twinkling eyes and lively personality, she made a good companion.

Then there was Professor Bastide's mother, the grandmere, a thin, formidable old lady, who always wore black. She liked to umpire our games of tennis. Spirited rallies and forceful serves would be brought to abrupt halts by an imperious cry from the chair, 'Une faute!' 'Mais bien sûr le bal etait sur la ligne!' the frustrated players would cry. Their protests were ignored and the score would be given as 'quarante-zero' in favour of her favourite grandchild, Roger. Monique would plead to no avail. The curt response from the chair was unwavering 'Quarante-zero. C'est ca. Jouez s'il vous plait'. As the game limped along, punctuated by argument, my partner's muttered 'Zut alors' was soon replaced by 'Merde'. And so I learnt to swear as well as score in French. It was a time of laughter, golden greengages and cider drunk from bottles kept chilled in the well. The rattle of trams, the sound of discordant brass instruments as a band marched through the town to the church on Sunday, the smell of Gaulloise cigarettes and the steady 'plip-plop' of a ping pong ball, all speak to me of Paramé in August 1939. We went to the local 'kermess' (fair) and won a rabbit. We fed it on damp lettuce leaves. This was a mistake. For days afterwards, Helen, proud of having mastered some French, greeted everyone with the news 'le lapin est mort'. We went to the tiny local cinema and saw Walt Disney's new film Snow White, dubbed in French. It was the first full-length cartoon and created a sensation in the film world.

We visited the old walled town of Saint-Malo and stepped down into the gloom of the Cathedral. In a matter of months, those ancient walls and little cobbled streets would be reduced to rubble. I am told that the town has been faithfully restored; but you cannot restore the spirit of history. Those little alleyways and medieval buildings had resonated to the voices of its inhabitants for centuries. They had witnessed the pageantry of ceremonies closely associated with the life of the town. The buildings and streets replacing them can never be more than lifeless stage sets. Oh the wicked senselessness of war!

Naturally, no day was complete without some time being spent on the beach. We would spread ourselves on the rocks and soak up the sun. After our swim, we would eat fresh, crusty bread, torn from a long baguette, with pieces of black chocolate, and feel very French. We had been warned about the surly group of men in charge of the horse-drawn beach cabins. They were Communists and, in the event of war being declared, had no intention of fighting for France. They particularly despised the English. The trouble was, Dermot relied on the beach cabins for his swim, as the sea was some way off. These uncouth ruffians made no allowance for his disability. Instead of leading the horse at a walking pace, they would goad the animal into pulling the rickety contraption at breakneck speed, across the sand, down to the water's edge, with a total disregard for Dermot's comfort. Once there, they would desert him, so that when he emerged from the sea, he was left stranded on the wet beach without either his sticks or his towels. Shivering with cold, he would give vent to his rage with an impressive command of colloquial French, but they just shrugged and turned away. Only on a further payment of several more francs, would they deign to respond.

We spent the evenings playing Monopoly with the Bastides. This was a game that had recently crossed the Atlantic from the USA and was very new in France. The properties were Parisian. The Rue St Honore and the Rue de Rivoli had been substituted for Park Lane and Mayfair. Euston Station became the Gard du Nord and so on. None of us had played the game before and trying to follow the rules in French was not easy. I found it very confusing and envied Roderick and his friends who could not be persuaded to join us. They were eighteen and the bright lights of Paramé called. One evening Mary sneaked out with them only to be sent home by Roderick. Her indignation could not be silenced. This was not the treatment she was used to. Subsequently, when questioned about what the lads got up to in the evenings, Roderick's evasive answers aroused suspicions. The cat was out of the bag, when Madame Bastide found a tram sign in one of the boy's bedrooms. Apparently, amongst other larks, they had become adept at switching the tram signs round at the terminus while the driver was having a chat with his mates. They would then watch with glee, the resulting confusion. They were all gated for a couple of nights. Calm was restored after apologies had been made to the Chef du Carnes (the tram master). Mary was satisfied. She had had her revenge. Helen and

I, meanwhile, had kept up our steady, rhythmic, endless, games of ping pong throughout the noisy recriminations.

On the political stage, recriminations were not just noisy, but dangerously threatening. The ranting tones of Adolf Hitler were becoming daily more strident. One afternoon, on returning from the beach, relaxed, sandy, and dishevelled, we found everyone in a high state of agitation. There had been a special news bulletin announcing the fact that Russia had signed a non-aggression pact with Germany. To appreciate the impact of this news, you would have to know that Stalin and the British Foreign Office had, for months, been in negotiations on how best to protect the Balkan States, should Germany invade Poland. All the while Stalin had secretly been planning with Hitler how to divide Poland between Russia and Germany *when* Germany invaded. The British Foreign Office had been well and truly double-crossed by the Russians. Stalin and Hitler spent the night of 23rd of August putting the final touches to their plan before breaking the news of their pact the next day. Hitler was convinced that as with Czechoslovakia the year before, Britain could be placated. But Neville Chamberlain had learnt his lesson. This time Britain would honour her pledge to help Poland if she was attacked. So this news bulletin meant one thing: war was imminent. Britain was immediately put on a war footing. All Service leave was stopped. Reservists were called up. Trawlers and merchant ships were recalled to the Admiralty for conversion into armed merchant cruisers. This time, Britain was determined to face up to Hitler.

We gathered in my mother's bedroom to discuss the situation. Without my father we turned to Dermot for advice. The question was, how long had we got before hostilities began? We were booked to stay another week. My mother did not like the idea of not getting our money's worth if we left early. Also it would be difficult to change our tickets for the ferry. To complicate matters, it was a weekend and the travel bureau would not be open before Monday. Dermot thought it likely that if we delayed, we would not get away at all. Roderick chipped in to say, he would be happy to stay and drive the trams. Dermot was adamant: we must leave at once, that very evening. I protested. This was not possible – our swimsuits were still wet. This was ignored. We hurried off to pack our cases. We said our farewells and took a taxi to the docks.

When we got there, we found the queue snaked all round the harbour. Apparently this was the last ferry out of Saint-Malo. The boat was built to take a maximum of three hundred people, but there were at least a thousand or more waiting to board. Our prospects did not look good. But this was to underestimate my mother. Leaving us in the queue, she went in search of an official. Seeing a man in uniform, she accosted him in her execrable French with the phrase 'Quand la guerre inevitable, vous me direz'? Continuing in French peppered with Swahili, she described her anxiety, with five children, no money and her desperate need to get away. The poor man became more and more confused, until Dermot came to the rescue. I believe it was the only time in his life that he used his disability to plead preferential treatment. The result was, we were all taken to the head of the queue and were amongst the first to board the ship. In minutes, every inch of deck space was covered. It was impossible to get a seat. In the scramble, we got separated and I found myself next to a drunk who vomited. To this day I cannot abide the smell of beer. My mother had managed to get a bunk for Dermot, but he could not be found. A beautiful blonde girl had befriended him. He spent the crossing cosily ensconced with her on a sofa in one of the lounges.

As we pulled away from the quay, we left a straggling line of 1500 people, with 500 people on the boat. We were well over the ship's legal capacity. These figures are lodged in my memory because my mother repeated them so often to everyone we met. As the ship got under way, everyone started singing. 'We're going to hang out the washing on Siegfried Line' was the favourite, followed by 'Run, rabbit, run, rabbit, run, run, run', and of course 'The White Cliffs of Dover'.

We made our way to Dublin, where we took rooms in a pretty regency house in Sandycove. Here, one week later – 70 years ago today – at 11.15 am, on 3rd September, we gathered round the wireless and listened in silence to the precise, clipped voice of Neville Chamberlain:

> *'I am speaking to you from the Cabinet Room at 10, Downing Street. This morning the British Ambassador in Berlin handed the German Government a final note stating that unless we heard from*

them by 11.00 that they were prepared at once to withdraw their troops from Poland, a state of war would exist between us. I have to tell you now that no such undertaking has been received, and that consequently this country is at war with Germany.'

We never went back to the convent in Crownhill Road. At a time when so many children were being parted from their parents as evacuees, our time of being orphaned came to an end. It was too late, though, for our brothers. Dermot was now a barrister at the Middle Temple and Roderick, after just one year at Cambridge, was called up. He served in the Coldstream Guards, and after fighting in North Africa and Italy, was wounded at Monte Cassino. Our childhood was over. A new chapter had opened in all our lives.

Postscript
Helen, my mother and I went back to the Manoir de Rivesleau after the war. The Bastides were still there. Jean and Roger had left home, but Monique and her husband were living with her parents. She was expecting their first baby which was born while we were there. They no longer took in students in the summer vacation; only the annexe was let. The four lads who had been with us in 1939 had all been killed in the war. Two of them had joined the navy as submariners.

Union Castle ship departing Capetown

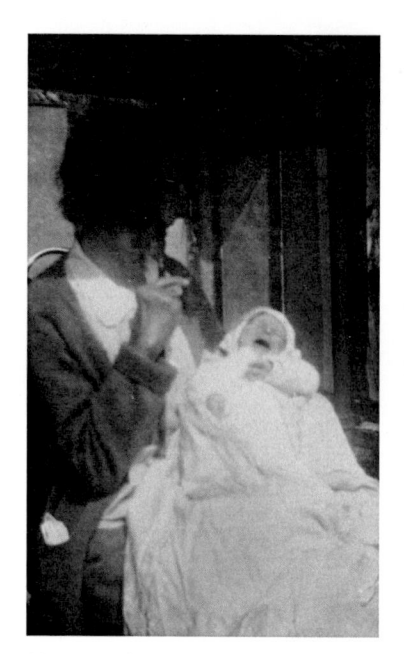

My sister Helen

Me at Three Bridges

The family at St Jacût de la Mer: standing, Peggy and Roderick; seated, my father, Mary, my mother, Dermot and me

Me aged four in fancy dress

130

Convent of Jesus and Mary, Willesden

Nuns on the beach at Southwold

Mary, Peggy and me at St Jacût de la Mer

Joe Sheridan and Peggy

My mother in her eau-de-nil dress

Dermot at Massbrook

Part Three

Nostalgia for Africa

Chapter 24

Freedom

After leaving France in August of 1939, we lived in Sandycove, on the outskirts of Dublin. Here, at Number 7, Eden Grove, we enjoyed the novelty of a proper family life. We acquired a dog. Foupi was a Basenji from the Congo, not unlike a miniature deer to look at. Basenjis have no bark. They make a delicate yodelling sound, which is rather endearing. We would attach his lead to the handlebars of our bikes and take him on expeditions to the top of Killiney Hill or day-long trips to Greystones and Brittas Bay. The freedom, after years of incarceration in the Convent, was intoxicating.

Helen and I attended a small day school in the neighbourhood. School hours were from 9.30 a.m. to 3.00 p.m. That was on a full day. Half days were Tuesday and Thursday when we would be back home by midday. I do not remember opening a single book while at St Anne's. Homework was unheard of. A thin man with a pencil moustache would occasionally lecture us on how to detect a gas attack. He was English, and seemed unaware that Ireland was a neutral country. The rest of the time was spent making plans for the afternoon. Could we afford the seven-penny ticket to see Charles Laughton in *The Hunchback of Notre Dame* at the Regal? Or maybe we might watch the boys (no girls allowed) diving at the Forty Foot. And then there was the fun of jumping on the little coastal train (now known as the Dart) as it slowed down, and seeing how far we could travel without a ticket. In Lent, we dared ourselves to enter Protestant churches, convinced that by doing so, we risked being killed by some kind of calamity. The roof might fall in; or perhaps we would die of fright on seeing the devil! My partners in crime were Deidre Doyle, Patricia O'Sullivan, sister of the Hollywood star, Maureen O'Sullivan, and Marie Cantwell, whose family gave wonderful parties from which I would have to be dragged away long after the clock had struck midnight. Like me, they must now be old women in their eighties. They are, however, locked in my memory forever, in all the noisy merriment and helpless laughter of twelve-year olds.

Any serious work took place at Miss Catt's School of Dancing in Lower Baggot Street. ('Proficient in the teaching of Ballroom, Tap, Classical Ballet & Greek – with the use of Skipping Ropes'). We took exams and performed in shows at the Abbey Theatre. Helen, in scarlet, tapped her way through a routine called 'The Military Tattoo'. I drifted before the footlights in yards of grey tulle as 'Smoke' in a ballet entitled 'The Bonfire'. And then of course there was the polka, during which our youthful enthusiasm had to be curbed by Miss Catt's stern commands.

While Helen and I were free as larks on a May morning, the same could not be said of Mary. She had been enrolled as a student in the notoriously strict Convent of the Sacred Heart in Leeson Street. She hated it, and used every opportunity to play truant. She asked permission to visit her aunt, Nellie Bourke, who she said was gravely ill in a nearby nursing home. Aunt Nellie was indeed in the nursing home, but for one night only, having an in-growing toenail seen to. Mary's visit was a surprise. Before the end of her first term, Mary decided she had had enough. She arrived home one afternoon and announced that she had informed the Headmistress she was leaving. Wild horses could not make her cross the threshold of that, or any other school, ever again. At the age of fifteen, she considered her education was complete. My mother received the news calmly. I suspect she was not unhappy at the thought of the saving in school fees. There was, also the thought that Mary would now be free to lend a hand in the running of the household. This was a task she was finding much harder than she had imagined without the help of her African servants.

There was another problem my mother had difficulty with. Having seen so little of us over the years, she found she hardly knew us. Her solution was to convince herself that each one of us must have a hidden talent which she would encourage, Alas! All three of us proved to be a disappointment. Mary, she decided, was artistic. With encouragement, she would, in time, rival Paul Henry, the renowned Mayo artist. An art teacher was found who taught her to paint white cabins in fields of turf bogs, against a backdrop of hazy, blue, mountains. At my mother's request, Mary painted this scene on the parchment shades of some table lamps used for dinner parties. This would provide an opportunity for her talent to be recognised by their guests. The result was disastrous.

The curve of the lampshades played havoc with her perspectives and then heat from the candles caused rivulets of paint to render the scene indecipherable. My mother's table lamps were ruined and Mary's future as an artist was quietly shelved.

As for me, my mother thought it reasonable to presume that as I had inherited my father's looks, I must also have inherited his vocal talent. Margaret Bourke Sheridan, a retired diva, erstwhile friend of Puccini's and cousin of my father's, was invited to tea. Before meeting her, it was thought to be a wise move for me to learn the aria 'One Fine Day' from Madame Butterfly. With my mother accompanying me at the piano, I practised earnestly; but try as I might, the climactic top A always eluded me. In the event, Margaret Bourke Sheridan was spared my ear-splitting screech. She refused our invitation to tea, but offered, instead, to take us to the opera.

We arranged to meet in the foyer of the theatre. She was easy to spot. Surrounded by a coterie of admirers, with her platinum blonde hair glowing under the lights, she basked in an aura of fame. The eyes of a fox from a fur stole stared balefully out from her substantial bosom. Her small feet were tucked into high-heeled shoes, making her appear taller than she actually was. She was the epitome of what everyone expected a diva to look like. On seeing us, she broke away from her friends and welcomed us with extravagant arm gestures. The scent of her powder made me to sneeze. She spoke rapidly, in soft, breathy tones. She would not be sitting with us, she explained. When *La Bohéme* was performed, the manager of the theatre insisted on beaming a spotlight on her as she sat in her reserved box. This was, she said, a tribute to her many performances in the role of Mimi. She was sure we would understand. We would of course, she added, meet afterwards. With that she turned to greet more of her aficionados, while we were ushered into our seats in the stalls. I remember little of the performance, but have a clear recollection of her, framed by the red curtains of her gilded box, bathed in the limelight, acknowledging the homage of the producer and cast as they took their final bows. We waited for her afterwards, but she did not appear. As the theatre emptied an attendant informed us that she had left by the Stage Door accompanied by the manager. My mother was furious. We had been well and truly snubbed. I, on the other hand, was dizzy with relief. My future as an opera singer was put on hold.

Instead of warbling through Puccini arias, I had piano lessons, which was a little easier to manage and not quite so hard on the family's sensitivities.

Helen was more problematic. After our years of institutionalised living, she had, out of all of us, the greatest difficulty in adjusting to family life. Her unpredictable rages were hard to control. My mother decided, wisely, to leave her to her own devices. She was categorised as 'the clever one' who one day would shine as an academic.

Towards the end of that July in 1940 we learnt that we had finally got our passages to Africa. Our Irish idyll was about to come to an end. I walked the length of Sandycove pier, and watched the powerful waves hurl themselves against the rocks, throwing the spume high into the air. Was it possible that in a few weeks' time, I would find myself back in the Africa of my dreams? Would the fronds of the palm trees still rattle? Would the sun be as hot and as golden as I remembered? Would the sea be azure blue and covered with sun-starts, unlike the foam-flecked grey that was now splashing over my feet? I looked at the rainclouds gathering over the Wicklow Hills and found it impossible to believe that soon we would be enveloped in the technicolour brilliance of Africa.

Chapter 25

Wartime Travel

Mary, Helen and I boarded the mail boat with my parents on a wet, stormy day and waved goodbye to Dun Laoghaire harbour. Over London, barrage balloons floated in the sky like suspended whales. In the streets people with grim faces hurried past mounds of sandbags. The Blitz was only days away. There was little traffic and hardly any buses. We found a taxi to take us out to Willesden to say goodbye to Mother Aquinas. The convent building was eerily silent. All the children had been evacuated to the country, leaving the school closed for the duration of the war. We stood in the all-too-familiar dark corridor, waiting for the grown-ups to end their tearful embraces. I felt no fear as I listened to my mother declaring her certainty that, as we were sailing without the protection of a convoy, we were bound to be torpedoed. For me, at that moment, any hazard was preferable to being incarcerated in the Convent again.

King's Cross Station was full of confusion. People in uniform pushed past us. There were no friendly porters with barrows; no helpful signs, only large notices warning us that Careless Talk Costs Lives. The noise and steam from the locomotives was deafening. Somehow we found our train, but had no information on our destination. All we knew was the name of our ship, the *Llangibby Castle*. No one would tell us which port it was sailing from. When the train pulled out of King's Cross, we had no means of knowing which part of the country we were travelling through. Blinds covered the windows of our compartment, and as an added precaution against spies, the stations we passed had had their signs removed.

We travelled through the night. The next morning, the train came to a halt in the middle of the country. This, we were told, was where we had to get out, but where 'this' was, we had no idea. Clutching our hand luggage, we made the long drop onto the track – not an easy feat for someone of my father's size. Then, stepping carefully between the rails, we followed the other passengers. Any sense of adventure I may have had earlier had by now deserted me. How could anyone be so foolish as to make us walk along a railway track! It's not easy stepping between sleepers, especially if you are carrying a suitcase. After walking some distance and just when I was beginning to feel I could bear it no longer, a line of parked coaches came into view. They were waiting to take us to our ship. We discovered we were not far from the banks of the Clyde. In fact it was just possible to make out the cranes of the dockyards, spiking the horizon.

As we drew near, the long-remembered pink funnels of the Union Castle Line became visible. Once through the dockyard gates, we found the quay lined with troops waiting to board a converted luxury liner, the *Star of Canada*. We waved to the young men, and shouted 'Good luck!' as, laden with equipment, they mounted the gangways, all unaware of the U-boat waiting silently out in the North Atlantic. She was sunk within hours of sailing; many of the young men who had cheerily acknowledged our greetings would have gone down with her.

The following evening, as the Luftwaffe dropped the first bombs of the Battle of Britain on London, we cast off our moorings and sailed down the mouth of Clyde, past the famous shipyards and out into the buffeting waves of the North Atlantic. It would be five weeks before we would reach the coast of Africa, and more than three months before we would land at Mombasa.

This was August 1940, when England was facing defeat. France had capitulated. It was barely two months since the humiliation of Dunkirk, and America showed no inclination to enter what they understood to be solely a European war. Even more worryingly, the Battle of the North Atlantic was going badly. The shipping losses were appalling. Admiral Doenitz's U-boats were creating havoc among the merchant ships, engaged in bringing vital supplies to a beleaguered Britain. Germany was winning on every front. It was no wonder that we were sailing without a convoy. A passenger ship on its way to the Southern Hemisphere was a low priority. There were simply no destroyers available to accompany us. Our only defence, apart from the one gun mounted at the stern of the ship, was to steer a zigzag course, which was one of the reasons the journey took so long.

Each night we put a pile of warm clothing at the foot of our bunks, in case of an emergency. Lifeboat drill was held twice a week and it was compulsory to carry your life jacket with you at all times. These were cumbersome contraptions, made of cork, covered with canvas, with long straps attached (this was before the days of plastic and velcro). One evening, in the dining saloon, mine caused me considerable embarrassment. We were sitting at the Captain's table, and instead of hanging my life jacket on the back of my chair, like everyone else, I left it carelessly on the floor. When the chief steward came by, deftly balancing a tray of food on one hand, his foot caught in one of the straps. To this day I can still hear the crash of crockery, coupled with the thud of his fall, followed by the appalled silence of the other dinner guests – even the pianist stopped playing. The steward examined his white coat, spattered with globules of meat and gravy, and I understood I was not his best friend!

The constant threat of U-boats meant that wireless communication had to be kept to a minimum, which left us without any regular news bulletins. To alleviate the anxieties of the passengers, who desperately wanted to know how the war was going, the purser, with Mary's assistance, invented bulletins. I was let into the secret and sworn to secrecy. Each day we would watch, with fascination, people jostling round the notice board to read a most colourful and entertaining account of the news. To my knowledge, no one suspected a thing!

The Mediterranean and Suez Canal were war zones, so our route took us down the West Coast of Africa, round the Cape and then, finally up into the Indian Ocean. We had just one port of call, the small, rocky, island of St Vincent, in the Cape Verde Islands, where a few intrepid travellers went ashore. After sampling the rough local wine, they had a difficult time negotiating their way back onto the ship up the rope ladder, much to everyone's amusement.

We gave little thought to our hazardous situation, and once we had found our sea legs, we began to enjoy the long days at sea. At night, when laying out my 'lifeboat clothes', I tried hard to envisage having to put them on in a hurry and race to our lifeboat station, ready to spend days at sea in a rowing boat. But the steady hum of the engines and the sound of the sea splashing against the hull outside the porthole as the ship sliced its way through the ocean gave such a sense of power and security that I just could not picture it. By day, my parents relaxed among their fellow colonials. Mary, when not writing news bulletins, played backgammon with the ship's officers. Helen and I played deck quoits, and when the weather got warmer, had fun in the canvas swimming pool. No dancing or gramophone music was allowed, because of the danger of the sound being picked up by the enemy. The only music the Captain permitted were the piano recitals that accompanied our meals. I fell deeply in love with the pianist, who reminded me of my favourite film star, Mickey Rooney. As he sat at the piano in the minstrel's gallery, wearing his white dinner jacket and black bow tie, I would listen to him playing, with rapt attention, letting the food on my plate grow cold. I fondly imagined he was playing his repertoire of Ivor Novello songs just for me.

At night we would stand on the deck, gazing at the beauty of the inky blackness of the sea and study the height of the Southern Cross above the horizon, to see how far south we had travelled. When dolphins and flying fish appeared and finally an albatross, we knew we were not far from land. Then one morning we awoke to see, through our portholes, the misty outline of Table Mountain. We had been at sea for nearly five weeks.

Slowly, the *Llangibby Castle* steamed into Table Bay, accompanied by the busy little pilot boat. We passed the old whaling station on our starboard side, where a group of Cape penguins stood sentry on the rocks. Leaning over the ship's railings, we watched strange jellyfish float by in the clear, green water. An albatross flying over the ship acted as our escort, as we sailed towards this southern tip of the African continent. Its huge wingspan cast a shadow over the deck. As we drew closer, the presence of Table Mountain dominated everything. A cloud drifted over its plateaued top, making it not unreasonable to imagine a giant tablecloth being spread in preparation for some mighty feast. Beside it the jagged point of Lion's Head resembled an unfinished work from a sculptor's yard.

The grandeur of this view has not changed over the centuries. The merchant sailors of the Dutch East India Company, after months at sea in their cramped wooden sailing ships, would have gazed in wonder on this bay. What excitement and what expectations they must have experienced on sighting this land! Capetown, which now sprawls over the foothills of the mountain, is their inspiration. Their footprint can be found in the pristine white farmhouses with their distinctive Cape Dutch gables.

Our excitement at reaching Africa and the prospect of going ashore to explore this beautiful city, bathed in sunshine, was tempered by the news that our ship was to be commandeered at Durban, our next port. It was required as a troop ship. Those passengers who held priority status would be flown by military aircraft on to Nairobi. The rest would have to make their own way back to Kenya as best they could. Our parents were classed as priority, but there was no provision for us children. The dreadful prospect of being abandoned once again did not last long. It was decided that Mary would accompany my father on to Kenya, while my mother would remain in Durban with Helen and me until she could get us a passage on another ship. So Mary, aged sixteen, who had never flown before, who was a stranger to Africa and knew no Swahili, stepped fearlessly on to the plane in place of my mother. Once in Nairobi, she acted as housekeeper, managing the staff, shopping, ordering meals and generally looking after my father until we arrived two months later.

Meanwhile, back in Durban, Helen and I were enrolled for one term at the Stella Maris Convent on the Beria Hill. My mother booked herself into a nearby hotel – the King Edward VII. Here she spent much of her day at her bedroom window, with her binoculars focused on the queue of shipping waiting to enter the harbour. When she eventually spotted the British India ship we were booked on, she was frustrated to see that day after day it remained at anchor, unable to get a berth. My poor mother! It was a dreadfully anxious time for her. Her finances were being stretched to the limit. And then, to add to her woes, Helen became ill with paratyphoid fever, and had to be hospitalised. When we finally boarded the ship, my mother refused to go ashore at any of the intervening ports until at long last we docked at Mombasa. It had been early August when we had sailed down the mouth of the Clyde. We were now into the middle of November.

Travelling on the ship with us, on this last leg of our journey, were Sir Delves and Lady Broughton. They were said to be on their honeymoon. With the romantic notions of a teenager, I studied them closely, as they walked round the deck. I judged them to be an ill-matched pair, with none of the attributes I associated with a honeymoon couple. They appeared to have little to say to each other, or indeed, to anyone else. She wore her platinum blonde hair in a shoulder-length bob. Her fashionable slacks spoke of money. He, in his Savile Row suit, was stiff and austere. With a receding hairline and bristling moustache, he looked old enough to be her father. Little did any of us imagine that this was the couple who would do more to blacken the name of the British in East Africa than anything the left-wing communist sympathisers back in Britain could ever dream up.

Delves Broughton was the 11th Baronet of Doddington Park in Cheshire. She had been Diana Caldwell of Hove – his mistress for the past five years. When his wife, Vera, abandoned him for Lord Moyne, he decided the time had come for him to leave the dangers and discomforts of wartime Britain and go with Diana to seek a life in the sun in Kenya, where he had a farm. When they got to Durban, they discovered that she could only get an entry permit to the Colony if she was his wife. Accordingly, they were married in Durban Registry Office on 5th November, 1940.

Within days of arriving in Kenya, after being welcomed into the bosom of the infamously amoral Happy Valley set, Diana Broughton began a torrid affair with the Casanova of the colony, Josslyn Hay, the impoverished 22nd Earl of Errol. This affair would lead to his murder, and Sir Delves Broughton, now pacing the deck with his bride at his side, would in six months time be brought to trial before my father, accused of the murder. A brilliant South African lawyer, Henry Morris, secured his acquittal. Cynics like to point out that his acquittal was assured, because it was unlikely that any member of the jury would want to convict the man of killing someone who might quite possibly have seduced his own wife! The culprit has never been named and the murder weapon was never found. One year later, Sir Delves Broughton was found dead in his bedroom in the Adelphi Hotel, in Liverpool, after taking an overdose of morphine.

This real-life Agatha Christie story refuses to die. Books continue to be written about it. A film on the subject, *White Mischief*, was received with great acclaim. Newspaper articles still appear, claiming to have discovered who the culprit was. At the time, the murder rocked the colony to its foundations. The shock, the scandal, the disgust, was compounded by the fact that it had happened at a time when Britain had its back to the wall. The sordid lifestyle of a few disgraceful reprobates, revealed over the course of the month-long trial, would, most unfairly, bring shame on the whole colony, the majority of whose population was exceptionally hard-working and upright. For my father it seemed that everything to which he had dedicated his life now lay in ruins. It was inevitable that a comparison would be made with the people of England who, at that time, were suffering terrible hardships and deprivation, my brothers among them. The impact on public opinion of, what came to be known as the Errol Case, would reflect forever on how badly the British behaved in Kenya.

Helen and I were at school at the time of the murder, and the nuns took care to see that no hint of the scandal penetrated the convent walls. Consequently when we eventually did hear about it, it meant little to us. It is true, I had met Lord Errol once briefly, when he came to sign the Chief Justice's Visitors' Book which lay open on our hall table. I remembered the occasion because, unlike anyone else who came to sign the book, he brought my mother a box of Cadbury's Milk Chocolate and insisted on giving them to her himself. Later, in the Easter holidays, we drove past the ditch on the Ngong Road where the Buick had been found with his body in it. And, of course, we had seen the Broughtons on our journey up from Durban. Apart from these slight encounters, the drama passed us by.

Mary and my mother, on the other hand, witnessed the daily drama of the entrance of Diana Broughton into the court. They joined in the collective sharp intake of breath of everyone in that packed courtroom, followed by the murmur of excitement that invariably greeted her appearance. People stood on tip-toe, craning their necks to gain a better view of what she was wearing. Each day it was something different. Her jewellery was spectacular. Her eye-catching hats all had a veil attached to them to hide her face. It was said that she and her Happy Valley friends treated the court as though it was the Ascot Royal Enclosure on Ladies' Day.

A few weeks after the trial, Helen and I had a chance encounter with Diana Broughton and her infamous friend, June Carberry. We were travelling home for the holidays to our house in Nyeri, on the branch line that linked Nairobi to the Highlands.

The train, which was of toy town proportions, was generally referred to as 'the Tram'. The name came about because Whitehall, fearful of inflicting the cost of another 'Lunatic Express' on the British taxpayer, had granted the money for the construction of a tramline, but not a railway. The Kenyan government, rather than argue with Whitehall over the unsuitability of a tramline through the African bush, chose instead to go ahead with the construction of a very small railway and call it a tramline. It proved to be an invaluable link for the farmers in the Aberdares, not only for their mail, but also for getting their animals and produce to the markets. Very few passengers used it, which was the reason Helen and I expected to have the compartment to ourselves.

To our dismay, we were joined halfway through our journey by two brassy blondes, reeking of perfume and swearing like troopers. Their car had broken down, so they had no alternative but to take the train. They threw themselves into their seats in a state of high dudgeon. In rasping, gin-soaked voices they raged against the Indian mechanic who was supposed to have serviced the vehicle. Ignoring our presence, they puffed furiously on their de Reszke cigarettes, while expressing their horror at the indignity of having to travel on what they termed 'this filthy cattle truck'. The atmosphere in the compartment soon became opaque with cigarette smoke. As the train had no corridor we were unable to escape: we were trapped.

Turning our backs on them we knelt on the seat under the window and passed the time by waving to the children who stood in all their gleaming brown nakedness on the banks beside the track. They watched in wide-eyed wonder the fearsome 'iron snake' clattering through the bush. We looked eagerly for our first sight of the Chania River winding its way through the red earth of the valley far below. This would indicate we were approaching our journey's end. It couldn't come soon enough.

I can't remember at what point we noticed a sudden silence in the compartment, followed by furtive whispering. This was broken by one of the women remarking in studied, dulcet tones, 'Don't they remind you of the two princesses, Elizabeth and Margaret Rose?' It was hard not to collapse into helpless giggles. Helen and I, in our ill-fitting school uniforms, were being likened to the daughters of King George VI, whose charming portraits decorated every chocolate box and biscuit tin! I turned round to find Diana Broughton's chill blue eyes fixed on me. They had worked out who we were from the luggage labels on our suitcases. From then on they did their best to engage us in conversation. 'Do you travel often on this awful train?' We protested that we liked the train. 'Do you like your school? Are the nuns nice to you? What do you do in the holidays?' And so the questions kept on coming, until, mercifully, we at last drew in to Nyeri station. All four of us stepped onto the platform together, the colour drained from my father's shocked face, when he saw who our travelling companions had been.

Chapter 26

Kenya Revisited

If, in 1940, someone had described Kenya as it is today I would have dismissed it as science fiction. The Kenya that we knew (pronounced 'Keenya') had no game parks, no package tours or tourist hotels. The camcorder had not been invented. We took photographs with box brownie cameras, not of game, but of each other. Big game was shot, not with cameras, but with rifles by famed white hunters. Nairobi was the size of a small provincial town, with no high-rise buildings. The shops, known as dukas, were mostly owned by Indians. There was a thriving African market with beautiful flowers and fresh vegetables for sale. This is where my mother and her friends liked to shop. Due to the war and petrol rationing, traffic was minimal. The lethal *mutata* (the African taxi of to-day) did not exist. Few of the roads were tarmacked and when the rains came, they were impassable without chains on your tyres. The coast, now a tourist paradise, was largely undeveloped.

There were no urban slums. Africans lived a pastoral life in the native reserves. Their thatched *rondavels* were built in family groups round larger huts belonging to the elders of the tribe. Africans who chose to work for Europeans (no African was ever compelled to work for a European) either lived with their families as dependant 'squatters' on European farms, or in the purpose-built servants' quarters adjoining town houses. In the latter case they generally left their wives behind in the Reserves. African men did not encourage their women to work in towns. Their job was to remain at home to work the *shambas* (smallholdings) and look after the children, (or *totos*.) In the town, Africans dressed in khaki shorts and colourful shirts, but scorned shoes. In the reserves, they retained their traditional dress of animal skins and beads. This included the Masai who had not at that time adopted the red plaid blankets they wear today. It was their haughty looks, their spears and their exceptionally long legs that distinguished them from other tribes, together with their passionate love for their cattle. They believe to this day, that at the dawn of Creation, God gave all the cattle in the world to them. This gives them, they would argue, the indisputable right to steal from their neighbour's herd. Recently they offered to advise the British Government on how to handle the latest outbreak of Mad Cow Disease in Britain. They were disappointed to have their offer rejected, for they consider themselves to be the world authority on how to care for cattle.

No one at this time foresaw the demise of the British Empire. Like Churchill, we felt certain that in a thousand years it would still be in place. My brother, Roderick, would never have dreamed of joining the Colonial Service after the war, if he had thought otherwise. Nor did anyone envisage the unprecedented population explosion of the post-war years. This, more than anything else, is what has shaped the Kenya of today. Poverty has driven a largely rural population to seek employment in the towns. This mass urbanisation of an uneducated, tribal people has given birth to slums like Kibera, one of the largest in Africa, with all their attendant lawlessness. Unchanged, however, are the vast skyscapes, the majestic panoramas, the red earth and brilliant sunshine, the suddenness of nightfall with its canopy of stars, the beauty and awesome power of its animals, the elemental secrets that lie at the heart of this great continent, along with the unquenchable optimism of the African people. All this remains as it ever was. This is the Africa that continues to bewitch and attract people from all over the world.

When we arrived in November 1940, the Colony was on a war footing. Mussolini's troops were penetrating Kenya's northern frontiers, and having broken through British Somaliland, threatened the country's eastern border. The Vichy French were also uncomfortably close on the island of Madagascar. After the fall of Singapore, the Colony faced another risk. Mombasa was now the Naval Base for the Eastern Fleet. From now on Japanese submarines would prove to be a deadly menace. They lurked in the Indian Ocean waiting to target troop ships leaving the port of Mombasa for the war in Burma. There were some truly dreadful casualties. The sinking of the *Khedive Ismail* with its complement of WRENS was one of the worst naval disasters of the war. Of the 1,511 people on board, 1,297 were drowned. My sister Mary was lucky not to have been on it. John Addington, (later my second husband, John Sidmouth), was in charge of the port at the time. With Singapore in mind, the War Office had issued him with a sealed envelope to be opened only in an emergency. It contained the authorisation for him to evacuate the port if and when events became critical.

At the outbreak of war, Kenya's defence force was woefully inadequate. All able-bodied men between the ages of 18 and 35 from a white community of 23,000 had enlisted in the Kenya Regiment. They were joined by the soldiers of the King's African Rifles – a military force whose rank and file were African. It had been formed in 1902 to assist the local askaris (police) to keep the peace. This combined force was hardly enough to defend the Colony. South African troops came to the rescue, and with their help the Italians were repulsed.

By a curious coincidence, the French island of Madagascar was liberated by a force of commandos led by my future brother-in-law, Tom Addington. He used to enjoy telling the story of how, after landing, the troops broke their way into the Mayor's Residence, which appeared to be deserted. Everyone had apparently fled. Upstairs, however, they discovered the Mayor in bed with his Madagascan mistress. Clutching the bedcover, and sitting bolt upright, the poor man pleaded 'I beg you, please, please do not tell my wife!' and then, recognising the CO, exclaimed 'Good Lord Tom! What on earth are you doing here!' The Mayor was none other than Monsieur Bonnet, Tom's French master from his preparatory school!

The crisis of war had one major beneficial outcome for the Colony. It served to draw a veil over the long-standing rift between the settlers and the Westminster Government. The war effort required that everyone must now pull together. With the men away in the army, the farms were managed by their wives. Thanks to these intrepid women the Colony was self-sufficient in food throughout the war. Their task was heroic, for farming in Africa bore little resemblance to agricultural life in Dorset or Somerset. In Karen Blixen's book *Out of Africa*, and Elspeth Huxley's biography of her mother, Nellie Grant, there are heart-breaking accounts of the problems they faced: the isolation, the loneliness, the hostile climate and the financial worries, together with the daily courage needed to face the constant danger of the wildlife. These challenges are forgotten in today's rush to condemn British colonialism. I learnt a great deal about the hardships these women endured from my school friends at Lumbwa, many of whom were brought up on these farms.

While the urgency of the war effort brought a new sense of unity of purpose to the colonialists, below the surface powerful nationalist forces were at work planning the overthrow of British colonial rule in Kenya. The air of permanence that kept the Union Jack flying over Government House was deceptive. After the war, East Africa would suffer a seismic change.

Jomo Kenyatta, the undisputed leader of the African National Union and later the first President of Kenya, was the product of Presbyterian missionaries. He saw a similarity between their Bible stories of the Israelites search for the Promised Land and the land grievances of the Kikuyu tribe. As a young man he was naturally drawn to the bright lights of Nairobi. Here he met other politically conscious Africans. With them, he joined the KCA (Kikuyu Central Association) and before long was elected to present the Colonial Office in London with their claim for title deeds to what they considered to be their land.

In London, although he was ignored by Whitehall, he managed to impress a group of left-wing intellectuals. He became the protégée of a wealthy Afro-American called George Padmore, a Comintern agent who took Kenyatta on a tour of all the major European cities, ending in Moscow, where he enrolled him in a school for African revolutionaries. After an induction course of eighteen months, Kenyatta returned to London where he began writing inflammatory articles for the communist Daily Worker, signing himself Comrade Kenyatta. He also gave lectures for the WEA (Workers Education Association). These lectures were full of colourful descriptions of how he had seen 'with his own eyes' his fellow countrymen put in chains by the British. (He later apologised for his many exaggerations). Britain at this time was too busy fighting World War II to take much notice, though some Labour politicians, like Fenner Brockway did take him seriously and supported him.

What the Government failed to realise, to their cost, was the fact that Jomo Kenyatta was no primitive, nomadic tribesman, as first encountered by the early pioneers. He was someone who had been groomed and moulded by the West. He and his friends were politically astute people, capable of forming trade unions and fomenting large-scale civil unrest. By the time Kenyatta returned to Kenya in 1946, after an absence of seventeen years, he was well equipped to lead the post-war national liberation movement.

That so much political unrest should have gone unnoticed for so long is a measure of how confident the British felt about their superiority and right to rule. The Union Jack continued to fly proudly from its flagpole, the Governor wore his ceremonial plumage with his accustomed regal authority, and things would continue that way forever, or so we all thought.

Chapter 27

The Daughters of the Chief Justice

I hated Nairobi. I hated the house. I hated the people. I hated the life. I was at odds with myself and my family. I counted the days to the end of the holidays. I longed to be back at our new school in Lumbwa. I was a typical adolescent, always angry, always in tears. Would it have been any different if I had been older, like Mary, or younger, like Helen? They seemed to have no difficulty in adjusting to our new life in Kenya. Admittedly, they rode, and I didn't. Helen, to my mother's delight, 'had a beautiful seat on a horse' and Mary looked wonderful in jodhpurs. I was put up on a horse once, where I felt horribly unsafe and was greatly relieved when the syce helped me to dismount.

Then there were the dogs. Mary had a thoroughbred dachshund, Porky, and Helen had Nellie, a lovable but strange-looking cross between a Labrador and a dachshund. I was considered too unreliable to own a dog. I would never remember to feed or exercise it. Certainly, I would never manage the daily ritual of de-ticking. I was far too squeamish to cope with the blood-sucking fleas, found in the long grasses, that burrowed deep into a dog's coat. These bloated creatures had to be picked off each night, and disposed of in a bowl of hot water, where they made a popping noise before dying. If this wasn't done regularly, the dog became seriously ill with tick fever. For this reason, short-haired breeds, like bullterriers and dachshunds, were the only kind of dog to have in Africa.

The criticism of me was fully justified. I was an idle teenager. To justify my label of being 'the musical one of the family' my mother decided I must have singing lessons. I don't think she understood that though I enjoyed music, and admittedly had quite a pretty, tuneful voice, I was never going to electrify an audience in Covent Garden or create a sensation at La Scala, Milan. In all honesty, there was little chance of my progressing beyond being able to entertain her friends by singing sad Irish ballads. Full of hope, she engaged a Polish aristocrat, one of the many refugees in the Colony, to give me singing lessons in the holidays. He was tall, with dark, glossy hair swept back from a pale, round face. He dressed formally, in a dark blue suit. Heaven knows what horrors he had endured under the Nazis, before crossing continents to find refuge in Kenya. Whatever they were, he never spoke of them. He would arrive each Thursday morning, click the heels of his well-polished shoes and bow, before presenting me with a bunch of red carnations. This caused much sniggering from my sisters. He talked a great deal about music, but little work was done at the keyboard. This was just as well, as on the rare occasions he coaxed me into vocal scales, my poor family suffered acutely; even the dogs objected. It was an uncomfortable arrangement. I can't remember how it ended. Did we dismiss him, or did he give us notice? His parting gift to me was a beautiful book on Rimsky-Korsakov, and a copy of his own composition of the Ave Maria.

Our house, situated on Government Hill, not far from Government House, was a disappointment. It had none of the ethnic charm of our house in Dar es Salaam. This one had been built for a businessman homesick for the pantiles of Surrey. When his business failed and he was declared bankrupt, the Government stepped in and bought it as the residence for the Chief Justice. This plain, red-brick villa with an oak front door and lattice windows owed nothing to African culture. The rooms, with the exception of the panelled sitting room, were small; the staircase lacked any distinguishing feature. Upstairs there were two bedrooms. Helen and I shared the guest room, which had all that a guest would expect - a cheval mirror, a large dressing table with a dressing table set, tie back curtains, and yes, pictures of Egypt on the wall, as described by John Betjeman in 'A Subaltern's Love Song'. There were none of the usual idiosyncrasies that characterise most teenage bedrooms: no books, no memorabilia, no teddies worn out by too much loving. When we returned to school, all trace of our occupation disappeared. My father's dressing room became Mary's bedroom. A second dressing room was used by my mother as a study. Hidden behind the house was the only concession to Africa: the thatched *rondavels* of the servants' quarters.

The garden had never been landscaped. It was no more than a rough field with one anaemic mango tree. Twice a year a gang of prisoners came to cut the grass. As they swung their pangas, they would sing a repetitive, hypnotic chant: one lead voice improvising above the rhythmic ground bass of the rest. Their male voices mingled with the call of the African dove. 'Geog...ra.. phee, Geog...ra..phee, Geog... ra..phee ', it would call, as if to remind us where we were. Indeed, these African sounds, together with the distant view of Mount Kenya, and the need for mosquito nets over our beds at night, went some way towards dispelling the whiff of Bagshot introduced by the sad businessman.

As our parents had been child-free for almoast decade, when we arrived in Nairobi, we created something of a stir. We became grist for the mill of the social columnist on the *East African Standard*, whose column went under the heading 'Miranda's Merrier Moments'. After being nonentities in a little-known convent in North London, we were now goldfish in a bowl. How we looked and what we wore mattered. Miranda was merciless. Her job was to amuse and entertain her readers. This she did with barbed comments that did little for my self-esteem: 'Lady Sheridan was there with her daughters; Therese, in purple taffeta, looking ill at ease beside her lovely elder sister, Mary, wearing a smart little number in rose pink with white accessories,' was typical.

Our clothes, including our shoes, were made in the Indian Bazaar. Our visits there were always an exciting experience. The scents were overpowering and the colours exotic. A good deal of bargaining was necessary before a price was agreed. When that was settled, all the *dhurzi* required were your measurements and a picture from a fashion magazine. You chose the material from the bales of cloth in the front of the shop. A week or so later you could expect to have a good copy of a dress from one of the London fashion houses. To have a pair of shoes made, the cobbler would ask you to place your foot on a sheet of paper. Squatting on the floor in front of you, he would draw round each foot. You then selected the leather from hides that hung in his very smelly yard; you gave him a pattern and in a few days you were the possessor of a new pair of really comfortable shoes. Whether they were a perfect match or not, depended on whether he had had to use two hides or one. Hats were important. My mother was clever at giving her old ones a makeover. The result was not always to our liking. On our way to Mass, one Sunday morning, Helen, enraged by my mother's orders to wear a particularly unbecoming hat, stunned us all by throwing it out of the car window. Secretly, I applauded her courage.

When the North African campaign opened, Kenya became a transit camp for the troops on their way to fight in the desert. The Mayor of Nairobi, Gladys Delamere, Lord Delamere's second wife, urged everyone to do their utmost to help entertain this influx of soldiers. Concerts, bazaars, receptions and dances were arranged. The Chief Justice with his wife and daughters were of course expected to attend them all. We waltzed with lecherous colonels, tangoed with passionate young officers, and fox-trotted with homesick airmen. We sat through endless recitals and helped at bazaars. The venues - Government House, Torrs Hotel, Muthaiga Club, the Race Course - became places of torture for me. What we wore and how we looked was closely observed and written up by the dreadful Miranda.

It didn't stop there. At home, there were guests to be taken care of. Jacqueline Hawkins was the fourteen-year-old daughter of an official in the Indian Civil Service. She and her elegant Parisian mother came to stay with us while waiting for travel permits to enable them to join her father in Cairo. Jacqueline, despite her age, was the ultimate sophisticate. She had picked up from her mother the trick of peppering her conversation with French *bons mots*, which I found particularly unnerving as I didn't speak a word of French. A bed was put up for Helen in the study, so that Jacqueline could share the guest room with me. As a result, I was spared no detail of her life in India: how much her fair hair was admired; how she was known as the Pearl of Poona; how amusingly and successfully she dealt with her many admirers, and much more beside. It was hard to keep up, but eventually their travel permits came through and we bade them farewell.

Prince Paul of Yugoslavia and his family presented a much trickier situation. They were despised by everyone. It was thought that he had done a deal with Hitler, and so was regarded as a traitor. The British had instigated a *coup d'etat* in Belgrade and got him deposed. Four days later, the Nazis invaded, causing terrible devastation. The family managed to escape to England. Churchill loathed him. He called him 'Palsy' and ordered that he and his family should be sent to Kenya and put under house arrest, under the supervision of my father. In recent years, there has been a reappraisal of his character. Far from being a cowardly, weak man, it transpires that he was unusually courageous. His aim as regent was to maintain the neutrality of his country. With this in mind, he stood up to both Hitler and Churchill. He travelled to Bertchesgarten and got Hitler to sign an agreement, (which Hitler failed to honour), guaranteeing the neutrality of Yugoslavia. Churchill, on the other hand, was determined to get Yugoslavia to declare war on Germany. This would give the British the pretext go in and attack 'the soft underbelly' of the Axis Powers. Prince Paul refused to comply. He knew this would spell suicide for his country. He was right. Churchill got his way by staging a coup d'etat in Belgrade, ousting Prince Paul who was declared 'an enemy of the state'. Churchill maintained 'It is the right of a great power to sacrifice a smaller neutral state for the sake of ultimate victory'. Many years later, Churchill, in his memoirs, apologised for his treatment of Prince Paul.

By the time he arrived in Kenya, Prince Paul, not surprisingly, was suffering from melancholia. Being a deeply spiritual man he found solace from his depression in his religion. My father was wonderfully sympathetic. He spent many an evening with this desperately sad man, praying with him in the Catholic Church in Nairobi.

The two boys, Prince Alexander and Prince Nicholas, would come over from time to time to spend the day with us. We were not allowed to take them anywhere: no cinemas, bike rides, walks or even shopping were permitted. Prince Nicholas was a year younger than me. I played cards and various board games with him, but he was not easy to entertain. He was easily bored and hated losing. His older brother, Prince Alexander, was much quieter. He appeared content to sit on the sofa and read. He was not much of a conversationalist. Poor boys! What a contrast it must have been from their life in the royal palace in Belgrade. After the war, Prince Nicholas became a close friend of Princess Margaret. He died in a car crash in Berkshire when he was still in his twenties. Prince Alexander married the daughter of King Umberto II of Italy.

Princess Olga, the boys' mother, invited me one day to have lunch with them in the house they had been allocated at Muthaiga. There was much debate in the family on whether I should curtsey to the Princess or not. The general feeling was you do not curtsey to someone who is a friend of Hitler. One thing was certain: I was not on any account to mention anything about Roderick fighting in North Africa.

I have two recollections of that lunch. The first was being greeted by two of the most elegant women I had ever met, either before or since. Princess Olga and her sister, the Duchess of Kent, were both wearing black. They were in mourning for the death of the Duke of Kent, who had recently been killed in a mysterious air crash in Scotland. I knew instantly what I had to do. I dropped a deep curtsey. The second recollection is of my surprising presence of mind when one of them asked where in England had I been at school? I realised it was not possible in that company to tell them about North London and the Convent of Jesus and Mary in Crownhill Road, Willesden. I found myself saying, in an impeccable French accent I was not aware I possessed: "With the nuns of Jesu et Marie, in London". They appeared impressed, if a little puzzled. They mercifully asked no more.

What no one told me, and what I have subsequently learnt, is that the two women, Princess Olga and her sister Princess Marina, Duchess of Kent, were Romanovs. Their grandfather was Tzar Alexander II of Russia, and they had been brought up with their cousin, Tzar Nicholas. Their uncle was the father of Prince Philip, later the Duke of Edinburgh. Moreover, the best man at the wedding of Princess Olga and Prince Paul had been the Duke of York, now King George VI of Great Britain. All in all, I think I was right to curtsey. My time at Miss Catt's School of Dancing had not been wasted!

My dislike of Nairobi and its society was due to a combination of things, but there is one dreadfully humiliating incident which stands out above all the others, and which colours my memory of that time. It was Christmas 1942, and the Amateur Dramatic Society were planning to put on *Cinderella* at the Theatre Royal. They were in need of someone to take the part of the Fairy Godmother. It was not a demanding role, but they would be required to sing the song made famous by Judy Garland in *The Wizard of Oz*: 'Somewhere Over the Rainbow'. The Committee considered the available talent in the town. Someone remembered that one of the CJ's daughters could sing. My mother was approached. She glowed with excitement. This was surely my first step on the rung of the ladder which would lead me to making my debut at La Scala, Milan. 'Yes, Therese has a lovely voice. She would be more than happy to play the part of the Fairy Godmother', and 'Yes, she knew the song well'.

I froze with horror when I heard the news; but as the proceeds of the show were going towards Christmas boxes for the troops, it was pointed out that it was my patriotic duty to perform. The audition went well and I made a passable sound at the rehearsals. Then came the first night. I tripped gaily on to the stage in my gauze tutu, covered with stars, and clutching my sparkling magic wand. Cinderella looked suitably impressed. The orchestra gave me my cue; I took a deep breath and opened my mouth – but not a sound came out. The orchestra tried again, and so did I – still no sound. On my third attempt, the whispering in the auditorium grew louder, growing ever more like a wind that presages a tropical storm. The conductor quickened the tempo in an attempt to jolly things along and Cinderella looked on in dismay at the sight of her Fairy Godmother, responding to frenzied instructions from the wings, leaving the stage in floods of tears. Oh the unforgettable shame of it!

Chapter 28

Lumbwa

Imagine you are standing on the veranda of a cedar lodge, on the top of a hill 9000 feet above sea level. It is evening and the vast canopy of sky is burnished with the changing colours of the setting sun, which reflect and stain the hills below. Far away, between the folds of the hills, you can glimpse an inlet of Lake Victoria, its waters shimmering in the last rays of sunlight. The air is crisp and cool. The only sound to break the silence comes from a tribesman in the valley thrumming on his native harp. In front of you the steps and terraces of an Italianate garden invite you to make your way down the hillside. Humming birds hover over the red-hot pokers, and cypress trees trick you into thinking you are in Umbria. This, with a few outbuildings that straggled over the brow of the hill, was the last school Helen and I attended.

The estate belonged to Count Tiele von Winkler, a German aristocrat who, on the outbreak of war, was unable to leave his home in Switzerland. His Kenya property was requisitioned for the use of the Loreto nuns and their one hundred and twenty pupils, who at the time of the threatened Italian invasion, were evacuated from their convent in Nairobi to Lumbwa, over 300 miles from the capital. To reach it necessitated an overnight journey in the famous 'Lunatic Express'. The train required two engines for the steep climb into the hills. With wood smoke billowing from both, it chugged its way over viaducts and bridges, across the floor of the Great Rift Valley and up the Escarpment, through some of the most spectacular scenery Africa has to offer. We never tired of staring out of the carriage windows at the grandeur of the scene spread before us. When darkness fell, it was time to tuck ourselves into the bunks made up with bedding from our kit bags, and be rocked to sleep by the slow rhythmic motion of the train.

The following morning, we stopped at Nakuru to breakfast at the Country Club. After re-boarding the train, we began the painfully slow ascent up into the forests. The drop in temperature became noticeable and we were glad of the warmth of our scarlet blazers. It was dusk by the time we reached the tiny station of Lumbwa. It was barely more than a railway siding. Here we clambered into the backs of lorries and were driven up into the Lumbwa hills. After a long bumpy ride, we rounded the final bend of a heavily wooded drive, and there before us, spread serenely over the highest hill, was the Count's hunting lodge. This would be our home for the next three months.

We played hockey on the lawn that sloped down from the front of the house (special skills were required to keep the ball in play) and we studied under cedar trees where wild crocus grew. Serious work went on in the classrooms, which were made of mud and wattle with thatched roofs and earth floors. We worked on slates, because due to the war there was a shortage of paper. Textbooks were also in short supply and had to be shared. Creepy crawlies and even snakes dropped from the thatch on to our desks. If it rained we were kept busy moving our desks around to avoid the leaks. Our lessons were never dull!

The drawing room, overlooking the view to the Lake, was converted into a chapel, but the library next door remained as the Count had left it. Here the Mother Provincial would entertain us on her annual visit with a recital of Irish ballads, accompanying herself on the boudoir grand. She was an accomplished musician with a lovely, contralto voice. As she sang, you became aware of the homesickness these brave women must have experienced, when reminded of their homeland. They had dedicated themselves to Africa in the knowledge that their rule, in those days, did not permit them to go home until they returned to die. It was not surprising that when she finished her recital there was barely a dry eye in the room.

Our own concerts were held in the dining hall. This was one of the more substantial of the outbuildings. The corrugated iron roof, however, had a drawback. If it rained, our performance became inaudible. This was frustrating, as a lot of work went into the production of such musicals as 'Columbus in a Merry Key' (composed by our headmistress); a choral piece entitled 'There Are No Birds In Last Year's Nest' and Liszt's Hungarian Rhapsody Number 2, arranged for eight hands. (The programme seldom changed from year to year). I reached the apotheosis of my school career, when I was not only Columbus, but also the soloist in 'There Are No Birds In Last Year's Nest', and, triumph of all triumphs, played the treble hand in the Hungarian Rhapsody. This was glory indeed!

The dining hall had an unusual feature. Ovens, accessed from the outside, were built into the brick walls. These were the inspiration of our beloved Polish housekeeper, Mrs Schlotawa. (She, along with the boudoir grand, was a legacy from Count Tiele's days.) She used the ovens to bake the crustiest, freshest, most flavoursome loaves of bread I have ever had the pleasure of eating. The ovens also provided the focal point of our midnight feasts. Clutching corns of cob, stolen from the kitchen garden, we would climb out of our bedroom windows and go in search of an oven still warm enough to cook the corn. Once the cobs were judged to be cooked – and this was always a matter of some dispute – we would stealthily make our way back to the grassy bank outside our rooms. There, we would lie on our backs, count the shooting stars, and tell each other stories while munching our smoky, half-cooked cobs. This, provided you didn't disturb a nest of safari ants, was total happiness.

The logistics of running a school in such a primitive place were formidable. A generator gave the main house electricity, but the outbuildings relied on storm lanterns. We had no flush toilets. At the start of each new term, the first essential was to discover the location of the newly-dug 'Long Drops'. A nocturnal visit to one of these required strong nerves. The African night is full of strange sounds and you could never be sure of what you might encounter. Snakes were our dread. But it was water that presented the greatest problem. We relied on a well, and the rainwater from barrels positioned to catch the run-off from the corrugated roofs. In times of drought, we went to a neighbouring farm in order to have a bath, nonchalantly swinging a sponge bag with a towel draped over one shoulder as we walked through the forest. A couple of inches of water poured from an old petrol can into a canvas tub was considered sufficient; but by the time we had walked back to the school in the heat of the day, we could well have done with another wash.

It was during one of these periods of severe drought that I found myself in, possibly, the most humiliating position of my life. We were in the habit of trying the taps in the bathrooms, before setting out on the trek to the farm, in the hope of finding that the water had been switched back on. On my bath day I had done just that, but was greeted by the usual gasp of empty pipes. Unfortunately, I did not remember to switch the tap off. The following day, we were gathered in a great arc on the front lawn to hear Mother Raphael announce, from the steps of the veranda, the name of the next Head Girl. To my amazement, my name was read out. I walked up the steps, with my head held high, to collect my medal, and bask in the applause as I returned to my place. Before we were dismissed, Mother Raphael had another announcement to make, concerning a matter of great seriousness. Someone had left a tap switched on in one of the bathrooms. As a result, when the water had been reconnected, several precious gallons had been lost. Would that person now, please, make themselves known. I don't know who was the more discomforted, Mother Raphael flanked by her Community, or me as I made my way a second time up the veranda steps, this time to receive a stern lecture on thoughtlessness. There was no applause as I made my way back across the lawn. A hundred and twenty pairs of eyes were fixed on my red face and the only sound I could detect was that of barely restrained sniggering.

These times of drought held another hazard: bushfires. We would sit on the steps of the terrace and watch giant flames leap from tree to tree on the surrounding hills in an awesome dance macabre. On more than one occasion plans were drawn up for the speedy evacuation of the school, but somehow our hill was always spared and the well continued to supply just enough water for our needs. The nuns firmly believed this was due to the power of our prayers, for these nuns knew all about prayer. (Did they draw their inspiration from the beauty of our environment, or were they naturally in tune with God, I wonder? Possibly both had a part to play.)

It never crossed our young minds for one moment to consider the daily challenge this little community of seven or eight nuns faced in caring for our welfare, our safety and on top of everything else, our education, under the most adverse conditions. I doubt if it would have been possible without the energy, drive and resourcefulness of those two remarkable women; our Mother Superior, Mother Raphael; and our Head Mistress, Mother Teresa Gertrude, otherwise known as MTG.

They were very different in character. Mother Raphael, it was rumoured, came from a family of Scottish aristocrats and it was also said that she had had a fiancé who had been killed in the Great War. What is certain is that her surname was Gordon. She came out to East Africa in 1921, with two companions, to found a convent for the IBVM (Institute of the Blessed Virgin Mary). One of her companions was killed in a car accident soon after their arrival. It was this tragedy that gave rise to the nun's custom of reciting a decade of the Rosary before travelling anywhere by car.

They opened their first convent in Nairobi and before long established themselves as highly regarded members of the Colony. The tall, slender figure of Mother Raphael commanded respect from the Governor down to the humblest kitchen *toto*. The success of the evacuation of the school up into the hills was largely due to her rapport with the Indian stationmaster at Lumbwa. I met him many years later, at Heathrow Airport, where he was working as a car park attendant. His memories of her were still full of the love and admiration she had evoked from everyone who met her.

There were very few Catholics in Kenya, so the main intake of pupils to the school were, nominally at least, Church of England. Mother Raphael assured the often bemused parents that before the children left the school, they would understand what it meant to be a member of the Church of England. True to her word, she not only provided them with a separate chapel, but also saw that they received instruction and were confirmed in their faith by the Anglican Bishop of Mombasa.

It was difficult to say what made her appearance distinctive. She had sharp intelligent eyes set in a face criss-crossed with lines. Her general expression was sombre, but when she smiled she became suffused with a captivating beauty. She spoke in a clear, gentle voice without any hint of hesitation. She emanated authority. It felt natural to drop a curtsey in her presence. On Sunday afternoons, we would gather under the cedar tree on the front lawn for her weekly address. It was an occasion when she chose rather to share her thoughts with us than address us with any formality. From her, we learnt the importance of other people. No one should be dismissed for being dull. If they were of interest to God, that ought to be sufficient. Before meeting someone for the first time, we should, if possible, discover something about them, so that we could make them feel comfortable with us. Sharing your conversation equally with those on either side of you at table was not just a question of good etiquette, it was ensuring neither person felt ignored. Good manners could not be put on, like smart clothes; they had to be adopted even when you were alone. In this way they became instinctive. A smile could bring a ray of sunshine into the bleak landscape of another person's heart. We must aim to bring light into this dark world (this was the 1940s). God had created us for this. These and many more gems from her store of wisdom were what Mother Raphael passed on to us, as we sat at her feet in the shade of the cedar tree.

Mother Teresa Gertrude, our Headmistress, while being in sharp contrast to her Superior, also complemented her. She was a small diminutive figure, bustling with energy. Her poor eyesight necessitated her wearing spectacles with pebble lens. The flat curve of her upper lip and the firm cut of her jaw, betrayed her fierce determination and scorn for those who fell short of her high expectations. She could be witheringly intimidating. We strained every sinew to please her, not out of fear, but out of a genuine desire to earn her praise. She was Irish. It was said that her brother was an active member of the IRA and that he was frequently on the run from the authorities. Just as in a Sean O'Casey play he would come knocking on the door of their home in the middle of the night, seeking shelter from the police. Whether these stories were true or false was difficult to say. Perhaps it was significant that she refused to teach us English History. She chose a European syllabus instead. Napoleon, Bismark and Garibaldi were her heroes.

We loved her because she was an enthusiast. She threw herself into every activity with a ferocious energy. During one term, walking on stilts became a craze. A few of us persuaded the school carpenter to make us some. We went everywhere on them; to meals and the classrooms. For MTG who was barely five feet tall, the idea was irresistible. She appeared on Sports Day with some of the younger nuns, each on a pair of stilts, wobbling unsteadily across the front lawn and shrieking with laughter.

One of the delights of the school at Lumbwa was the number of unexpected holidays we enjoyed. It seemed that any excuse was good enough to declare the day a holiday. It might be the visit of some dignitary, or perhaps there was good news from the war front. There were, too, the familiar Feast Days as well as the nuns' individual feasts. Whatever the reason, the day would be an opportunity for one of MTG's renowned bush treks. These expeditions were not for slackers. She would chose a group of girls she considered to be old enough and fit enough to accompany her. We would set out early in the morning, equipped with a bottle of water and a packet of Mrs Scholtawa's sandwiches. MTG, with the folds of her white habit hitched into her leather belt and sporting a topee over her black veil, kept up a terrific pace throughout the day. She seldom looked back to see how we were faring. Regardless of the state of our tunics – this was before the days of jeans – we crawled through dark tunnels of tangled thorn bush, stepped across rushing streams, used ancient pathways to clamber up nearly vertical hills and frequently lost our bearings. We stopped, briefly in a forest clearing, to eat our sandwiches, but soon hurried on, fearful of losing sight of our diminutive guide. We were stretched to our physical limits. It was the nearest we came to experiencing what it must have been like to be an African pioneer. The next day, while we, with our scarlet, sunburnt faces and aching limbs, were hardly able to move, MTG was her usual bustling self, untouched by fatigue.

She was a lively teacher. She taught us English and Biology, along with History. She also enjoyed preparing us for formal debates in front of the school and community. But it was in RE that she excelled. When I arrived in London, aged eighteen, I was amazed at how little my well-educated, Catholic contemporaries knew about their faith. MTG had given us a clear, overall view of what made Catholicism distinctive. The Mass was the cornerstone of our belief. In those days, it was always referred to as the Holy Sacrifice of the Mass. We studied its history from the predictions of Melchisedech, through to St Paul, Constantine, and on to our present day. We explored the relationship of blood-sacrifice and religion, and the pre-cognition of Catholic beliefs in other religions. We discussed the relationship of human love in the context of Divine Love. Natural Law, Original Sin and the Ten Commandments were explained. We were given logical reasons for the Sacraments and Grace. This and so much more besides, was what she taught us. Above all, she taught us how to think.

Mother Raphael was sensitive to the impact the presence of the school was having on the local Africans. The Wa-Lumbwa tribe had had very little contact with Europeans. They still wore animal skins and decorated their bodies with coloured beads threaded onto coils of copper wire; – probably the same wire stolen by their forebears from Mr Preston's railway workers in 1901, and now treasured as tribal heirlooms! To satisfy their curiosity about us she invited them to come and show us how they danced. The occasion was only partially successful. The ground shook as they leapt and stamped and whirled about, ever more ferociously; but throughout the performance it was noticeable that they were inhibited by our presence. There was a cautious look in their eyes, as they chanted and 'whooped'. They were uncharacteristically hesitant, with some dropping out and attempting to hide their embarrassment with giggles. This was nothing like the exuberance and wild abandon of a wedding ngoma we had once witnessed on the coast.

She had more success with the chapel, which was always open to them. There was one old man who spent hours in silent prayer in front of the Blessed Sacrament. A number asked to be baptised. On those occasions we were often invited to stand in as godparents.

The Convent also provided a respite home for exhausted missionary priests, one of whom made a life-long impression on all of us. Father Daniel Morrissey was a Holy Ghost father. He was twenty-seven years old and had only recently been ordained. Soon after arriving in Africa, he was diagnosed with Bright's Disease, a rare form of cancer. He came to Lumbwa to die. He was a living example of someone resigned to God's Will. He enchanted us with his beautiful tenor voice and was an authority on plainchant. We learnt from him the subtleties of its phrasing, the rise and fall of its cadences and how to read the notation. I never hear the Missa de Angelis without thinking of him. His stories, told in a quiet, gentle voice, with just a hint of a brogue, were full of merriment. This was laughter in the face of adversity brought to perfection. He taught us to pray the rosary. We would compete to see who could recite the most rosaries on his behalf. Indeed, I would say, he taught us how to pray. His retreats were memorable. When he died, tenderly nursed by the nuns, we knew a saint had been among us.

In our final year we put our names forward to be enrolled in the Sodality of the Children of Mary. This meant we accepted Mary as our role model for life. We promised, under her protection, to always remain faithful to Christ. Wearing white dresses and carrying lighted candles, we processed into the chapel. After making our solemn promises, we received the wide blue ribbon with its silver medal, together with the Sodality's manual of prayers. It was an impressive little ceremony, which meant a lot to us.

These golden days had to come to a close. The time came for us to take our Cambridge Higher Certificate. Our slates were put aside, and substituted with precious sheets of A4 paper. Throughout the exams, we were fed like prize fighters on Mrs Sholtawa's special delicacies. The rest of the school regarded us with respect and awe. We were given ample time to study and allowed to relax in the gardens with our wind-up gramophone - 'Oh for the Wings of a Dove' and 'In a Monastery Garden' were our favourites. We sat under the trees and on the steps of the terrace, immersed in our books. We felt terribly important.

Those who were likely to get the required number of credits in the exams were urged to think about applying to Rhodes University in South Africa. MTG discussed the matter with my parents. She thought I had a chance of doing well and that I ought to think of taking an English degree. My mother, however, was adamant: if I must go to university (Dermot had, rather naughtily, pointed out that my parents owed me a university education for having sold the Kaiser's gold fob watch, given to me by Ali bin Salaam all those years ago!) then, she said, I must read for a Music degree. No matter how hard MTG pleaded, she remained firm; it was a B.Mus. or nothing. The trouble was neither my piano nor my singing were up to standard. I had been taught by dear old Mother Mary, a much-loved member of the Community. Not only was she partially deaf, she loved reminiscing about her time in Poona. It was easy to distract her from the glaringly obvious fact that I had practised not a note since my last lesson. Although an examiner for the Associated Board of Music in the form of a handsome young RAF officer, with the appropriate name of Ivor Keys, had kindly allowed me to scrape through my Grade IV piano exam, this was hardly sufficient to imagine I had the potential to read for a music degree. But the alternative, of remaining in Nairobi and taking a secretarial course was too awful to contemplate, so I agreed to apply to the university with the intention of taking a degree in Music. Of course, it all depended on my results.

Before we left, MTG as our Headmistress had one more duty to perform. She took all seven of us 'leavers' individually for a walk up the drive in order to explain the Facts of Life. Using illustrations of the male and female sexual organs, she explained the process of copulation in a straightforward, matter-of-fact, graphic manner. She described the varied heightened emotions and the importance of the context of marriage. She was of the opinion that it was a brilliant, generous idea of the Creator's to ensure we would enjoy the business of procreation. In this way He safeguards the future of the human race. We must always be aware of the beauty and the privilege of being partakers in God's Great Plan. She then fielded our questions with aplomb. Afterwards, we compared notes, and came to the conclusion that, as a nun, she had done a good job.

Our exam papers were marked in England, so it took some time for our results to come through. Because of the hazards of war, we had used carbon paper to make copies, in case the papers were lost en route. What had been overlooked, however, was the impact our bracelets and bangles and rings made on the carbon. Unfortunately, the ship carrying the papers was sunk, and the papers lost. Consequently, we were judged on our indecipherable carbon copies. In a generous gesture, the Cambridge Board of Examiners gave us the benefit of the doubt: we all got the necessary number of credits to go to University. Three of us chose to apply. And so, armed with these dubious merits, a new chapter of my life opened. Closing this one, though, was very hard. Our emotions ran high as we said goodbye. I shall forever be grateful to those wonderful nuns for showing us the path to true happiness, by living the Faith they taught us.

Chapter 29

Escape from Nairobi

The country around Nyeri, close to the foothills of Mount Kenya, was an area my parents were particularly fond of, and with thoughts of retirement in mind they bought a plot of land beside a tributary of the Chania River. They engaged an architect, Mr Zukermann, who was Lebanese, to draw up plans for a house. Mr Zukermann was not only a talented architect, he also understood African culture. His design was beautiful in its simplicity and use of local materials. The main building sat under a steeply pitched roof, facing the mountain. Two cottages, built on the arc of a circle, faced the house in a manner reminiscent of a native settlement, where the huts cluster round the much larger hut of the tribal chief. The rough stone and timber construction with the grey cedar shingle roofs harmonized gracefully with the landscape. We loved it.

There was no electricity so in the evening we sat close to the Tilley lamp on the table, to read, sew or knit. The only sound that filled the gaps in our idle conversation was the gentle hiss of the pressure lamp. It could be cold at night so a wood fire burnt in the grate. Njoroki, our cook and general handyman, would come in from time to time to put another log on the fire. He scorned the bellows, preferring to use his own lungs, blowing gently on the flames while squatting on the stone hearth. We used storm lanterns to light our path to our bedrooms in the cottages. As we walked over the gravel, the night air would be punctuated by strange sounds. The mad laugh of a hyena was common; a repeated rasping noise, not unlike an old man clearing his throat, meant that lion were about. In the crisp freshness of the morning, the presence of the mountain made itself felt. From it we learnt to predict the weather for the day. Some mornings we would awake to find that during the night it had had a fresh fall of snow on its twin peaks. We noted all its moods, its changing colours, the way it wrapped itself in a duvet of clouds in the rainy season, only to emerge sharp, bright and forceful when the mists cleared. It came as no surprise to learn that two Italian prisoners of war, from the nearby camp, had become mesmerised by the mountain. They felt impelled to make their escape and attempt a climb to the summit, regardless of the fact that they had little experience of mountaineering and precious little equipment. After a traumatic week, they were happy to report back to camp and had no objection to their punishment of solitary confinement where they were able to recover from exhaustion and catch up on lost sleep.

Our nearest neighbours were people called Doig. We would walk several miles across the grasslands to their farm each day to collect our milk, remembering always to carry a stick as snakes could be a problem. The announcement that you were 'Going to the Do(i)gs' became a regular family joke. Most days, Mary and Helen would ride. Though they were always accompanied by the syce, my mother would still go through paroxysms of anxiety if they were not back by a prescribed time. She would stand by the stables, watching for their return, a storm lantern in one hand and her rosary in another, preparing herself for tragedy. We spent a lot of time down by the riverbank exploring and picnicking among the profusion of arum lilies. It was a pity none of us were anglers, for there were trout to be had in the stream. Jiggers – fleas that burrowed into your toes – were a hazard if you wore sandals. They would lay little sacs of eggs, which we became expert at extracting, without breaking the skin, using a sterilized needle.

The road to our property was little more than a dirt track. In the rainy season, even with chains on the tyres, the car slithered and slid from one side of the road to the other. When it was dry, corrugations were a problem. My mother's method was to drive at speed over them, causing the car to bounce and rattle alarmingly. My father believed in treating each ridge with a change of gear and a measure of respect. This slow rocking-horse method not only added time to one's journey but also left passengers feeling distinctly queasy.

Our inaccessibility meant we had few visitors, which was a welcome relief after Nairobi. Elspeth Huxley would ride over occasionally when she was staying with her redoubtable mother, Nellie Grant. Then there were the Sherbrooke Walkers, who owned the Outspan Hotel in the Aberdare Hills. My parent's friendship with them went back over many years. Lady Bettie was a Catholic, so when they arrived in the Colony in 1926 on the Soldier/Settlement Scheme, with very little money, my father felt obligated to help them. From then on a natural affinity developed between the two families. It was possibly because of them that my parents chose to settle in the Nyeri district.

They made a surprising couple. Eric was tall, vain and debonair. He invariably wore a blue shirt to emphasise the blue of his eyes. Lady Bettie, one of the seven daughters of the impoverished 9th Earl of Denbigh, was, by contrast, a small matronly figure who, had little time for fashion. She was a merry, matter-of-fact, straightforward person, of enormous courage and intelligence, who must have been very pretty in her youth. I suspect he had the ideas and imagination, while she, in her practical way, kept the show on the road.

Eric was a born raconteur, and had some thrilling tales to tell. There was nothing he liked more than to reach for the atlas, and show us how he had walked halfway across Europe in his many escapes as a prisoner of war during the First World War. If there was a pretty girl in his audience, then he would enjoy embellishing his tale. One of his escapes had been facilitated by Lord Baden-Powell, the founder of the Boy Scout movement, who had sent him a pair of wire cutters hidden in a leg of ham in a POW parcel. Eric had been his personal assistant before the war and was appointed the first scoutmaster of the movement. When Eric and Bettie opened their hotel, the Baden-Powells invested in the venture and bought a house in the grounds with a wonderful view, overlooking the gorge of the Chania River. It is here that Baden-Powell died in 1942.

In 1914, Eric had joined the Royal Flying Corps. He was shot down over Germany early on in the war and imprisoned. When he at last managed to escape successfully, he enlisted to fight with the British Military Mission alongside the White Russians against the Bolsheviks. The White Russian Army were so grateful, they gave him two decorations: the Order of St Anne and the Order of St Stanilaus. He then went to fight in the Crimea and was awarded the MC for outstanding bravery in the Battle of Ushun. It was soon after this that he met Bettie. Neither of them had enough money to marry, so he started a bootlegging business, smuggling liquor into America during Prohibition. His book, *The Confessions of a Rum Runner*, is about this period of his life. He wrote it under the pseudonym of James Barbican.

Eventually he and Bettie had enough money to marry and embark on their life in Kenya.

In 1928, they purchased seventy acres of land in the Aberdare Hills, where they built the Outspan Hotel. It was an immediate success, due in part to the beauty of the site, but also to the personalities of the Sherbrooke Walkers and the hard work they put into the project. Their African staff loved them and were proud of the skills they acquired under their tuition. Initially they needed a great deal of training and supervision. The gardeners, for instance, found it hard to grasp the purpose of growing flowers, only to cut them and bring them into the house, where they died. For them the soil was a place to grow food. (Interestingly, the cut-flower industry is today one of Kenya's most profitable exports.) Despite their different outlook on this and several other issues, the staff remained loyal to their employers for many years. They were a major contributor in helping to produce an atmosphere of calm efficiency that led guests to recommend the hotel to their friends.

In 1932, Eric dreamt up the idea of building a tree house in the forest, some twelve miles from the hotel, for viewing game. Tree Tops, as it came to be known, is what put the Outspan Hotel on the international map. The house, which was little more than a hut, was built in a giant fig tree, overlooking a salt lick. A couple of decades later, this was the unlikely site of a significant moment in English history. Princess Elizabeth and Prince Philip were spending the night in Eric's tree house far from any telephone or wireless communication. It was the night of 5th February, 1952: the night her father, King George VI died. As the popular saying went, 'she climbed into the tree a princess, and came down the following morning a queen.' But it was not until she returned to the hotel that she became aware of this.

In 1939, with the advent of the Second World War, Tree Tops was closed for lack of visitors. Four years into the war Eric became increasingly worried about what state the tree house might be in after four years of neglect. He decided to make an inspection, and set about planning an expedition. Honor, their eldest daughter and a school friend of mine, invited me to join the party. I was thrilled to be asked. We reasoned that the animals, having had no visitors to disturb them for several years, would probably have become accustomed to turning up at the salt lick in some numbers. We reckoned we were in for an exciting night.

We set out at midday. This was deemed to be the safest time because the animals seldom exerted themselves in the noonday heat. We walked in single file. We were a small group. Two Africans led the way, beating a tattoo on empty petrol cans, their bare feet impervious to the hazards on the ground. Eric followed carrying his rifle; then Honor and me with Bettie behind us. Two more Africans, also armed, brought up the rear, carrying our provisions. We were all wearing dark clothing. I had been warned not to bring anything coloured. We spoke softly in whispers. Every so often, Eric would point out a rickety ladder attached to a tree, for us to make our escape by, should the need arise. I did not fancy the idea, as most of them had missing rungs, and it was a long way up, for the trees of the Aberdares are tall with little undergrowth. The heavy canopy of leaves meant that little light penetrated through to the forest floor, making it threateningly dark. But trees on the equator have their own individual seasons, so when we came across a group of trees in hibernation, their leafless branches allowing the sunlight through, we would stop for Eric to make notes.

It was late when we arrived at the clearing. Pools of water on the wide sweep of the salt lick reflected the last of the light. The bole of the tree was massive. It towered above us. The wooden steps up through the branches to the tree house were in a dreadful state of disrepair. Eric and two Africans went up gingerly, leaving us strict instructions to stay close to the tree until he said it was safe for us to follow. They returned rapidly. The place had been colonised by a troop of colobus monkeys, and if that was not enough, the chimney of the stove was blocked by a swarm of bees. It was too late and too dangerous to turn back. Camping in the open was out of the question. It was decided that an attempt must be made to scare off the monkeys, and to seal up the chimney. Armed with every kind of stick - fallen branches, walking sticks, camp-bed poles - Eric and the Africans returned to do battle. The noise was alarming. Monkeys when they are angry roar and shriek in a terrifying manner. Thank goodness they managed to seal the chimney before the bees became disturbed.

It seemed an eternity before we got the all clear. Eric had rigged up a rope to help us negotiate the broken steps. Even so it was tricky. It was dark by this time so we had to find our way up through the enormous branches by torchlight, clinging to the rope as we went. Lady

Bettie was one of those comfortably-built women whose agility was restricted. She did not find it easy, but once in the tree house all her customary good humour returned, despite the devastation that surrounded us. The monkeys had smashed everything including the paraffin lamps. We couldn't use candles because of the risk of fire. We stumbled about in the dark, using our torches sparingly. There were just two rooms, running the width of the tree, plus the viewing balcony. It was difficult to make out anything distinctly. One or two outraged monkeys attempted to regain territory, which caused pandemonium. With their white faces and long capes of white fur draped over their backs they made ghostly intruders. We saw them off by banging saucepan lids. They continued however to sit in a nearby tree, glaring menacingly at us. They were not a comfortable presence.

There was no chance of cooking supper with the stove out of action, so after an unsatisfactory meal of spam, bread and chocolate, Honor and I fell asleep on one of only two camp beds. Bettie promised to wake us if any animals appeared. Meanwhile, the men spread more salt round the muddy edges of the spring in order to entice the animals to stay as long as possible. Eric was worried that after four years the animals might for one reason or another have abandoned this area of the forest and moved to another tastier spring elsewhere.

He need not have worried. We were woken by Bettie around midnight. It was cold on the balcony. The Aberdares are nearly 7,000 feet above sea level. Eric had rigged up a sort of dimmer switch using a terminal, yards of cable, a trout reel, a jam jar and goodness knows what else, to imitate moonlight. It was very Heath Robinson, but it worked. He could make the pale light come on very gradually and then make it fade as though it had been obscured by a cloud. And there, in this simulated moonlight, just below us, was a family of rhino enjoying themselves at the edge of a muddy pool. They were joined by one or two warthogs. Then one of the Africans pointed out a black shape crouching beside the water, to the left of our balcony: a big cat of some sort. We thought it might be a panther, but this was not likely. It was coal black and very beautiful. We subsequently discovered it was a very rare sighting indeed of a black leopard. Are there any left I wonder? More rhino arrived, and then, just as the party was getting under way, we heard the unmistakeable sounds of the approach of the big boys on the block. The rhinos also picked up the sound. As they lifted their heavily armed heads, their little ears waggled in alarm. The crashing of trees and the excited falsetto trumpeting of the elephants grew louder and louder. They made their dramatic entrance out of the darkness of the forest stage left, facing the rhinos on the opposite side of the clearing. Neither set of pachyderms was happy about sharing the pleasures of the salt lick. At times it looked as though there was going to be an all-out battle. The rhinos started urinating with panic and fear. But it didn't come to that. The elephants spread their great ears and pretended to make charges, but were never more than obstructive and downright rude, trumpeting loudly to tell the rhinos to move over. The rhinos tried to ignore them, but eventually could bear it no longer and sulkily sloped off into the forest with a cheeky posse of young elephants at their heels forcing them into a brisk trot to safety.

The African dawn broke slowly, lighting up the cushions of pink blossom of the cape chestnut trees, nestling jewel-like among the variegated foliage of the forest. The elephants reluctantly moved off, leaving the churned-up mud as testimony to the revels of the night. The salt lick was deserted, except for one young elephant, who had recently mastered the skill of rooting up saplings with his trunk. He was not in a hurry to join his family. Weary, hungry and cold, we started to pack up. But oh, what a night it had been!

As a result of our reconnoitre Eric rebuilt Tree Tops and renewed all the escape ladders. Unfortunately this was later destroyed by the Mau Mau who made the forests of the Aberdares their headquarters. Today if you visit Tree Tops you will find it a few miles off the main B5 road. You will spend the night in a fifty-bedroom lodge with ensuite bathrooms and mains electricity, built not in a tree but on wooden stilts. The forest has given way to parkland with the lights of houses visible through the bush. There are no rhino. The elephants have won the day; and they have a concrete reservoir of fresh water to drink from. All in the name of 'progress'.

Chapter 30

The Coast

If you lived on the equator, 6000 feet above sea level, it was considered advisable for health reasons to go down to the coast at least once a year. Conveniently for us, the date for the annual Court of Appeal Sessions in Mombasa coincided with our August school holidays. So each year we would rent a house on the coast, near enough to Mombasa for my father, after the travails of the week, to come and relax with us at weekends.

We travelled by train from Nairobi in the luxury of the Chief Justice's coach. This had a sitting room, with vases of cut flowers on polished tables, chintz curtains and comfortable armchairs. There were three bedrooms and a bathroom. The kitchen and staff quarters were in an adjoining coach. We brought our own staff: Njoroki, our houseboy, and our cook, Kumau. We were fortunate in Kumau, who was an exceptionally good cook. On our return from school we looked forward with greedy anticipation to his *chef d'oeuvre:* a crème caramel encased in a bird's nest of delicately spun sugar. It never failed to impress us. His reference book (*kipandi*), revealed that his previous employers had been people who liked to entertain on a lavish scale. Under their tuition, he had learnt a lot and had come a long way from the cooking pots stirred by his wives in the Native Reserve. The most coveted cooks in the Colony were those from Mauritius. They learnt their culinary skills from the French and, as a result, were the equal of any chef to be found in the capitals of Europe. Understandably, they were not only expensive but also difficult to come by.

Kumau, however, had one weakness. He was a bad timekeeper. He invariably caught the train at the last minute, causing us all untold anxiety. The clanking and squeaking of brakes, the noisy emissions of clouds of steam, the excited toots on the whistle, would all indicate that the train was about to leave, but there would be no sign of Kumau. My father's Indian clerk, Mr. Narriman, would be dispatched to tell the engine driver to hold his horses until the Chief Justice's cook could be found. Then, when my mother's exasperation was about to peak, Kumau would emerge from the crowd, grinning from ear to ear. With the agility of a cat, he would leap on board and join Njoroki in the kitchen, where he would cheerfully await my mother's wrath.

As the train pulled out of the station to begin its three-hundred mile journey to the coast, my parents would settle into the armchairs beneath the official portrait of King George VI. My father would undo the pink tape holding his case papers, and with his spectacles perched on the end of his nose, would concentrate on the complex minutiae of that great British institution that underpinned the Empire:- the Common Law. My mother, after remonstrating with Kumau, relaxed with a copy of *The East African Standard*, while Helen and I drew our chairs up to the windows to watch the herds of game roaming over the vastness of the Athi Plain. 'Have you seen anything interesting?' my mother would ask in the absent-minded way of someone who has seen it all many times before. 'No', we would reply, 'only wildebeest and zebra'. Poor wildebeest, with their long, sad faces, wispy beards and hunched shoulders, they were too ugly to be worthy of comment. They liked to graze in a companionable way with zebra, whose jolly stripes did a lot to cheer up their own dismal appearance. We never thought to remark on the antelope and beautiful Thomson's gazelle as they went bounding over the scrub, away from the smoke and noise of the train. To us they were as common as the deer in Richmond Park. What we were waiting for was giraffe and possibly lion. The latter are difficult to detect because their fur is the same dusty brown as the savannah grass. I saw a pride of lion only once. The male was lying lazily in the shade of a thorn bush, watching his cubs tumbling on top of each other, playing like puppies. The jigsaw pattern of giraffe, on the other hand, is easy to spot. They loved the train. They would stop nibbling the tender shoots at the top of the acacia trees and canter over towards the railway with all the awkwardness of lopsided rocking horses. At the risk of getting wood sparks in our eyes, we would lean out of the window and watch them try to keep pace with the train. When they realised the train was winning, they would come to a halt at the side of the track, admitting defeat, and stand, gazing sadly at us disappearing into the distance, before ambling back to the thorn trees.

The moment the sun went down, night replaced day. There are no lingering sunsets in equatorial Africa. This was the time to fix mosquito screens over the windows and draw the curtains. Njoroki, who had changed out of his khaki shorts and bush shirt into a red fez and white embroidered waistcoat, or kanzu, came in to tell us 'Chakula tiari' ('The food is ready').

We sat at a table laid with crisp white linen. Napkins, cutlery and plate all bore the logo K.U. R.& H., (Kenya and Uganda Railways & Harbours), surmounted by an imperial crown. Njoroki had difficulty in serving the dishes, for by this time the motion of the train was uncomfortably bumpy. We had left the plateau of the Highlands and were entering the Taru desert. Here, the intense heat of the day followed by the chill night air of the desert caused the rails to buckle. Occasionally there was a derailment, as happened once, some years back, when my mother had been travelling with Mary, her new-born baby. Fortunately they suffered no injury. This was a rarity, for the train seldom exceeded twenty-five miles per hour.

Once in bed, it was difficult to sleep. There was a lot of clanking and jolting throughout the night as we stopped at little wayside stations to take on water. It was sobering to recollect that we were tracing the same ancient route taken by the Arab slave traders. It was poignant, too, to know that the rails we were clattering over were the very ones laid only fifty years ago by Mr Preston, the engineer in charge of construction, and his workforce of Indian labourers, all of them strangers to the unexplored interior of Africa. In the early hours of the morning we would pass through Tsavo, where a hundred and forty of the workforce were killed and eaten by two marauding lions. After months of agony and terror, the lions were eventually shot by one of the engineers, brave Lt-Col Patterson, who wrote a thrilling account of the incident in his book *The Man-Eaters of Tsavo*.

So with sparks from the engine throwing up specks of light into the enveloping darkness, the train, a tiny symbol of the might and power of Empire, threaded its way through the secrecy of the night, like a determined glow worm, towards the busy port of Mombasa.

We were woken in the morning by the sound of African voices exchanging greetings in the languid tones of coastal Swahili. The train had stopped at Mackinnon Road, a small station named after the

Glaswegian businessman who had been the first to envisage a railway into the interior of Africa, in order to confront the issue of slavery. This was as far as he got. His company, the Imperial British East African Company, went bankrupt. He had spent seven years and £250,000 building just ten miles of track; hundreds of miles short of his goal of reaching Lake Victoria. The project was taken over by the British Government in 1888.

Our next stop was a halt at Mahji ya Chumvi ('Water of the Ocean'). This was picture-post card Africa. We pulled down the window and breathed in the hot, tangy air. Coconut palms jostled for space in the sandy soil with groves of bananas. Shafts of sunlight made patterns on the small, tin-roofed shed that passed for a station building. Young women, swathed in yards of colourful cotton, carried babies on their backs and baskets on their heads. Their features were sharper and their skin paler than those of the up country tribes, revealing their Arabic ancestry. The men wore white kanzus, small, cotton hats, and leather sandals. They were lean and wiry and walked with an air of authority. With consummate grace, the women approached the train, proffering their baskets of fruit. We leant out of the window and reached for some mangos, dropping the money into the basket balanced delicately on the woman's head. We were watched all the while by her solemn, wide-eyed baby, who appeared untroubled by the number of flies buzzing round its curly head.

Soon we were rumbling over Salisbury Bridge (renamed Macupa Causeway), the bridge that connects the island of Mombasa with the mainland. There was no time to admire the beauty of the Old Harbour, or to applaud the sun sparkling on the sea. We snapped close our suitcases, combed unruly strands of hair into submission and stood ready, as the train tooted its way into the terminus, to step into the heat, the noise, the colour, the scents and the bustle of the ancient city-port of Mombasa.

After leaving my father at the Club, we drove north out of the city over Nyali Bridge on the unsurfaced Malindi road. One year my mother rented a cottage from a Swiss farmer, Mr Markwalder, who owned a sisal estate not far from the coastal resort of Nyali. Apart from a few Africans walking in the traditional manner – the man in front, jauntily swinging a stick, followed by his wives carrying large bundles on their heads – the road was deserted. Today, I am told, it is busy with taxis and buses and crisscrossed with access roads that lead to hotels, beach houses and holiday apartments. On the verge where, seventy years ago, kapok trees and mangrove bushes grew, there are now billboards advertising restaurants, deep-sea diving resorts, marine parks and other tourist attractions.

We kept a sharp lookout for snakes, especially black mambas, which were common in the area. They could be dangerous. They would whip themselves onto the bonnet of a car, climb in the window and create havoc. One morning, when we were driving into Mombasa for Sunday Mass, we drove over a python. As I was sitting in the back of the car I did not see it, but I most certainly felt the bump.

When we reached Mtwapa Creek, not far from Killifi, we boarded a unique, hand-operated ferry. Although this 'singing ferry', as it was called, has today been replaced by a bridge it is still remembered in many tourist manuals. We would drive the car on to a simple wooden platform with handrails. We were then hauled across by a team of men, pulling on a chain, fixed to the jetty on the far side. As they pulled, the men kept up a rhythmic chant; the lead singer extemporising with elaborate lyrics describing their passengers. The chorus would pick up the refrain, repeating the last line. You needed to be proficient in Swahili to enjoy the fun. My father, for instance, was an important man – 'a bwana mcubwa'. He was also a large man – a 'mkubwa bwana' and very heavy to pull. But he was also a rich man with lots of money - 'mingi pesa' - so they must pull hard 'harambe, harambe, harambe,' and then he would surely pay them well. My father loved the attention and would always reward them generously, ignoring my mother's pleas for restraint.

When the vegetation gave way to acres of cactus, we knew we had arrived at our destination. And sure enough a tall, arched wrought-iron gateway proclaimed that we were indeed at the Vipingo Sisal Estate. We turned into the drive leading up to the house. Mr Markwalder was there to greet us. He was a genial, heavily-built man in his early forties, who spoke English with a strong Swiss accent. We collected the keys and found our way to the cottage. Built like the main house in the simple vernacular style of the coast, it was a well-planned, sturdy little building, looking out over the sea. The ragged line of surf breaking on the reef was some way out, but the incessant, thunderous boom of the ocean pounding on the coral shelf made it sound much closer.

It did not take Helen and me long to find the path through the bushes to the beach. This is where we would spend every hour of every possible day of that sun-soaked holiday. Apart from the Markwalders' ridgeback dog, Pluto, there was not another living soul to share our paradise. When the tide was out, we spent hours in the lagoon studying the brilliant stripes and colours of the tropical fish, darting in and out of the fretwork of their coral pools. We discovered that the perfect way to eat a juicy mango was in the sea. We would spend so long in the water that at the end of the day, our eyebrows and eyelashes would often be white with encrusted salt. My mother joined us occasionally. She was no swimmer, and would sit on a cushion in the shade studying her Red Cross manual, not because she anticipated disaster, but because her chosen war work was to be a volunteer Red Cross nurse. She had hoped that simply wearing the uniform at certain official functions might be enough, and was dismayed to discover that she would have to take an exam.

In the evenings, we changed into long, cotton dresses, known as 'housecoats', for dinner with the Markwalders. This was inclined to be an awkward meal. My mother was not only irritated by Mr Markwalder's hearty good humour, but she was also nursing a suspicion that he was overcharging her. Then there was the business of Friday abstinence. She had explained to him that as Roman Catholics we did not eat meat on Fridays. Now the Markwalders, with their Muslim staff, were well aware of the sensitivities of religious fasts. They were careful to see that their staff were not overburdened with work during Ramadan, and even went to the trouble of giving them extra vitamins after sundown, to help sustain their strength during the day. They were, it appeared, sympathetic about our Friday observance. The only trouble was Mr. Markwalder was under the impression that my mother was talking about fasting, not abstinence. Consequently, when we appeared for dinner at the usual time on the first Friday, they looked surprised. Unfortunately, Mr Markwalder was away that evening, and neither Mrs Markwalder – a shadowy figure at the best of times – or the manager – a weasly little man, who Helen and I were convinced was a spy – spoke much English. We explained as best we could that we would like some food. Eventually we were, somewhat reluctantly, served with a banana fritter. And from then on, this was our standard Friday fare: one banana fritter each.

After the ritual game of cards, we would walk back down the sandy path to the seclusion of the cottage. On the evenings when the light of a full moon fell on the surf, turning the reef to silver and forming a path of rippled gold over the lagoon, it produced a sight of such beauty that it etched itself on our memories forever.

My father joined us at the weekends. My sister, Mary, who was serving in the WRENS in Mombasa would also come when she could get leave. On one occasion she was accompanied by an Admiral and his handsome Flag Officer. We discovered, however, that it was not 'Flags', who was smitten by Mary's charms, but the Admiral. As the tide was in, Mr Markwalder decided to entertain our guests by organising a pre-prandial swimming party. Pluto, by this time Helen's and my faithful companion, joined in the fun. There was much laughter and splashing and throwing of a large multi-coloured rubber ball. My mother looked on with amusement from the steps of the house. Helen was the only one of us who refused to be impressed by the dashing Admiral. She confided in me afterwards, that she had noticed he swam by keeping one foot on the ground.

Among the things we looked forward to at the weekend were the letters my father brought with him. We would spend all week replying to them. Helen and I cherished those we received from our school friends, and the remarkable ones sent by our saintly school chaplain, Father Daniel Morrissey. I remember one in particular on how to pray the rosary. Then there were Roderick's accounts of the battles in North Africa, and Dermot's blue lettercards with his almost indecipherable scrawl, telling of his struggle getting through the bomb damage of London to the Inns of Court. It was difficult enough for an able-bodied person, but for a person with Dermot's disabilities, it was unimaginable. He never complained, and was always amusing and full of praise for other peoples' courage. Fascinating letters also arrived from my father's close friend, Sir O.B. Daley, the Chief Justice of Bermuda, giving vignettes of life with the Duke and Duchess of Windsor. His abject devotion for her was, he said, like that of a lapdog. Poor woman! It was not the life she had envisaged, and he apparently was dreadfully homesick.

As the Court of Appeal in Mombasa wound up its business for another year, so our holiday drew to a close. This time my father decided to return to Nairobi by car. A friend of his, a Holy Ghost Father from the

Catholic Church in Mombasa, was looking for a lift to the Italian mission station up in the hills above Voi, and my father was happy to oblige. He had a lot of admiration for the work of the missions and would not, if he could help it, miss an opportunity of visiting them. He always looked forward to his annual stay in Uganda with the White Fathers, so called because of their white habits. They were a French order renowned for their good works and their pungent, homemade cigars.

As there had been a muddle over the booking of train tickets for my mother, Helen and myself, (two had been booked, instead of three), it was arranged that I should accompany my father and the priest in the car. There was some doubt about me being able to spend the night in the male preserve of an Italian monastery, but the priest from Mombasa assured us this would not be a problem. The monks were not known to turn away travellers, be they male or female. It would, nevertheless, prove to be a memorable journey.

When we reached the Taru desert, the spiralling dust devils made visibility difficult. The conversation between the two men became desultory as they concentrated on the road ahead. My father was at the wheel when through the clouds of red dust we saw a lone bull elephant at the side of the road. He stood with his huge ragged ears stretched out like sails, a sure sign that he was alarmed. My father stopped the car as the angry elephant stepped on to the road in front of us. He stood stock still for several moments with his small eyes focused on our car. Then after deciding we were not a threat after all he folded his ears back against his head and slowly lumbered off. We breathed a sigh of relief and wished him well.

Soon after this incident we took the left hand turn towards Taveta and started to climb into the hills. The sun slipped below the horizon and my father turned the knob to switch on the headlights. He clicked the switch several times with no response. The priest got out and opened the bonnet. He fiddled with some wires and was rewarded with a beam of light. Alas! It was a temporary fix. As soon as the ignition was turned on the lights went off. We were not well prepared. We didn't even have a torch. The ever-resourceful priest produced a box of matches and peered once again into the engine. Even I could see this was not a good idea. We begged him to keep his matches for some other emergency. My father who was wearing a white linen suit pointed out that as he would be visible in the dark he could walk ahead while the priest drove. So driving very slowly behind this larger than life Winnie-the-Pooh figure, the priest negotiated the most terrifying hairpin bends of a road that never stopped climbing and at some points was barely twelve feet wide, while my father kept on steadily walking uphill in front of us. The dark was intense. There was no friendly moon to light our path. We did arrive safely; but how long it took, I cannot say. I only know that the words 'Nearly there' were never more meaningless.

Our welcome was heartfelt. The good monks had been anxious. There was certainly no question of me being turned away. To the contrary, I was given the room generally reserved for the bishop! In the morning I was woken by the sound of sheep and bells and looking out, I had my breath taken away by the view. We could have been in the foothills of the Bavarian Alps. The air was crisp. The light was amazingly clear. It was good to be alive.

After breakfasting in my room on warm, freshly baked rolls and a big bowl of coffee, I went out. The monastery, built by the monks with their own hands, was a simple cedarwood construction with open cloisters. They spent their day, praying, farming, and caring for the local tribal people. There were so many questions I would love to have asked them, one of them being 'Could I please stay here?', but alas, I had no Italian. I need not have worried. Their smiles and gentle voices said all that needed to be known: they had found their way back into the Garden of Eden and walked with God.

Our car, as well as our spirits had been repaired. My father was none the worse for his marathon the night before. We thanked the monks for their hospitality, made our farewells, and set off for Nairobi.

Chapter 31

I Spread my Wings

'You have only to smile at people' said my travelling companion, with wonder, 'and they'll do anything for you!' Expanding on this heartening discovery, I recalled how our parents, in order to get anything done, always felt it necessary to make a conspicuous fuss, 'when', I mused, 'just a simple smile would do.'

Sally Irvine was an old school friend. At the age of seventeen, we were innocently unaware that it was our youthful good looks that turned the baggage handlers of Nairobi's Eastleigh Aerodrome into our willing slaves. We must have made a pleasing contrast: Sally with her blue eyes and peaches-and-cream complexion, and me with my trim figure and glossy black hair; both of us aglow with the anticipation of adventure. We were about to fly to Grahamstown in South Africa, to enrol as undergraduates at Rhodes University. This would be our very first flight. We could barely contain our excitement as we walked over to board the little Avro Anson plane parked on the dirt runway. The interior was scarcely bigger than a saloon car. There was room for just five of us including the pilot. We were joined by a faded woman of indeterminate age and an uncommunicative businessman, who quickly buried himself in the back seat, apparently impervious to our youthful charms. The pilot introduced himself and pointed out the sick bags. We laughed: not for us, surely!

The plane taxied over the bumpy ground with increasing speed. Then, as in a dream, we found ourselves in the air. We were flying! The great Athi Plain, patterned with game, spread out below us. Etched on the horizon were the misty, blue outlines of the Aberdare Mountains, and far ahead, the bulk of Kilamanjaro. For a few brief moments I experienced the pure joy of flying – an experience never, alas, to be recaptured.

It was as we flew over the shoulder of Mount Kilamanjaro that the dream turned sour. I felt a stabbing pain in my ear. I tried to ignore it by concentrating on the snow-covered rocks just beneath us. They seemed perilously close. Then, without warning, we were thrown up and down like a leaf in an autumn gale. This went on continually as we flew over the interminable forests of Tanzania, where the equatorial thermals took a vicious delight in tossing us around like a paper kite. We tried desperately to stabilize our heaving stomachs. The sick bags were now no longer a laughing matter.

Mercifully, we had to come down every two hours to refuel. Our first stop was an air force base in a clearing in the forest near Dodoma. Before we could leave the plane to stretch our legs and inhale lungfuls of fresh air, we were ordered to stay in our seats, while we were disinfected with DDT. This pyrethrum-based chemical was pumped into the cabin, to destroy any malarial mosquitos that may have hitched a ride. I can well believe, from its effect on us, that it was lethal for mosquitos.

We spent the night in a ramshackle hotel at Lusaka, the capital of what used to be Northern Rhodesia, and is now Zambia. The following morning after breakfasting off thick slabs of ham we returned to the airport. It was 5 a.m. but there was no sign of a beautiful African dawn. The sky was dark with black thunderclouds. Our pilot spent some time consulting with airport officials. My hopes were raised: perhaps we would get a reprieve? Surely it would be wise to wait for the weather to clear? However, the sight of another plane taking off decided him. We reluctantly boarded the plane and took our seats once more.

Within minutes we were being tossed and buffeted by the fierce winds of a tropical storm. Claps of thunder were followed by shafts of forked lightning. The rain spat viciously against the windows. Our misery was now compounded by fear. As the pilot battled with the controls we felt our little plane was no more than a plaything for the enraged elements of Nature to hurl out of the skies. I don't know how long the drama lasted. At the time it seemed endless. Fear is an emotion outside time.

Skilfully, our pilot managed to negotiate his way out of the maelstrom. To his dismay, however, he realised that we had been blown off course and had lost radio control. He had no idea where we were and there was nothing in the carpet of forest below, stretching as far as the eye could see, to indicate our position. He scoured the featureless landscape with mounting anxiety, aware that our fuel was running low. Then with a shout of relief he pointed to a silver ribbon of water snaking its way in a great arc through the jungle. The Zambezi River was the landmark he had been looking for. Now he would have no difficulty in plotting our route due east to Salisbury (Harare), the capital of Southern Rhodesia (Zimbabwe). We followed the bend in the river and as we approached the waters of Lake Kariba the pilot pointed out the Victoria Falls. He asked if we would like to have a closer look. Without waiting for a reply he put the little Anson into a steep dive, swooping down over the Falls and causing a nearby herd of elephant to stampede in panic. I do wish I could say I had seen this spectacular wonder of the world, but I am ashamed to say I kept my eyes tight shut. One glimpse of the ground rushing up to meet us, together with the sensation of zero gravity, robbed me of any urge to sightsee.

Rhodesia at that time was the 'breadbasket of Africa' and Salisbury, where we landed, reflected that wealth in its staid, solid architecture and wide, tree-lined streets. There was nothing flashy about its prosperity. It embodied many of the characteristics of its inhabitants: quiet, dependable, hardworking and rather dull. Its colonial history went further back than that of Kenya, having been founded by Cecil Rhodes while he was still an Oxford undergraduate. Its people, both black and white, thought of themselves as 'Rhodesian' rather than 'British'. This gave the country a greater sense of stability than that of either Kenya or Tanzania. But as we know, all that was to be swept away by the 'wind of change'. It is now one of the poorest nations on the planet and a focus for famine relief. We probably wouldn't recognise the place today.

It was here in Salisbury that we said goodbye to our bucking bronco Anson and after an overnight stay, transferred to a Dakota DC3 for the last leg of our flight to Johannesburg The DC3 was a new type of Dakota so there were a lot of interested people gathered round it at the airport. There were several press photographers, some booked to travel with us. This time our distress would be recorded on film and shown in tomorrow's newspapers. The plane was destined for the South African Air force and had been fitted out as a troop carrier. The cabin windows had been blacked out and the passenger seats were arranged facing the aisle with their backs against the fuselage. This last was particularly uncomfortable, as we experienced all the noisy judderings and vibrations of the aircraft through our spines whenever we leant back in our seats.

There was also the fact that despite being in a more substantial plane than the Anson, we were still unable to fly above the thermals and so escape the sickening effect of being in an out-of-control elevator. Thankfully, it was a short flight.

We were met at Johannesburg airport by a friend of my father's, Hans Winkelmann, the Dutch Consul, known affectionately as 'Winkie'. Winkie's kindness and generosity of spirit were legendary. It was typical of him to offer to put us up for the night and to shepherd us onto the Grahamstown train the following morning. What made this gesture of hospitality doubly impressive was that, at this time, he was under a great deal of personal stress.

The previous year, 1943, he and his family had been on holiday in the Netherlands, visiting their relations. Pressure of work had necessitated him returning to Africa earlier, leaving his family to follow on later. He never saw them again. Soon after returning home, he received the news that his Jewish wife, together with his children, had been arrested by the Nazis and sent to an 'internment camp'. It was only during the last days of the war, when the Allied Armies of Liberation revealed to a stunned world the horrors of the concentration camps, that he learnt how his wife and children had perished. To us he never gave the smallest hint of the anxieties he was battling with. He was, it seemed, concerned only for our welfare. He was gentle and courteous. Nothing was too much trouble for him.

That evening we dined at the Country Club as guests of the de Beer family. Fortunately, Sally and I had packed evening dresses in our hand luggage (our heavy cases had gone by sea as Luggage in Advance). Unfortunately, I had forgotten to pack evening shoes. Rubber-soled leather sandals were not what the sophisticates of the Country Club were expecting to see on my feet. Dainty satin slippers were *de rigueur*. Not only were my sandals a disastrous fashion statement, they were also highly unsuitable for dancing. Each time my partner attempted to steer me through an elegant turn, my feet remained glued to the floor. Whenever I tried a graceful glissade, the unrelenting rubber squealed on the polished parquet. In addition to the embarrassment of being wrongly shod, three days of bumpy air travel, coupled with the novel experience of drinking champagne, induced a worrying sensation of unsteadiness. The floor appeared to be rising and falling alarmingly.

Poor Winkie, I hope we didn't disgrace ourselves too badly! As we left, Sally made an effusive speech of gratitude to the doorman, while making several attempts to shake his hand. It was all too evident that we were not accustomed to mixing in such high society.

There are two reasons for remembering the train journey to Grahamstown. First, the shame of finding myself penniless and unable to buy my train ticket. It was Sunday. The banks were closed and I had been unable to collect my South African rands. Alas! Cash dispensers were way off in the future. I had no option but to borrow a large sum of money off Winkie. And then there was the intense heat. I don't know what the thermometer readings were; I only know I could not raise my arm to brush away a fly without breaking into a sweat.

The journey took all day. We skirted the monumental grandeur of the Drakensberg Mountains and travelled over miles of parched veldt, peppered with giant anthills and scrubby trees festooned with the curious hanging nests of the weaver bird. It was late in the day when we got our first sight of Grahamstown – a small town, tucked into the folds of the 'bundu' or wild bushland. The gothic spire of its parish church gave it the appearance of an English market town in the shires. It was a place we would become very fond of in the ensuing months. But for now, we were overwhelmed with a sense of relief that, after four days of turbulent travel, we had finally arrived.

Chapter 32

Rhodes University

Today, Rhodes, is still the small, intimate university it was in my day, although now it is, of course, multi-racial. The policy of the governing body, since its foundation in 1904, has been to foster academic excellence, rather than increasing student numbers. It has the smallest ratio of students to tutors of any of the South African universities. This intimacy is reflected in the layout of the campus. The main buildings were designed by Herbert Baker, the Edwardian architect celebrated for his Government Buildings in Pretoria. He is less celebrated for the unfortunate siting of his design for the Secretariat Offices in Delhi, built during his unhappy partnership with Sir Edwin Lutyens. Here, in Grahamstown, free from the constraints of the architecture of Empire, his work expresses a delightful Italianate *jeu d'esprit*, a contrast to the staid buildings of the academic town that spawned the University. The central clock tower and the arts centre – reminiscent of a campanile and a Roman villa – are particularly charming. The halls of residence, echoing the white stucco and red pantiles of the main buildings, are scattered over the hillside, close to the Botanic Gardens. The approach to the campus from the town is up a steep incline, along a wide drive lined with jacaranda trees, with the clock tower providing a focal point.

I found my way to the admissions office and despite knowing how ill-prepared I was for such a course, I enrolled for a B.Mus. It was on this condition that my parents had agreed to my going to Rhodes. Now I had to live up to their label of being 'the musical one' of the family. Was my ability to sing sad Irish songs and my pass in Grade IV on the piano going to be enough to build on? I did not feel confident.

The music department was at that time the Cinderella of the University faculties. Now, it is at the heart of the biggest Arts Festival in Africa, hosted annually by the town. In my day, the department was housed in a dilapidated structure which was soon to be demolished and replaced by the impressive buildings that stand there today. The Head of the Department was a Professor Hartmann, who bore a striking resemblance to Laurent de Brunhoff's Babar the Elephant. He and his wife were Austrian refugees from Vienna. She was a golden-haired *hausfrau* whose comfortable shape owed much to her love of homemade *apfelstrudel*. The Professor was a chain smoker. He liked to punctuate his lectures with long, silent pauses, during which he would blow perfect smoke rings. Was this to demonstrate his skill at blowing smoke rings, or an aid to gathering his thoughts? It was difficult to tell. I got the impression that, at such moments, as he critically studied the drifting rings of smoke, his thoughts were also drifting - possibly to matters unrelated to the subject under discussion. He had a lot on his mind.

The townsfolk did not like the Hartmanns. Many of them were Afrikaners, who, with their long memories of the Boer War, had no love for the British. They weren't just anti the Allied war effort: they were pro-German. V.E. Day, as far as I was aware, was not celebrated in the Eastern Cape. They did not take kindly to the presence of refugees in the town, and it was not long before they found a peg to hang their grievances on. It was rumoured that under the guise of lecturing on music, Professor Hartmann was actually giving lectures on sex. The Afrikaners' puritan sensitivities were scandalised. They advised the Chancellor of the University to dismiss him from his post forthwith. The Professor was furious. He refused to alter the content of his lectures and filed a suit for defamation of character.

It was Professor Hartmann's propensity to emphasise the difference between major and minor keys in terms of gender that gave rise to the accusation of his lectures being pornographic. He liked to contrast the dominant masculine character of the major key with the gentler, feminine tones of the minor. He would illustrate the point on the piano, showing how skilfully Mozart resolved the dominant masculinity of a major chord into the delicate femininity of a minor key by use of one pivotal note. In a lecture on the atonality of the twelve-tone scale, he used the analogy of skiers on the Austrian Alps. The figures in their ski suits all moved with equal grace and prowess on the slopes, making it impossible to distinguish male from female. Similarly, in the music of Shoenberg, the distinction between a major and minor key was lost. He was of the opinion that contemporary music would continue to reflect the growing equality between men and women. On a good day, he could be a rivetingly good lecturer. His sexual innuendos, however, were too much for the burghers of Grahamstown. The legal wrangling went on for months. The case went to appeal. I have no idea what the outcome was, for by that time, I had left Rhodes. Discussing the matter with South African friends some years later, they felt that it was more than likely that the Professor would have lost his case. In those days, the Africaaners were very powerful.

Mrs Hartmann gave me singing lessons. From her I learnt, but never mastered, the difficulties of singing lieder. She was not suited to academic life. She used to sigh a lot and lessons would be arbitrarily cancelled. The only time I saw her laugh was when she discovered that the smell of burning in the room was coming from me. She had an electric fire positioned on a chair beside the piano, to keep her hands warm – it could be quite cold in winter. On this occasion I was standing in front of it, and as I was concentrating on the intricacies of Schumann's 'Die Nussbaum,' I was unaware that the back of my skirt was about to burst into flames. Shaking with laughter, she removed the fire, threw a glass of water over my bottom, and ordered me to continue singing. The fact that I had to walk some distance back to my hall of residence with a large hole in my skirt was of no interest to her.

Then there was my piano tutor, Hubert du Plessis, a young dandy who was first and foremost in love with himself, and secondly, in love with the fiancé of the girl he had been asked to look after while the fiancé was away fighting the war. He was worried that he might possibly be falling in love with the girl, and so in danger of betraying his true love, the fiancé. All this had to be discussed at length with his pupils. He liked too, to show his virtuosity on the piano by playing the Bach Chaconne, written for solo violin, using his left hand only. How I, or any of his students, were progressing, was of little interest to him. This was possibly because there was little likelihood of any of us making much progress between one lesson and the next, there being no practice rooms. The only pianos available to us were those used for tuition; and as time for these was limited and the demand heavy, it was not uncommon to turn up for a lesson without having touched a keyboard for a week or more. Altogether the Rhodes Music Department at that time was not fit for purpose. We should have complained, but that was unheard of.

In those days students were a subservient lot. Was it any wonder I put in the minimum amount of time permissible at the Music Department, and succumbed to the temptations of the social life of the University? I must confess to spending many too many golden days by the swimming pool; playing squash; gossiping in the University Kaiffe (Café) and planning picnics in the *bundu* (countryside). How to flirt and have a coterie of boyfriends was a game I was eager to learn how to play.

It did not take me long to grasp the unwritten rules and stratagems necessary to gain the attention of the opposite sex. Back in John Koetze House, our hall of residence, we talked of little else. I soon realized that in this game of boy meets girl, much more skill was required than in the management of Professor Hartmann's major and minor keys! For a start, as a girl, you never made the first move. At most you were permitted to semaphore complicated eye messages in the direction of the man you fancied. Once you had him hooked, you had the difficult task of keeping him attentive, without letting him think he was the only one in the world for you. It was vital to keep other arrows to your bow, for no one, in those days, was prepared to complicate their youthful lives by entering into such a thing as a serious relationship. It would have been scandalous to have thought otherwise. Today it is all about 'respect'; in those days 'self-respect' was what mattered. It was up to the girl to see that things did not get out of hand. It was helpful to learn how to smoke, for one of the tactics to cool your beau's ardour was to teasingly blow smoke into his eyes (there was even a popular song at the time entitled 'Smoke Gets in Your Eyes'! Composed, of course, by a poor frustrated chap). It was a game of fine judgement and consummate finesse. It was also terribly exciting after all those years in a convent.

My first date took me unawares. I received a phone call from someone calling himself Nigel Mandy. He said we had met at the Freshers' Social. I said 'Oh yes, I remember' – but I didn't. The line was not good and I was not yet tuned into the South African accent. I thought he was inviting me to meet him in somewhere called St Louis. I asked him for directions, adding that I was not familiar with the town. There was a pause at the other end. I thought he may have hung up. Then he said something about a 'bioscope', which really confused me. I was soon to learn this was the South African name for a 'cinema'. He was inviting me to see a film called *Meet Me In St Louis*. He would pick me up at an agreed time and we would walk into the town together to the bioscope.

There was a great deal of curiosity among my friends to find out what my conquest looked like. I was as curious as they were, as I had no recollection of ever having met him. As the time drew near, I hovered in the vicinity of the front door, while my friends positioned themselves strategically close to windows in order to get a good view. I seem to remember a lot of nervous giggling. Then the doorbell rang and I opened the door to a serious-looking young man. He was tall, dark and, in the opinion of all, very handsome indeed. The only problem was the accent. It was not long, however, before I was able to translate it and even adopt it as my own.

Nigel was reading Engineering. He was a fine athlete and was forever in training for one event or another. His passion was hurdling. He liked me to watch him training. Never having seen hurdling before, I was, initially, impressed by his performance. The stride, the awkward angle of the back leg, and above all the speed required to clear the barriers, amazed me. But after a while, the role of being a solitary spectator palled. It became harder and harder to feign interest. The end of a beautiful friendship was in sight. But not before I had received from Nigel my first romantic kiss. Is there anything more thrillingly beautiful for a young girl of seventeen than this first exquisite pledge of unreserved love? I had been kissed before, by Michael Trafford, when I was staying with his family on their Rift Valley farm. His father had been on the fringes of the notorious Happy Valley set. It was surprising that my father gave permission for the visit. Possibly the Traffords were now deemed to be reformed characters. The encounter happened between the landrover and the trailer, while the grownups were occupied in loading the day's trophy of dead gazelle. My shocked reaction was to respond in the way I had seen Judy Garland deal with Mickey Rooney in one of their films, I gave the poor boy a resounding slap across the face. He was just sixteen – one year older than me. I was not asked to stay again! Now two years later, walking in the lovely, moonlit Botanic Gardens with the scent of peach blossom drifting on the night air and the strains of Debussy's 'Clair de Lune' coming from the nearby Music Department, the kiss was an altogether different affair. Oh the exquisite bliss!

I met Nigel's replacement at one of the university balls. These were organised by Ian Smith, President of the Students Union and later Prime

Minister of what was then Rhodesia, now Zimbabwe. While serving with the RAF in the war, he had been shot down. As a result of his injuries he had partially lost the sight of one eye and was invalided out of the air force. After his discharge, he decided to take a postgraduate degree at Rhodes. He was a popular President of the S.U. and an energetic fund-raiser for the nearby Fort Hare, a college for Further Education for Africans. He raised considerable sums of money through rugby matches, fetes, 'hops', fancy dress balls, etc. (At the Lancaster House independence talks for Rhodesian Africans, the media liked to give him a sinister appearance by focusing their cameras on the injured side of his face. Propaganda!) The balls were the high point of the University's social calendar and it was at one of these that I met Claud Reynolds.

Claud Reynolds was neither tall nor good-looking. He was a law student, with a quiet, arrogant, quick-witted charm that was very attractive. He was at the centre of a group of equally intelligent, witty law students. His popularity could have had something to do with the fact that he owned that incredibly rare thing, a motor car. No matter that it was little more than a battered old banger, that petrol coupons were hard to come by, and when he did have any petrol, he liked to use the car to drive out to the golf course rather than give his friends a lift into town: the mere fact of owning a car was enough to set him apart. I had other boyfriends who must have appealed to me because of the oddity of their names. There was Ben Downe, and his brother Neil Downe (later on, in London, I would have an admirer called Robin Hood!). There was Bunny Curran who wore a white dinner jacket at parties. He came by his name because a rabbit had run in front of his parents' car, causing his father to brake suddenly. As a result he had been born prematurely. They were all fun to be with, kind-hearted and generous. I was very fond of them.

Claud, however, was the most stimulating company of them all. He taught me to widen my horizons. From him I learnt something of the complexity of South African politics. He told me how unimpressed many South Africans were by the adulation their President, Jan Smuts, was receiving in London, when so many problems at home were being ignored. Given the critical times we were living through, it is astonishing to recall how ill-informed most of us were, and how incurious. On a personal level, I had, of course, shared in my family's anxiety over my brother Roderick, fighting in North Africa and the Italian campaign. When he was invalided out of the army after narrowly escaping death in the awful battle of Monte Cassino, we were all relieved to know that he was recovering from his injuries in a hospital in Rome, where he was being treated with the new wonder drug, penicillin, and that for him the war was over. The bigger picture of the final stages of the war was of little interest to us. We were cocooned in our self-centred bubble of Youth. Anything on the periphery was not our concern. If we thought at all, we didn't doubt that the Allies were about to win the war. Then everything would be as it had been before. Winston Churchill and the British Empire would, of course be around for the foreseeable future.

It is true that in those days there was nothing like the communication of world news that there is today. There were few South African newspapers and those that were available were chiefly concerned with sport. We did not even have access to the BBC's only news bulletin at 9 p.m. Portable radios were in their infancy. They were difficult to tune and reception was patchy. Our main source of news came from the Pathé Newsreels, shown in the cinemas before the main film and we paid scant attention to these. They were not what we had come to see.

There was, however, one newsreel that could not be ignored. We were well and truly shaken out of our self-absorption when the first pictures came through of the liberated concentration camps of Belsen and Auschwitz. We gasped. The horror was too much. We attempted to shield our eyes from the piles of corpses. The hollowed eyes and skeletal bodies of the survivors stared off the screen at us. We found it impossible to focus on the Hollywood blockbuster that followed. We couldn't find the words to speak of what we had seen. Surely there must have been some mistake. It could not be real. Dummies perhaps? We suffered nightmares. It was a horror that stood grotesquely on its own. There was no resolution to it, no explanation. Just the question 'Why?'

But soon, even this as yet unnamed atrocity faded into the recesses of our minds. It had happened far away in another country. It was nothing to do with us. Soon we were busy making plans to spend the coming spring vacation at the coast, at a place called Bushman's Creek. The academic year was divided into four terms with three short vacations of ten days or so, and one long one at Christmas. There was no question of students from East Africa going home for the short vacations. It was far too expensive. Sometimes we would be invited to stay with friends who lived nearby, but mostly we stayed in college. It was a good time to catch up on work. This September, however, we planned something more adventurous.

Bushman's Creek today is a popular holiday resort. Since the advent of electricity and a main road in the 1980s, the place has become unrecognisable from the remote hamlet we had known in 1945. Now it is crowded with villas and tourist centres. Then it was little more than its name would suggest – a settlement of two or three Africaaner farms, close by the mouth of Bushman's River. There were no shops, not even any of those colourful wayside markets Africans like to set up at the side of the road. We had to take all our provisions with us. We were fortunate to have Ruth Lany in charge of planning. Her family were pioneers who lived in Tanganyika. They were the first people to take parties of mountaineers up Mount Kilamanjaro. Ruth's knowledge of the African bush and her competence were inbred.

To keep the costs down we needed a minimum of two dozen students. We hired two lorries with reliable African drivers. We were careful to check the drivers' references. The year before a lorry carrying a group of students to the coast had overturned, causing a number of fatalities. We arranged for a farmer to let us rent a couple of shacks for a week - one for the boys, the other for the girls. The journey of thirty-seven miles from Grahamstown to Bushman's Creek can be done in under an hour today, by car over good roads. In a lorry, over corrugated dirt tracks, it took a lot longer. It was also a lot less comfortable.

We slept on camp beds on open verandas. We became accustomed to the nocturnal rainstorms. We slept through them and next day dried our bedding on the washing line. We ate mounds of spaghetti and sausages. We spent the day attempting to surf the enormous rollers that crashed on to the blindingly white sand, with makeshift surf boards. If you fell off – and you frequently did – you were churned over and over, until you were spewed up on the beach, gasping for breath. The wind was a fierce competitor in all our games. It would try to push us backwards as we attempted to walk to the nearest headland. Swirling round unexpectedly, it would blow you over. We sheltered in the sand dunes, soaking up the heat of the sun. In the evenings, we danced in the bothy with the farmers and their sturdy wives, to Voortrekker tunes thumped out on a honkytonk piano. The farmers were enormous, patriarchal Afrikaaners with long flowing beards. They spoke no English. Gripping you with their huge hands, they whirled you round and round, lifting you in the air and only occasionally allowing your feet to touch the floor. There was so much laughter. It was the most energetic, wildly happy holiday I have ever experienced.

Chapter 33

The Journey Home

Sally Irvine and I were in agreement: we would not be travelling back to Kenya for the Christmas vacation by air. Our flight to South Africa at the start of the year was an experience we had no wish to repeat. Our adventurous friend, Ruth Lany, invited us to join her on an overland trip. She was planning to see how far she could travel on the partially completed Cape to Cairo railway. She felt sure it had got as far as the Congo and that there was a branch line to Albertville (now Kalemie) on the shores of Lake Tanganyika. After crossing the lake on a steamer to Kigoma in Tanganyika, it would be possible to get a train to Dar es Salaam, where she lived. We would then board a ship to take us up the coast to Mombasa where we could take the train home to Nairobi. We hesitated before turning her down. She made it sound so easy, but the distances were vast and the heart of Africa had changed little since the days of Stanley and Livingstone. We had no urge to explore. We just wanted to get home as quickly and easily as possible on tickets we could afford.

We booked our passage on a ship due to sail from Port Elisabeth at the beginning of December. The shipping agent assured us the journey to Mombasa should take no more than ten days at the most. A third girl, also a Rhodes undergraduate, decided to join us. She was a jolly, easy-going personality, and would prove to be a good travelling companion. Until we arrived at the docks in Port Elisabeth, we had assumed that our ship, the S.S. *Joliet Victory*, was an ordinary passenger liner. Imagine our dismay on discovering it was a small, rusty cargo ship. Our hearts sank even further on learning that we were to be the only passengers. It meant nothing to us that the Victory ships were considered by some to have been America's finest contribution to the war effort. We had never heard of them.

In 1943, the situation at sea had been desperate. The German U-boats had decimated both the British and American merchant navies. Vital supplies were not getting through to Britain. To replace the losses, the Americans decided to embark on an ambitious shipbuilding programme. In two years, six Californian shipyards delivered 550 ships. At one point they were constructing one a fortnight. These mass-produced vessels were known as Victory ships. They were built entirely from steel and were armed. Their design and engine power made them faster and more manoeuvrable than the standard cargo ship. They were highly successful. Today, there are just three left. They are open to tours in a Californian dockyard as museum ships. The other day, I impressed a London taxi driver by telling him I had sailed on a Victory ship. He refused a tip, because he said, I had made his day!

We were welcomed on board by the First Officer. This kindly man would be our guardian angel over the coming weeks. He showed us our accommodation: a hut on the metal deck at the stern of the ship, directly under the funnel. The plumes of smut-laden smoke, together with the heat, were things we would have to get used to. We did not sail on the appointed day. We soon learned that there was no such thing as a timetable for dates of arrival and departure. A lot depended on the whim of the Captain. We spent the time exploring the docks, gazing enviously at the other ships moored along the quay. One afternoon, as we were strolling back to the ship along the quay, we were approached by a pretty auburn-haired girl. She was from Capetown University and was trying to get back to her home in Lourenco marques (Maputo), but had had her bag, with her passport, tickets and money, stolen. She asked if we would be willing to smuggle her on board our ship, and find somewhere for her to hide. After some debate, we decided we must help her. It was easy enough to get her on board; the sailors were used to seeing us come and go, and they did not notice on this occasion that we were four girls, not three. There was enough room in the hut for a makeshift bed on the floor, and as the *Joliet Victory* was an American ship, there was food in abundance. We had no problem bringing her something to eat after our own meals. The steward understood we were hungry adolescents who needed constant replenishing. The difficulty came at the ports, when passport officials came on board. We would hide her in a small cupboard while one of us stood in front of it. The other two would then persuade the men to examine our papers on deck, 'where the light is better'. We held our breath, knowing that at any moment they might ask to search the hut for contraband. Thankfully, they never did. It was a relief when she left us at Lourenco marques.

There was one other passenger with whom we had very little contact. She was the ship's tart or 'lady of the night'. She appeared only at meal times. Being an Africaaner, she was forbidden to wear make-up, but made up for this lack with a wardrobe of startlingly provocative clothes. She was there the evening the Captain invited us to his cabin for a drink. Despite the fact that the *Joliet Victory* was a 'dry' ship she was very drunk, as was the Captain. We were offered Coca Cola, which we accepted with trepidation, never having drunk it before. It was rumoured that one of its secret ingredients could cause addiction, but the First Officer assured us it was quite safe. His own family had drunk it without any ill effects. It was certainly a strange taste. We vowed, privately, to stick to orangeade in the future. On our way back to the hut, our faithful escort, the First Officer, advised us not to accept any more invitations from the Captain. He explained that he, along with several members of the crew, were all desperate alcoholics. When they were unable to get hold of a bottle of alcohol they would drink their after-shave lotion. He offered to take it upon himself to make our excuses. We accepted his offer gladly.

The ship crawled up the east coast of Africa, calling at every port. Days were spent loading copper at the port of Beira. Here, the law instigated by Cecil Rhodes, making it illegal to use any machinery in the port and thereby ensuring employment for the unskilled Africans, was still in operation. So it was a long, tedious and very dirty operation. In Portuguese Mozambique, we swam off the beach reserved for members of the Country Club. The netting supposed to keep out sharks was in shreds, but this did not deter us. We learnt to play liar dice and poker. But mostly we were too hot to do anything. The days passed frustratingly slowly. Then, on the last lap of our voyage, just off the island of Pemba, we were struck by an electric storm. Is there anywhere else in the world where so much awesome energy is demonstrated with such drama, as in equatorial Africa? Forked lightening rips through inky, black skies, accompanied by shatteringly loud claps of thunder. This terrifying spectacle is repeated over and over again, instilling a primitive fear in man and beast. Mercifully there was no wind, so the sea remained calm. But the ship, being made of steel, had most of its instruments put out of action by the storm. For the next two days we drifted on 'a painted ocean' with the scent of cloves wafting on the air from the island of Pemba. It was an anxious time for the crew and their relief when we were once more under way was palpable.

What joy it was to see at long last the tree-lined coast of Mombasa and to pick out the old familiar landmarks, Fort Jesus, the Club and Ali bin Salaam's lawns sweeping down to the waterfront! The harbour was busy. There were no free berths, so we weighed anchor in the bay and waited for the tenders to come alongside to take us off. What happened next has never been believed by anyone, least of all our parents.

Two or three tenders came and left, taking various officials and members of the crew off, but always refusing to take us. When we complained, the sailors said ours would be coming shortly – but it never did. We were standing disconsolately by the gangway with our cases, when we saw the First Officer. He, who was always so calm and in control of events, was now distinctly agitated. He hustled us along the deck to the hut, explaining as we went that the Captain was very drunk and was armed with a gun. He was determined not to let us leave the ship and had given orders to the sailors to prevent us boarding any of the tenders. When we reached the hut, the First Officer ordered us to lock the door, and to remain quiet. We were not to come out until he told us the coast was clear. He would see what he could do to get us a launch. We were beginning to sense that we would never be able to get ashore. It was difficult not to panic.

We had hardly turned the key in the lock, when we heard angry voices approaching. There was a ferocious banging on the door accompanied by a stream of foul language. We froze with terror, hardly daring to breathe. We listened to the sound of heavy, shuffling footsteps circling the hut and the Captain's slurred voice shouting for us to open the door or he would shoot. Thankfully the windows were high up, so he could not see in. There were more voices and more banging, and then it all went quiet. We waited for what seemed ages. It was dreadfully hot. Eventually, we opened the door very carefully. There was no one about. Just as we were wondering what to do next, we saw the First Officer by the gangway. He beckoned us over. Clutching our cases, we stumbled towards him, and saw, to our immense relief, a launch by the bottom step. It was a hurried goodbye. We tried to express our gratitude, but he would have none of it. He handed our luggage down to the boatman, and then, our guardian angel, turned on his heel and disappeared through a hatchway. That was the last we saw or heard of him. I can never forget his kindness, though I am saddened that after a lapse of sixty-six years, I cannot recall his name.

We arrived home in Nairobi on Christmas Eve. How we had longed for this moment! At last we could share with our families the story of our odyssey. On the train journey up from Mombasa, we had spent time speculating on how our parents would react to our traumatic experience with the drunken Captain. We envisaged the headlines in the *East African Standard:- CHIEF JUSTICE'S DAUGHTER & COMPANIONS TAKEN HOSTAGE ON AMERICAN VICTORY SHIP*. I was hardly through the front door, when, choking with emotion, I launched into a feverish telling of our adventures on the S.S. *Joliet Victory*. But no one was prepared to listen. The war was over, and Mary, newly, demobbed from the WRENS, had come home with an engagement ring supporting a diamond to rival the Koh-I-Noor. She was to be married in London in May. There were, too, retirement parties for my father - so much to arrange – AND it was Christmas – why had my journey taken so long? I persevered. But when I came to the incident with the Captain, the family burst into peals of laughter. Things like that didn't happen. What a vivid imagination I had!

Our house in Nairobi

Our house at Nyeri

Sheridan family at Vipigo with the Admiral, his Flag Officer and Pluto the ridgeback.

Loreto Convent, Lumbwa

Lumbwa classroom

Father Morrissey

Lumbwa nuns, 'MTG' 2nd from right

Rhodes University

Me at Rhodes University

Epilogue

We arrived in Plymouth in early March of 1947 to find Britain bathed in the pale, uncertain light of spring, after suffering one of the coldest winters on record. The railway embankment on the journey to London was studded with clumps of primroses. Newborn lambs skipped merrily over the buttercups in the little green fields. Rosy-roofed farmhouses snuggled into the folds of the Devon countryside. It was a child's picture book image of spring. For us, accustomed to the vast landscapes of Africa with herds of zebra and wildebeest roaming over the savannah, it could not have been more of a contrast.

In London we were brought face to face with the grim evidence of the suffering endured in the war. The effect of the Blitz and the V2 rockets was everywhere. There was hardly a building left unscathed by bomb damage. Many shops were boarded up. There was very little traffic. People in shabby coats and worn shoes queued patiently for the buses which were few and far between. A few people sat in deck chairs in the parks enjoying the sunshine. They looked wan and weary compared to our African friends. Food rationing was still in operation, so while obesity was not a problem, lack of vitamins was. And yet there was a buoyancy in their step. The cheeky cries of the cockney news vendors and barrow boys lent an air of merriment to the drab streets. London was like the winner of a marathon; bent double with exhaustion, having given every ounce of energy to win the race, but filled with elation by victory. A feeling of optimism was palpable. London was the place everyone wanted to be. It was the centre of the world. To us Kenya was now no more than a backwater. It was no wonder then that when my parents returned to live in their home in Nyeri after Mary's wedding, we all chose to remain in what was still called Great Britain.

Mary's marriage to Ben Faller took place in May of that year in the Church of the Assumption, Spanish Place. Their love and devotion for each other over more than sixty years was something that impressed everyone who knew them. They had three children: Juliet Hunter-Tilney; Simon, who died at the age of ten, and Clare Copeman. Ben died in 2009. Roderick married during the war. His bride was the beautiful Lois (Lola) Green. After the war he joined the Colonial Service and their eldest child, Kevin, was born in Zanzibar. Their daughter, Tara Brazier, followed a couple of years later. Roderick outlived Lola, dying, aged 92, in 2013. Dermot resisted marriage for many years, believing it would be an imposition to ask anyone to marry a disabled person. He finally succumbed and in his late fifties married a Kenya friend, Marion Donnelly, who brought him much happiness in his last years. He became Chief Justice of Uganda in 1970. He died at the age of 64.

Before returning to East Africa, my mother enrolled Helen in the sixth form of Farnborough Convent. She believed that someone of Helen's intelligence should finish her education at a reputable academic establishment. After leaving school, Helen went to work in the Syrian Embassy in London, and in 1955 married Peter Orchard, the youngest son of a prestigious Downside family. Peter became Chairman of De La Rue. He died prematurely of a heart attack in 1993. He was only in his early sixties. They had four children – Rupert, Timothy, Maryanne Hopton and Josephine McCormack. My mother continued to insist on my musical education. A Mr Myers Foggin was engaged to give me piano lessons (I got the impression he was pleased to have the money!).

I rented a room in the Queensbury Club in Egerton Gardens. There I met Gaybrielle Belloc. With another friend, Mary Coppinger, Gay and I moved into a flat, 82 Queen's Gate. To help pay the rent (£6.00 per week) I worked at Harrods in the Active Sportswear Department.

And then my godfather, Anthony Lytton, introduced me to the Pollen family. After that my life changed utterly. In 1950 their eldest son Francis, and I, married at Westminster Cathedral. We enjoyed thirty-seven years together.

Our children, Clare, Kathy, Rosie, John and Louise – to whom I dedicate these memoirs – are a constant reminder for me of the blessings and the joys of those singularly happy times.

Bibliography

Anderson, David. *Histories of the Hanged*. Phoenix, 2006
Best, Nicholas. *Happy Valley*. Secker & Warburg, 1979
Darwin, John. *Unfinished Empire*. Allen Lane, 2012
East African Standard. 1933
Fox, James. *White Mischief*. Jonathan Cape, 1982
Huxley, Elizabeth. *A New Earth: an experiment in Colonialism*. Chatto & Windus, 1960
Huxley, Elspeth. *White Man's Country: Lord Delamere & the Making of Kenya*. Chatto & Windus, 1935
Huxley, Elspeth. *The Mottled Lizard*. Chatto & Windus, 1962
Huxley, Elspeth. *Nine Faces of Kenya*. Collins Harvill, 1990
Miller, Charles. *The Lunatic Express*. Macdonald, 1972
Murray-Brown, Jeremy. *Kenyatta*. Dutton, 1973
Pakenham, Thomas. *Scramble for Africa*. Abacus History, 1993
Paice, Edward. *Lost Lion of Empire*. Harper Collins, 2001
Travelaid. *Guide to East Africa*. London, 1993